MW00830690

Tracking God

Tracking God

An Ecumenical Fundamental Theology

IVANA NOBLE

S. Switankowsky
received May, 2010.
reviewed Oct, 2010.

WIPF & STOCK · Eugene, Oregon

TRACKING GOD
An Ecumenical Fundamental Theology

Copyright © 2010 Ivana Noble. All rights reserved. Except for brief quotations in critical publications or reviews, no part of this book may be reproduced in any manner without prior written permission from the publisher. Write: Permissions, Wipf and Stock Publishers, 199 W. 8th Ave., Suite 3, Eugene, OR 97401.

Wipf & Stock
An Imprint of Wipf and Stock Publishers
199 W. 8th Ave., Suite 3
Eugene, OR 97401
www.wipfandstock.com

ISBN 13: 978-1-60608-700-8

Manufactured in the U.S.A.

The book is based on the earlier Czech version: *Po Božích stopách: Teologie jako interpretace náboženské zkušenosti.* Brno: CDK, 2004.

A basic translation of the Czech original by Angela Radiven was adapted for an English-speaking audience by Ivana Noble and the language corrections were done by Tim Noble.

This study was supported by the Protestant Theological Faculty of Charles University and by the International Baptist Theological Seminary in Prague and is a part of the project "The Hermeneutics of Christian Tradition, in particular the Czech Protestant one, in the Cultural History of Europe." (MSM 0021620802).

All Scripture quotations are taken from Common Bible: New Revised Standard Version Bible, copyright 1989, Division of Christian Education of the National Council of the Churches of Christ in the United States of America. Used by permission. All rights reserved.

Contents

Preface

THE BASIS FOR THIS book came out of a course I have taught in different versions since 1994, first at the Institute of Ecumenical Studies in Prague, which was founded by several theologians from different confessions after the fall of Communism, and later in the Theology of Christian Traditions program of the Protestant Theological Faculty of Charles University in Prague. In 2003 it was submitted as my habilitation work at the same faculty and a year later published in Czech by the Centre for Democracy and Culture (CDK) publishing house under the title (translated into English) of *Tracking God: Theology as an Interpretation of Religious Experience*. My main question then was how to introduce students from different backgrounds to theology in a setting that is skeptical to institutional religiosity, but nevertheless interested in spiritual life.

Four years later, thanks to the encouragement and interest of several of my colleagues from both Europe and America, I started to consider an English translation. With some time having passed and after a careful rereading of the book, I have decided to change the subtitle. While the experiential basis is still important to me, I was increasingly aware that we never share pure experience. Instead, it is always mediated by some, at least fragmented, tradition of interpretation, or even by fragments from a number of different traditions. These are as important to theology as the initial experience since they are already at work when we name what has been experienced to ourselves, and even more so when we ask about the authenticity of the experience, and when we seek for a language that could communicate it to others. The new subtitle, *Ecumenical Fundamental Theology*, highlights two aspects of the book. It deals with basic themes that keep re-emerging in any reflection on how Christians have experienced their relationship to God, to the world, and to each other. At the same time, it approaches these themes from within a plurality of traditional and contemporary perspectives.

The new subtitle also expresses the task already present in the Czech original, to introduce students from different church backgrounds to

Christian theology as a field that they would share in together from the beginning, including the historical development as well as the ever-present plurality of perspectives as something that could be their own. By this I mean that, for example, Protestant students studying the Church Fathers would recognize them as their sources too, as would Catholics studying Luther, or the Orthodox reading the Catholic theologians of the Second Vatican Council. In order to avoid misunderstanding, this does not mean that their differences would be eliminated. Rather, they would be recognized and studied with an effort to understand the other tradition as well as their own while acknowledging the mutuality and interdependence of them all. In this sense theology could be studied as an ecumenical discipline from the start, not as a meta-tradition harmonizing the differences and avoiding points of conflict.

The traditions represented in this study, the Orthodox, the Catholic, and the Protestant,[1] need to be allowed to remain valid besides each other, and as such to participate in the cumulative search of how the following of Christ has been understood and enacted down the centuries. In this search treasures old and new can be discovered as something we can meaningfully share with each other across Christian traditions and even beyond, with people of other faiths, as well as with our secular and post-secular contemporaries. In this search we are also confronted with the fact that what was considered as family silver by some of our ancestors has subsequently turned into dry leaves. Worse still, we have to face what has been humanly damaging and violent in our traditions. In these negative discoveries, however, it is necessary to retain the same level of mutual connection, solidarity, and responsibility as when we appropriate the peaks of another spiritual tradition, form of ritual celebration, intellectual insight, or example of practical wisdom.

My further teaching of international students, and especially of students at the International Baptist Theological Seminary in Prague, has extended my horizons towards evangelical Christianity. But here I have an apology to make. As most of the text was written before I was more engaged with them, their voice is not sufficiently integrated into the choir.[2]

---

1. I speak here about traditions as broad types that include several institutional representations.

2. I have tried to include the evangelical voice in my forthcoming book, *Theological Interpretation of Culture in a Post-Communist Context: The Central and East European Search for Roots*, to be published by Ashgate.

Still, I hope that *Tracking God* will be useful for them as an introduction to other theological approaches and methods, which could extend their own understanding and stimulate their response.

The need for an adapted English translation of the book was further stimulated by my work in Societas Oecumenica, the European academic society for ecumenical theology. Conversations with my colleagues there, and recent conferences we have organized, have made me even more convinced that it is necessary to reach beyond presenting ecumenical theology as the process, methods, and results of dialogues between different ecclesial bodies. However important and useful such studies are, they seem to excite only a small audience. In my view, they need to be integrated into a wider program of studying and teaching theology as ecumenical from the beginning to the end. It does not have to mean that every person will manage to grasp all Christian traditions at the same depth, or, as I mentioned above, that a kind of meta-tradition could be constructed. It is enough to encounter some of the other traditions more deeply, to understand how related each is with my own. Thus, without giving offence to others, one becomes open to a different type of identification of what belongs to a Christian heritage, to the heritage I and we are gifted by and responsible for.

There are many who deserve thanks. I am indebted to my Czech students at the Institute of Ecumenical Studies and to both the Czech and international students at the Protestant Theological Faculty in Prague for their engagement and interest, and for teaching me about their traditions from within. Further I want to thank to my colleagues there, and the faculty as a whole, for supporting me during this project and financing the translation. Many thanks belong to Angela Radiven who undertook the translation. I would not have considered the English version of the book without the interest and encouragement of my colleagues from Societas Oecumenica, whom I also want to thank. I would also like to express my gratitude to my colleagues at the International Baptist Theological Seminary for their long-term interest in the project and for practical support in finalizing and editing the English text. Most of all, special thanks belong to my husband Tim, who not only did the language editing, but has also been a supportive, critical, and loving partner during the whole writing process. Without him the adapted English version of this book would never have seen the light of day, and it is to him that I would like to dedicate it.

Ivana Noble
Prague, August 2009

List of Abbreviations

Athanasius, *DeIncarn* – Athanasius, *De Incarnatione*

Augustine, *Conf* – Augustine, *Confessions*

Augustine, *DeBapt* – Augustine, *De Baptismo*

Augustine, *DeCiv* – Augustine, *De Civitate Dei*

Augustine, *DeTrin* – Augustine, *De Trinitate*

Augustine, *DeVeraRelig* – Augustine, *De vera Religione*

Clement, *Strom* – Clement of Alexandria, *Stromata*

DS – Denzinger, H.; Schönmetzer, A. *Enchiridion symbolorum, definitionum et declarationum de rebus fidei et morum.* Editio XXXIII. Barcinone; Friburgi Brisgoviae; Romae; Neo-Eboraci: Herder, 1965.

DV – *Dei Verbum* Dogmatic Constitution on Divine Revelation, Vatican II

Gregory of Nyssa, *ContrEun* – Gregory of Nyssa, *Contra Eunomium*

Gregory of Nyssa, *Treat* – Gregory of Nyssa, *Treatise on the Inscriptions of the Psalms*

Gregory of Nyssa, *VMos* – Gregory of Nyssa, *De vita Moysis*

GS – *Gaudium et Spes*, Pastoral Constitution on the Church and the Modern World, Vatican II

Ignatius, *Eph* – Ignatius, *Letter to the Ephesians*

Ignatius, *Smyr* – Ignatius, *Letter to the Smyrneans*

Irenaeus, *AdvHaer* – Irenaeus, *Adversus Haereses* (Against the Heresies)

Justin, 1Apol – Justin Martyr, *First Apology*

Justin, 2Apol – Justin Martyr, *Second Apology*

LG – *Lumen Gentium*, Dogmatic Constitution on the Church, Vatican II

Origen, *DePrinc* – Origen, *De Principiis*

Tertullian, *DePraescr* – Tertullian, *De praescriptione haereticorum*

Theodore of Mopsuestia, *Commentary* – *Commentary on Galatians*

Introduction

A S THE MAIN AIM of this book is to offer an ecumenical introduction to theology, I need to explain what I mean by this. In order to do so, I want first to distinguish between ecumenism, ecumenics, and ecumenical theology. They do not signify the same thing.

Ecumenism is an attitude of interest, openness, and good will towards Christian confessions other than one's own. This attitude is discernible in modern convergence movements, motivated by a desire for cooperation in the fields of mission, social work, work for peace and justice, as well as in the desire to overcome historical schisms and achieve the full visible unity of the church, expressed liturgically, doctrinally, and canonically. The particular expressions and visions of ecumenism as an attitude towards others have developed and diversified, yet in some ways its forms refer to the foundational dream of unity.

Ecumenics is a discipline specifically dedicated to the study of the ecumenical movement, its organizations and documents, the history and methods of bilateral and multilateral dialogues, and the typology of the churches involved (or refusing to be involved) in such dialogues. It is important to recognize that, though an important part of ecumenical theological education, it is not the only part. After almost fifteen years of experience teaching ecumenical theology, I have to say that ecumenics, although taught to all our students, usually really interests only a small number of them, despite the fact that a majority would say that they are interested in ecumenical theology.

By ecumenical theology they and I would mean something else than what might be termed the formal side of ecumenism. In the following pages ecumenical theology will be seen not so much as a theology of the dialogues and other documents supporting Christian cooperation and desiring unity, but rather the studying of Christian traditions in their plurality as our common heritage. Ecumenical fundamental theology, then, will be understood as a common investigation of the roots and the main themes that have contributed to theology both as a science and as a spiritual journey—even if always lived and reflected in a particular setting.

Ecumenical theology, as I understand it, challenges the usual and to a large degree artificial denominational perspectives of theology. In the lived context of my students, my fellow teachers, and even my own, we do not encounter the sort of "pure" Catholics, Protestants, Orthodox or Hussites with whom the church documents operate. Not only would we experience a wide plurality of positions within each of the confessional families, with similarities and differences grouped across them, but also that practicing in more than one of them subsequently or simultaneously would be common. In teaching ecumenical theology we have to take into account both the fragile permanence and the existent multiplicity of religious belonging in our context, however much we might feel that encouraging people to be clear confessional types of Christians is a part of our job. Maybe it is not, at least not in ways that prefer ideas to real people, their search, and their commitment.

This takes me to the next important point, namely that the search for meaning, for authenticity of life, and for God is not limited to people who are rooted in the traditions of religious practice, Christian or other. The societies in which we live often display paradoxical movements. On the one hand, secularization is growing in countries that, prior to and for most of the twentieth century, would have seen themselves as Christian, such as England, Belgium or Holland. On the other hand, in those countries where secularization was a part of the official ideology, it has already passed its peak. In the Czech Republic, Estonia, or Bulgaria, countries that statistically display the smallest presence of traditional religions, as well as mistrust of institutions (including religious institutions), and a tendency to privatized world-views (including religious ones), there is a big shift away from atheism and towards new forms of religiosity.[3] Ecumenical theology, if it is to be true to the traditions it interprets, needs to be open to the searching of people who do not belong to any of them, to listen to their experiences, and to offer in exchange the symbolic mediation of meaning and wisdom of discernment.

Including the major Christian traditions and the post-institutional search as the sources that ecumenical fundamental theology relies on and critically examines requires a specific methodology. First, a suspension

---

3. I have dealt with these changes in Noble, *Theological Interpretation of Culture*.

of judgment concerning which of the positions included is the best one. Instead, the different positions make a kind of cumulative case, to use Newman's terminology,[4] for the meaningfulness of human experiences and relationships in the light of beliefs, hopes, and love associated with God. The cumulative approach to different contributions does not exclude their tensions and aporias. They remain. Sometimes they can become more understandable in relation to the contexts in which they arose, but not always. The search for meaning, whether Christian or other, always also includes encounters with meaninglessness. There are the painful and violent moments of traditions. Just as we have learned to appropriate the best in all Christian traditions as our own, we need to accept that the worst of what different Christian traditions have contributed also belongs to us. We need to find a responsible attitude to those who oppose Christianity for this reason, rather than blaming someone else for involvement in religious wars, the Inquisition, witch-hunting, anti-Semitism, the oppression of women, of strangers, etc. Without this attitude we will remain outsiders to the forms of Christian spirituality, liturgy, theology, or philosophy that we admire, as they are the other side of the coin of the struggles, even of the failures. If ecumenical theology wants to make its home in the different traditions, this has to include also solidarity with their weakest moments, so that instead of passing sentence on them, we engage with them to help them to find liberation for a new life. Such an attitude, or at least the desire to have such an attitude, is indispensable for ecumenical theology.

Now let me move to the structure of the book. The main themes I concentrate on in the book include theological method, divine revelation, authorities and their overlaps and clashes in Christianity, the historical and cultural contexts of theology, and theology's roots in religious experience. Each theme has a biblical and patristic part, and then contemporary discussion involving Catholic, Orthodox, and Protestant theologians.

In the first chapter, while offering historically developed definitions of theology both as a science and as a spiritual journey, I ask what makes theology distinct, and in what way it is related to other forms of searching for God, and other ways of knowing. Three notions of theology as existential, dialectical, and historical science, each of which in different

---

4. John Henry Newman uses the concept of "cumulative case" for a number of interdependent criteria, external and internal, that build together right Christian belief and practice. See Newman, *Grammar of Assent,* 408.

ways determined its classical methods, will be complemented by more recent phenomenological, hermeneutical, and epistemological approaches. Both the classical and the contemporary methods will then be employed in the following chapters.

ch. 2.   The second chapter focuses on how theologians of different times and traditions have understood divine revelation, and the claims and promises inherent in the texts testifying the experience of revelation. Starting from the questions concerning the nature of the knowledge of God, of the world, and of our place in God's plans with the world in the Scriptures and in tradition, we gradually move to the present. Here a Christian theology of revelation amidst agnosticism or claims to revelation by other religions needs to spell out in what sense it belongs to its foundational requirements to be open to a dialogue of all people of good will while holding on to the unique revelation of God in Jesus Christ.

ch. 3   The third chapter examines the grounds on which we take our beliefs, values, and convictions as authoritative, but also the problems stemming from the corruptibility of such grounds. Offering a mosaic of historically developed authorities, both external, such as the Scriptures, tradition, or the church, and internal, such as human conscience, reasonableness, or inner peace, I track how each of these authorities is related to the supreme authority of God. Then I look at the kind of hierarchies that have been at work when different conflicts of authorities took place, such as that between the authority of the church and human conscience, or between tradition and scientifically defined reasonableness. Arguing for the positive and constructive role of the authorities sketched above, I also have to investigate their shadows, the ideological abuse of authority that makes claims on human life, as if it were itself divine. Here my main questions are how the ideological potential in the authorities can be prevented from growing into manipulation or fanaticism, and how different traditions can help each other in this task.

ch. 4   The fourth chapter deals with contexts, historically and culturally understood. Arguing against the theory that it is possible to isolate a core of Christianity by peeling off the skins that have grown over time around the pure a-historical and a-cultural essence,[5] I show that the foundations of Christianity are embedded in the historically and culturally conditioned ways in which people have grasped divine revelation. If we take

---

5. For a theory that sought to isolate the essence of Christianity, see, e.g., Harnack, *What is Christianity?*

the incarnational principle seriously,[6] this historical and cultural conditioning would become an advantage and a source of wealth for Christian traditions. At the same time, however, we need to abstain from cultural imperialism, and from the conviction that we can determine what in history is progress and what regress.

The fifth and final chapter investigates the role of religious experience for theology. It offers a narrow and a broad definition of religious experience, one emphasizing the specifically Christian symbolic grasp of spiritual experience, the other understanding the whole of human experience from the transcendent—or the holy—foundations of life. In showing how these two notions of religious experience were present in the Scriptural and traditional accounts of faith, and how discernment between what is authentic and what is inauthentic cuts through both, the ground is prepared for the modern and postmodern discussion. This traces how religious experience has been rehabilitated as a subject of scientific investigation. While looking at religious experience from a contemporary theological point of view, it relates it back to the themes of the previous chapters. It asks about the proper theological methods of investigating religious experience, about what or who it reveals and on what authority it is trustworthy, about how its interpretation develops with the personal development of those who underwent it, as well as with the development of the contexts of its future audiences.

In the conclusion I come back to the ecumenical character of the fundamental theological themes as examined above. I spell out basic tasks inherent in teaching and studying theology ecumenically in a time when Christians in their surrounding societies and cultures encounter an interest in spirituality and in non-institutional religiosity, as much as a growing ignorance concerning confessional differences and a lack of interest in traditional forms of religious life.

I hope that this book will be helpful not only as an introduction to theology that works simultaneously with Catholic, Orthodox, and Protestant traditions, but also in its emphasizing that theology needs to be approached as a common heritage and a common presence. In testifying to the multilayered web of theological discourse I hope that not only

---

6. By the incarnational principle I refer to the Chalcedonian dogma saying that the divinity and the humanity in Christ are without any commingling or change or division or separation (See DS 302). This principle has been more broadly applied also to the presence of the divine in the human world. See, e.g., Sobrino, *Jesus the Liberator*.

tolerance towards the other can be found, but also acceptance, forgiveness where needed, understanding, and the desire for communion with the other, where exchange of gifts and solidarity in need can happen and be extended to those who search without belonging to any religious tradition themselves.

Theology and the Problem of Method

Thomas said to him, 'Lord, we do not know where you are going.
How can we know the way?' Jesus said to him, 'I am the way,
and the truth, and the life.'

JOHN 14:5–6A

We must begin with the mistake and transform it into what is true.
That is, we must uncover the source of the error; otherwise hearing what
is true won't help us. It cannot penetrate when something is taking its
place. To convince someone of what is true, it is not enough to state it; we
must find the road from error to truth.
I must plunge again and again in the water of doubt.

WITTGENSTEIN[1]

THOSE WHO WANT TO pursue theology seriously are subjected to the process of which Wittgenstein talks in the introductory quotation. They have to confront the question as to whether the security that has held their faith so far is a real security, or whether it has been a crutch that must be left behind on the way to the One who is the truth and life. This process is necessary, but it is not easy. It is accompanied by doubts with which the emerging theologian must learn to deal. Immediate experiencing of faith has to be subjected to testing. The time when it felt as if God spoke through everything one encountered can appear in this process as a lost childhood paradise, now exchanged for a period of insecurity. At the same time this loss of security opens up a new stage on the journey to a deeper understanding of who God is, how God interacts with us, what

1. Wittgenstein, *Remarks*, 1e.

truth about Godself, about the world, and about ourselves God discloses to us, what God has in mind for us, and what God asks of us. On this journey we will encounter again and again what we left behind, like clothes a child has grown out of, but from a new angle, in new forms integrating new experience and new knowledge.

We will discover en route that theology is not a language, but a plurality of languages. The people who speak them strive more or less for mutual understanding, and look for traditional connections and topicality in regard to the problems with which they are confronted by their times and society. What is the role theology plays and can play? What is its view of itself? What are its tasks, agendas, methods? What role does it play for the Christian faith and for the human quest after truth?[2] We are going to focus on these questions in this opening chapter on theological methods. First, I will outline a definition of theology. Then, having elaborated it further, I concentrate on the issue of the scientific approach to theology, before finally dealing with the variety of methods that theology employs.

WHAT IS THEOLOGY?

Theology is generally understood as a science that focuses on God and religion. This simplified definition of theology is widespread, despite two substantial problems. First, in what sense is God the object of that which theology scientifically investigates? We cannot inquire into God the same way we would into a stone or bacteria, plants or animals, the human soul, or human society and its culture. In this sense God resists being treated as an object. Whenever theologians try to speak about God in terms of evidence for an object, they sooner or later find themselves acting out of their depth. What methods would they use to pin down their Creator and the Lord of the Universe, to master their Master?

However, if we attempt to escape the problem of whether it is possible to speak directly about God and say that theology is teaching about religious ideas and practices in which notions of God emerge, we face another problem. It is true that religion can be at least partially grasped historically or typologically. However, the science concerned with religion is not called theology, but religious studies. In reducing theology to the study of religion the specificity of theology is abandoned.

---

2. Geffré and Jeanrond, "Why Theology?," viii.

In this chapter I will introduce alternatives to either insisting that God alone, fathomless, other than anything we know, is the subject of theology, or to saying that God-discourse is always relative to its religious mediation, which alone is the subject of theology. I will introduce theology as an investigation of God's traces. The focus on the traces of God will make it possible to hold on to the mystery of God through a direct as well as a mediated relationship. God's self-revelation will be examined from the point of view of a relationship that has transformed human lives, has been witnessed and handed down in holy texts and communities of faith, and has left its marks on human history and culture, whilst also transcending all these and remaining the other that we cannot pin down and edit.

Origins of the Concept

The word "theology" comes from Greek, *theologia,* made up of the words *theos* (god) and *logia* (sayings). Sayings about God (gods, divinity) did not start with the beginning of Christianity, nor were they taken over exclusively from the Jewish background. Although the Jews believed in one Lord God, the Greeks also had their discourse about gods. Before the Greeks there were the Egyptians, the Sumerians, and other ancient peoples. Their discourses varied: some of them were pantheistic, others polytheistic, and still others monotheistic. The concept of theology is first found in written form in Plato's *Republic,* where it signifies patterns and norms of speech about the gods, so that the true quality of divine goodness would not be lost.[3] For Plato, theology works with a plurality of styles and a variety of insights. Within and through them it sought to prevent the dissemination of any belief that the gods desire war, or do harm to anyone, or participate in vices. Aristotle was the first to define theology as a divine science.[4] It shares with other sciences the pursuit of wisdom, or, in Aristotle's terms, the investigation of principles and causes. However, theology deals with universal principles and prime causes, with facts separated from matter and immovable. Even if not the most practical, it is the noblest science because it desires knowledge for its own sake.[5]

---

3. See Plato, *Republic* 2.379a.

4. See Aristotle, *Metaphysics* 1.983a. Divine science is conditioned by "(a) all believe that God is one of the causes and a kind of principle, and (b) God is the sole or chief possessor of this sort of knowledge." Then Aristotle concludes: "Accordingly, although all other sciences are more necessary than this, none is more excellent." (Ibid.)

5. There are still other concepts of theology. In Plutarch's Stoic philosophy, theol-

Biblical Greek lacks the concept of theology as such,[6] but it can be found in the Church Fathers who adopted it from the Greek philosophical tradition and adjusted its meaning to the discourse about God, handed down in the Scriptures, and in what was called the *regula fidei* (the rule of faith), or creed (Gr. *symbolon,* Lat. *credo*). So, according to Irenaeus, Clement of Alexandria, Tertullian, Hippolytus, and Origen, it represented the basic articles of the Christian faith, preserved and handed down by the church.

This understanding of theology then spread across the whole of church teaching and practice, which together with the Scriptures possesses the authority of the authentic tradition of the Christian faith and way of life. Talking about God is bound up with talking about people, about the world in which they live and struggle for faith, hope, and love. Theology includes its own history, as well as the cultural plurality and diversity of the environment out of which it arose. The Church Fathers further elaborate the requirements of a Christian theologian. Here we can find the need for "inner *katharsis*, contemplation, veneration of the divine mystery."[7] Clement of Alexandria writes: "For only to those who often approach them [the Scriptures], and have given them a trial by faith and in their whole life, will they supply the real philosophy and the true theology."[8] In the fourth century, during the ongoing struggle with Arianism, the words *theologia* and *theologos* became related to the correct understanding of the Trinity, incarnation, and redemption. However, the emphasis on the purification of life as a condition for understanding God's revelation remains: "[A]nyone who wishes to understand the mind of the sacred writers must first cleanse his own life, and approach the saints by

ogy is at the top and is often related to sacred ceremonies; according to Plotinus, the theologians are those who discuss the birth of Eros; Proclus speaks of four levels of theology: symbolic, metaphorical, inspirational and scientific. See Ventura, "Teologie jako duchovní cesta," 26.

6. On the other hand, the New Testament works with the term *gnosis* (knowledge), especially as *epignosis* (fullness of knowledge). This is related to a spiritual enlightenment as well as to an intellectual understanding. In both cases the fullness of knowledge stipulates the love relationship (Rom 3:20; Eph 1:17; Col 2:2; 2 Tim 2:25). *Gnosis* as a knowledge for its own sake creates nothing (1 Cor 8:2–3), guarantees nothing (1 Cor 13:2). The term *gnosis* further appears to signify false knowledge—a heterodox teaching of Gnostic origin (1 Tim 6:20).

7. Ventura, "Teologie jako duchovní cesta," 26.

8. Clement, *Strom* V.9.

copying their deeds. Thus united to them in the fellowship of life, he will both understand the things revealed to them by God and, thenceforth escaping the peril that threatens sinners in the judgment, will receive that which is laid up for the saints in the kingdom of heaven."[9]

Theology as a Triple Critical Reflection

Theology originates in experience. In continuity with the patristic tradition, we can say that it is an experience of encounter with God, and an experience of the believing community that, with all available help, strives to hold together orthodoxy (the correct way of belief) and orthopraxis (the correct way of life). Theology reflects on that experience, and on the tradition that the experience both initiates and continually challenges. Furthermore, this reflection is critical. It means that theology not only collects data about the experiences but also examines the patterns or norms implicit in the experiences and measures them against its own accumulated principles. In the Christian tradition a special place has been given to the triad of faith, hope, and love. This triad has given a symbolic vocabulary to express people's experiences of the anchorage of their being, of trusting that God who is with us today will be with us tomorrow, of receiving that inspired gratitude and generosity towards God, towards other people, and the whole of creation.

The triad of faith, hope, and love can already be found in the New Testament. For instance, the letter to the Hebrews urges its readers: "Let us approach with a true heart in full assurance of faith, with our hearts sprinkled clean from an evil conscience and our bodies washed with pure water. Let us hold fast to the confession of our hope without wavering, for he who has promised is faithful." (Heb 10:22–24). Christians have considered faith, hope, and love to be the fundamental expressions of Christian existence;[10] tradition even called them "cardinal virtues" or "theological virtues." This means they are "imparted by God," not gained by any human effort. Despite the changes of the meaning of the terms during history and in different cultural backgrounds, I will try to interpret instances of faith, hope, and love in ways that are accessible for contemporary readers, and in which they can recognize their own experience connecting God's gift and human actions.

---

9. Athanasius, *DeIncarn* IX.57.

10. See 1 Cor 13:3; 1 Thess 1:3; 5:8; Eph 1:15–18; Col 1:4f.

A Reflection of the Experience of Faith

What is the basis on which we decide what is and what is not faith? Traditionally the meaning of these terms was handed down in the culture in which people were raised. However, today most Europeans (not to speak of others) live in cultures that, in general, are not marked by religious faith, and thus any meaning concerning faith is passed on without roots in a living tradition, or at least they have lost access to the roots. This fact makes any cultural discernment between faith and non-faith less reliable. In order to speak about a Christian experience of faith, we have to seek where such faith is found. It originates in the relationship with God, when God speaks through the Scriptures, tradition, history, culture, other people, nature, or even through a silence that can be full of meaning. The human being responds in prayer, speaks through prayer, but also through what he/she does and lives, and God responds. Such experiences and attitudes of faith are found in the biblical narratives. To understand what faith is we need to immerse ourselves in their symbolic wealth.[11]

Let us start with the story of the cure of the blind man near Jericho.[12] He has been given a chance. Jesus is on his way to Jerusalem for the last time, to die there on the cross and rise again from the dead. The beggar does not let those who want to have Jesus for themselves brush him away. His trust is deeper. He is asked to name the main problem of his life. Where to start? He is short of so many things. Where is the root of all his problems? What can become the main turning point? The blind man wants Jesus to give him back his sight. Jesus praises him not only for "wanting" it, but also because he is open to a new possibility, to being cured.

In Luke's gospel, this story about being given sight to be able to follow contrasts with the blindness of the followers who do not understand where Jesus is going and do not believe his journey can open a new life for them. The blind man is willing to consider his relationship with Jesus as more important than his personal misery. Perhaps he understands

---

11. If we were to follow the terminological analysis, the narratives would be chosen according to their use of the Hebrew *emunah*, usually translated as faithfulness or trust (see, e.g., Gen 15:6; Exod 14:31; 1 Sam 2:35) and its Greek equivalent *pistis* (see, e.g., Matt 9:22; 15:28; Rom 4:5; 1 Cor 2:5; 13:13; 15:4; Gal 5:6; Eph 4:5; Heb 11:1; Jas 2:14). But instead we will follow the characters who believe, seeking for similarities between their situation and ours.

12. See Luke 18:35–43.

that God is acting here, perhaps his blindness did not penetrate his inner being. In contrast, the disciples are stuck in their momentary situation, trying to "bury the talent" they were given, as is obvious from one of the following parables.[13] The effort to secure their faith destabilizes the faith they were given and takes away their freedom for God. Faith liberates. The blind man is free and that gives him a chance to "regain his sight, follow Jesus and glorify God." (Luke 18:43)

Jürgen Moltmann stresses the liberating power of faith, where faith is not understood just as a formal consent to a set of convictions, but rather as something that concerns us personally. As such it can stand at the beginning of a freedom that restores the whole of life. In this sense faith "conquers the world." (John 16:33)[14]

The critical reflection of such faith must take into account an important distinction between faith as an act, as was shown in the story from Luke's gospel, and the content of faith, which we pass on to be able to perform the next act of faith. Theology has traditionally differentiated between *fides qua creditur*, faith by which we believe and by which we are able to enter into a relationship with God, and *fides quae creditur*, faith in which we believe, the formal structure of faith.[15] The two types of faith cannot be confused, but at the same time are interdependent. An act of faith, *fides qua creditur*, is linked to the fact that we as Christians are people of the covenant. We refer to the covenant of Abraham, fulfilled in Jesus Christ for us. Furthermore, we know about this covenant because of the tradition that testifies to events to which we have no immediate access. As the people of the covenant, we profess faith in God and share God's revealed knowledge.[16] The event of Jesus Christ's death and resurrection, constitutive for Christianity, has a particular content that the church safeguards and passes on from one generation to the next as a treasure of faith (*depositum fidei*). But it is important not to reduce this treasure of faith to doctrine alone, but to preserve the interdependence between the content of faith and human conduct.

The experience of faith, reflected by theology, features both. Except for the particular narratives testifying the experience of faith, such as the

13. See Luke 19:11–27.
14. See Moltmann, *The Spirit of Life*, 114.
15. See Alfaro, "Faith."
16. See Deut 6:20–24; 26:5–9; Josh 24:2–3; Pss 78; 106; 135; 136.

story about the blind man from Luke's gospel, the New Testament also offers general guidelines on what faith is. Furthermore, it is necessary to complement the figurative particular meaning with the non-figurative abstract meaning. For example, according to the apostle Paul, to believe means to accept Christ's redeeming death and his resurrection.[17] The gospel is the "word of truth" (Col 1:5) that comes through the faithful proclamation of the apostles and those who received faith from them.[18] To give some more meaning to these statements, they must be lived and *PARADOSIS* passed on by living people, with their yearnings and endeavors, their feelings concerning the truth of God's words, and their experiences of God's activity. According to the Johannine tradition, to believe means to recognize Jesus as the Son sent by and from the Father, who both advocates and is the truth.[19] The early church expressed the content of faith using special formulas[20] that have continued to have their place in Christian life. The confession of faith in Christ and eventually in the Holy Trinity formed a part of the baptismal liturgy.[21] Thus ritual participation in the event of faith and the belief that its content is what it signifies united *fides qua creditur* and *fides quae creditur*. Human action, however, also includes other dimensions than the ritual-liturgical. Theology as a critical reflection of the experience of faith needs to investigate how believing in the reality of an event, such as Christ's redemption, fills and is filled by a moral life, social and political life, cultural life, or even other forms of spiritual life that are not exhausted by the liturgy and by ritual. As we do that, we also encounter the shadowy attitudes and contents that deform faith, or are already testimonies of a deformed faith, as we could see, for instance, in the attitude of the disciples in Luke's story. But these distorted attitudes themselves belong to the narratives of the lives of people experiencing faith and its growth.

A Reflection of the Experience of Hope

Tracking the experiences of hope, of openness towards the future, and trust that the future with God is good will also take us through the valleys

17. See Rom 10:9–10; 1 Cor 1:1–19; Phil 3:10–11; 1 Thess 4:14.

18. See Rom 10:8; Gal 1:23; 3:2.5; Eph 4:5; Acts 6:7; 13:8.12.

19. See John 3:1–13.31–36; 8:14.18–32.40–46; 14:5–6.12.20; 17:3.21.23.

20. See 1 Thess 1:10; 4:14; 1 Cor 1–8; 12:3; Rom 1:4; 10:9; Phil 2:5–11; Acts 8:37; 1 John 2:23; 4:2.15; 2 John 7.

21. See Lampe, "The Origins of the Creeds."

Provenance- place or source of origin

of hopelessness. We will encounter experiences of suffering, of failures, uncertainties, and fears, perhaps such as those addressed in the mythical accounts of the origins of the world, of creation, and fall. Hope arises when the goodness that was from the beginning[22] is tested, and when people are tired of questions about the provenance of evil and death. The Scriptures depict hope as a still deeper insight into God's promise, an insight that does not necessarily come up with coherent solutions, but functions as medicine for a wounded life without future. Noah, Abram and Moses are typical characters who set off on a journey from an old order of things to a new one, marked by a promise and a hope. Noah sailed on the face of the waters together with the creatures that he had rescued, in the ark he had built according to the Lord's command. Abram, called by the Lord, left Ur of the Chaldeans to become a new numerous people in a new, promised land. Moses led these same people, by the Lord's power, out of Egyptian slavery and across the waters and the desert to return to their promised land.[23]

Hebrews links faith with the people of faith, those who, out of faith, do something hopeful: "faith is the assurance of things hoped for, the conviction of things not seen." (Heb 11:1) They all followed a promise of things yet unseen and thus allowed hope to break into hopeless situations.[24] This trust grew out of the past, the hoping person remembered God's powerful deeds, and became open to the possibility that God could act like that again. In the New Testament, this trusting hope involves believing that certain events are true.[25] According to Romans: " . . . in hope we were saved. Now hope that is seen is not hope. For who hopes for what is seen? But if we hope for what we do not see, we wait for it with patience." (Rom 8:24–25) Christian hope arises in anticipation of the coming kingdom of God: with Christ's coming, it is already here in our midst,[26] but not yet in fullness,[27] and not only the creation, but we ourselves groan in

22. See the chorus of the creation story from Gen 1, "God saw that is was good." (vv.12.18.21.25.31)

23. See Gen 6–8; 12–24; Ex 3–15.

24. Compare to Pss 40:4; 62:8; 71:7; 73:28. The Hebrew word for hope, *bataha*, means both "to rely on" and "to make sure."

25. The Greek word for hope, *elpis*, connects hope and faith together, as we have seen in Hebrews.

26. See Matt 12:28; 19:24; 21:31; Luke 6:20; 17:21.

27. See Luke 13:29; 17:20; 22:16.18; Acts 14:22.

a world where we have to struggle with evil, where it is so difficult not to sin.[28] Hope gives us an orientation towards God, and anchors our desire to live by faith. Scholastic theology speaks in terms of *spes docta* (learned hope), which symbolizes a non-naive openness towards reality.[29]

Jean Daniélou, in his book *The Christian Today,* reflecting the situation after two World Wars, says that a positive attitude towards time is the essence of hope. This positive attitude leads to trust in the future, more precisely, the trust that God will be with us in the future. Such trust does not have much in common with enthusiastic rhetoric about progress. Christian hope as a non-ideological option over against skepticism is seen, then, as a theological virtue. It depends on God, and on God's promises, and not on our plans for how the future should be. Such hope is present everywhere that genuine prayer is present, and where people in and despite their helplessness call to God. [30]

Jürgen Moltmann links Christian hope with creative desire participating in changing the future. What the future with God means can be seen in Christ's resurrection. What is possible is fundamentally extended there. The boundless new life is not limited by the past although it is a response to it. A Christian hope that dreams the messianic dream, in which all is healed, complete, and alive, is not escapist. It does not lead people away from this world and its history, but leads them to new possibilities for this world, ones that transform history. Moltmann stresses that we ought to approach theology eschatologically, recognizing God's coming in the history of the world. God leading us out of slavery, bringing us back from exile, giving a future to his creation, standing by us, this is what gives hope, and what is central to our theological enquiry.[31] If we study in detail the life-stories of our Scriptural or ecclesial fathers and mothers in faith, if we pay attention to the lives of our contemporaries and reflect deeply enough on our own life-story, we will find that hope is born in the struggle with despair. It is confronted and tested in precisely those hopeless situations from which it arises as a non-causal, inexplicable, other dimension.

---

28. See Rom 7:14–25; 8:20–23.
29. Compare Thomas Aquinas, "De Spe," in *Summa Theologiae* II.2. xvii.xxii.
30. See Daniélou, *The Christian Today*, 114,116,123.
31. See Moltmann, *The Spirit of Life*, 119–20.

A Reflection of the Experience of Love

Love puts the experiences of faith and hope into the context of relationships with others. In this light, what anchors and orients my life is not given just for me. There is not an isolated "I", but an "I" in an endless net of relationships, moving out further and further from the closest ones till there is nothing left unrelated. Those who are not me claim me from outside. They do not steal my "I", but give me opportunities to be what the experiences of faith and hope confirmed, a human being in relationship with God and with others. Thus the others give me also something from themselves, a gift that further inspires my gratitude and generosity. And yet, love, like faith and hope, stands outside of causal relationships. It is an extra quality, a presence or, to use the classical theological language, a virtue. Other things flow from this fact.

Abraham loved the Lord and therefore he set out on his many journeys. Most of the time he withstood the tests, the situations where his love was overwhelmed by fear. Nevertheless, the Scripture writers, in witnessing to his love, do not neglect the moments of weakness. His struggles, even his falls and risings, belong to the presentation of Abraham as an example. The writers take us on a journey with Abraham, till finally he has enough love, faith, and hope not to deny the Lord his son Isaac. Thus the Abram who set out to a promised land is not infinitely distant to us. When hunger comes, he descends to Egypt. When he is afraid the Egyptians will kill him to get his beautiful wife, he pretends that she is his sister. Abram is in a hurry to fulfill the promise and fathers a child with the slave girl, Hagar. Rising from falls teaches him faithfulness and the confrontation with the fruits of his egoism teaches him love.[32]

Love in the Old Testament comes as the imperative of a relationship that is holistic, connecting physical and spiritual relationships and including intimacy and social support.[33] The same is true of the relationship between a man and a woman, parents and children, and friends, too.[34] Love even appears as a claim that goes beyond all natural relations. The imperative to love my neighbor as myself (Lev 19:18) applies to the stranger who stays in the land as a guest (Lev 19:34). Human love ought to

---

32. Compare Gen 12:10–20, 16:1–16, and Gen 22.

33. In Hebrew, besides *ahabah* (love), we find used, less commonly, *hesed* (manifesting gracious love), *hen* (grace), *raham* (true loving, mercy), *chalet* (forgiving love) and *'emeth* (faithfulness).

34. See Gen 22:2; 24:67; 29:18; 37:3; 1 Sam 20:17, Song 1:3.7; 3:5; 5:8; 8:6–7.

be an image of God's love. We read of God's love for his people regardless of whether they deserve it or not.[35] God tries again and again to inspire the desire for mutuality in love, and gives this mutuality a permanent expression in the covenant with Israel, where both God and the people are on the giving as well as the receiving side. They have claims on each other.[36] Belonging to the Lord even has its physical sign: circumcision.[37]

Loving the Lord is manifested in loving certain values that are personified in the Old Testament. It is possible to love justice, wisdom, art, good, truth, peace, the name, the law, the commandments, witness, or salvation.[38] However, love can take on perverted forms as well. It is possible to love wealth, slumber, vanity, money, false prophecy, or even death.[39] This does not mean, though, that there is a polarity of two loves only: one right, the other wrong. There is a plurality of right and wrong loves, and moreover, it is not always crystal clear at the beginning, or in the process, which love is right, and what is a perversion of love. Both the Old and the New Testaments recognize this plurality, as well as the fact that our judgment of what seems right and what seems wrong can be easily misleading if we apply too harshly our legal minds to the untidy web of life.

Despite this, in the history of Christian theology there has been a tendency to reduce especially the New Testament accounts of love to one form of love only, *agape*.[40] This covers the love of the Father for the Son,[41] of God for God's people,[42] of God's people for God and Christ[43] and it radicalizes the commandment of love that now, besides strangers, also

---

35. See Deut 23:5; Hos 3:1.

36. See the prayer, which has perhaps a similar place in Judaism as the Our Father in Christianity, *Shema Yisrael*, in Deut 6:4–9.

37. Gen 17:10–14.

38. See Pss 11:7; 33:5; 37:28; 45:8; 70:5; 119:97.127.132; 146:8; Prov 12:1; 29:3; Amos 5:15; Mic 3:21; Zech 8:19.

39. See Ps 4:3; Prov 8:36; Eccl 5:10; Isa 56:10; Jer 5:31.

40. Paul Tillich claims that in our modern languages the plural expression of love has disappeared. In Greek, there was *epithymia* (vital longing), *philia* (friendly love based on personal relation), *eros* (creative, uplifting love aiming towards good, truth, and beauty), *agape* (the selfless, giving love). See Tillich, *Perspectives*, 200. A good popular attempt to rehabilitate this plurality is in Lewis, *Four Loves*.

41. See John 3:35; 5:20.

42. See John 3:16; 14:23; 16:27; Heb 12:6.

43. See John 21:15–16; Rom 8:28; 1 Cor 8:3; 1 John 2:19–21.

includes enemies.[44] As such it will be a continuous reminder that this type of self-giving love is not a romantic sentiment, but the "fruit of the Spirit." (Gal 5:22) But it does not lack mutuality. It is not a love that does not want response in love. Furthermore, it does not push away other genuine forms of love, as can be seen when we read that God in us teaches us to love.[45]

Having said all this, however, if love is reduced solely to a sacrificially interpreted *agape*, it is not only unfaithful to the multiple understandings of love in the scriptural texts, but it very easily becomes its own parody. It can produce a sentimental pity that, under the mask of meekness, lowers a person to the position of helplessness and rejects positive human values, such as friendship, sexuality, art, science, or seeking justice in this world. In this sense we can agree with Tillich, when he says that Nietzsche[46] rightly criticized this type of "Christian" love that claims to be unselfish, apparently wanting to sacrifice itself for another. In reality, it puts others in the position of weaklings needing protection. "This is a love of the weak man for the other who once lived from his strength, and it is a form of love which exploits the other. This kind of self-surrender has the unconscious desire for exploitation."[47] In a theology that wants to be a critical reflection of love, we have to bear in mind this shadow in the Christian understanding of love. This sentimental romantic caricature is widespread.

In the New Testament, the still present plurality of love prevents this ideological reduction. Love can be found there in its non-preferential as well as preferential forms. Jesus loves his friends, Martha, Mary, and Lazarus (John 11:3–5); he has a beloved disciple (John 19:26); the Apostle Paul speaks about love between husband and wife (Eph 5:25–33). As in the Old Testament, there are also many perverted forms of love, stemming from a fear of giving, as if giving means losing and destabilizing one's life (Matt 10:37). There is a distorted self-love that leads to "love of the seats of honor" (Luke 11:43) or to "love of mammon" (Luke 16:13).

Taking concepts of love as the sole traces of the experience would have another disadvantage: it would exclude those instances where love is at the centre of what is happening, even if the verbal identification is missing. Nevertheless, the hesitant commentary on the voluntary self-

---

44. See Matt 5:43–48; Luke 6:27.28.32–36.

45. Rom 5:5; 2 Cor 5:14; 1 Thess 3:12; 1 John 2:5; 4:8.16; 5:3.

46. See, e.g., Nietzsche, *Thus spake Zarathustra*.

47. Tillich, *Perspectives*, 200.

giving, on the longing for acceptance and for a loving response, on the sharing beyond utilitarian motives, is closer to how we understand love today than general statements without any particular action. For example, when John the Evangelist speaks of how Jesus washed his disciples' feet, he does not use the word *agape* except in the introductory note that Jesus "loved his own who were in the world, he loved them to the end." (13:1). Similarly, when we read about the Last Supper, Jesus' love for the disciples and for the world he came to save is what grounds the narrative, yet Jesus, giving himself for others, does not speak of love, but enacts it.[48] Jesus' voluntary readiness and his desire to share with others what he is and what he has presents an interpretive key to the passion events and to meeting the Risen One raised by the Father's love back to life.

Theology as a critical reflection of love cannot settle either for the worship of love as a concept, or for the promotion of love as a uniform behavior that more or less aggressively removes the "otherness" from the other, divine or human. We can comprehend love only when we see those who love so much that sharing of what they are and what they have makes others better people, cultivates their behavior, gives them a chance to overcome their selfishness, provokes the desire for justice; or when we see the absence of these qualities and realize a need for love in situations where it is absent. In both cases, it is necessary to avoid sentiment and to combine emotional experience with other theologically relevant themes such as discipleship, spiritual life, and the striving for justice.

Theology as a triple critical reflection seeks, deciphers, and puts together traces of God in the transfiguration of human ways of being. Such theology has a vital interest in the experience of authentic manifestations of faith, hope, and love. It seeks that which gives roots to people and helps them to be open towards the future and the gift, the possibility of sharing what we are and what we have. Those who engage in theology must in some way learn to speak out of faith to faith, out of hope to hope, out of love to love, and, as Athanasius emphasized, those who want to understand the holy writers of the Scriptures must purify their lives in advance to be united with them. Then they will be ready to understand what God reveals and participate in what they understand.[49]

---

48. See Matt 26:26–29; Mark 14:22–25; Luke 22:14–20.
49. See Athanasius, *DeIncarn* IX.57.

THEOLOGY AS A SCIENCE AND ITS OBJECTIVES

When we speak about theology as a science, we have to keep in mind its double foundation. As a science, theology is answerable to demands for clarity, historical and conceptual accuracy, interpretative and systematic coherence, just as other sciences are. But at the same time theology, as a triple reflection of the experiences of faith, hope, and love, has to seek adequacy with regard to its subject. As such it remains answerable to the inner rules of faith, hope, and love, which include coherence and fragility, understanding and non-understanding, light and darkness.

The tension and fertility of the relations between science, on the one hand, and faith, hope, and love on the other, has been recognized in theology since the earliest days of Christianity. The Apostolic Fathers (Clement of Rome, Ignatius, Polycarp, Hermas, the authors of the *Didache*) struggled to grasp accurately the relation between Christianity and Judaism. The first Apologists (Quadratus, Aristides, Justin Martyr, Athenagoras) strove to make Christianity intelligible for a philosophically-oriented Hellenic culture. The anti-Gnostic theologians (Tertullian, Clement of Alexandria, Irenaeus of Lyon, Hippolytus) were responsible for the theological method that organized formulas of faith on the basis of interpretation of the tradition. Origen laid the basis for the scientific exegesis of Scripture and elaborated the first systematic theory of religious knowledge.

Thus the early Christian theologians demonstrated that a scientific approach to the Christian community's experience of faith, orientation to hope, and practice of love is possible. This approach, similarly to the manifestations of faith, hope, and love, was subject to changes in the surrounding context. Both the symbolic language that ordered the experience and the methods of scientific investigation underwent development, as did the church and the world in which the church lived, as it moved from being a persecuted minority to a bearer of the official religion, culture, and power, and then through the Enlightenment to secularization, and to today's post-Christian revival in religiosity. Theology as a science became a collective term for a number of different schools and approaches. Here, we will not concentrate on giving a complete chronology of these, or even of the various types. Rather, using some representative examples, we will try to answer questions about the scientific principle of theology and the basic methods it uses today.

The Nature of Science in Theology

The Enlightenment and the branches of science that have since undergone a massive development put this question to theologians rather strongly. Such phenomena as space research, investigations into the smallest particles of matter, the use of new knowledge in technology and medicine, all these seem to serve as the beginnings of the realization of Descartes' dream of the human master who knows all the laws of nature and could thus rule over nature.[50] Science has been used as a tool in this process. That does not mean that many scientists were not religious people too, but they did not make links between their faith and their science. Often, they considered a rational reflection of their faith to be something additional, or even dangerous.[51]

Theology is not a science in terms of the natural sciences. This does not mean, however, that it is not a science. Its methods are not aimed towards the subjugation of nature or of people, but towards the understanding of nature, people, and God. Its scientific approach lies in its adequacy: strictly speaking in a double adequacy—with regard to its subject and its audience. If we previously defined theology to be a critical reflection of attitudes and experiences of faith, hope, and love, this means the scientific form of these reflections stands and falls with the approach to the field it investigates.

In other words, theology can hardly be done by a person who has no experience with the anchoring provided by faith, with the freedom opened up by hope, and with receiving what is unmerited, and with the giving, out of love, of what one is and from what one has to God and to neighbor. Without such experiences people will always have at their disposal only material, such as texts, excavations, architecture, statues, paintings, or pieces of music. They will be learning to understand from the outside, without actually having the key to the inside of theology. Perhaps they can become religious studies scholars, but not easily theologians.

The other adequacy concerns communication with the audience to which theology as a science turns, whether it is an academic or church

---

50. See Descartes, *Discourse on Method*, VI.2.

51. As an example we can mention Pascal (1623–1662), whose system separated the scientific field and the realm of faith. He used rationality in arithmetic and in physics, and defended religion against it. He is the author of the well-known statement: "The God of Abraham, Isaac and Jacob is not the God of the philosophers and scientists." *Penseés*, 309.

audience, or society as a whole.[52] Theology is not an esoteric science, an impression one might gain from walking through our bookshops. Its scientific approach consists in its ability to interpret and communicate God's word and the acts testified in the Scriptures faithfully in different generations and different social and cultural settings, taking on board insights from other sciences with which theology shares common interests.

Three Classical Approaches

In the history of Western theology three conceptions of theology as a science have played a prominently influential role. There is Augustine's existential approach, showing the relationship between knowledge and wisdom. Then we have Thomas's dialectic approach, adopting Aristotelian teaching on knowledge and applying it in terms of scholastic method. Thirdly there is Schleiermacher's historical approach. This perceives Christianity as an empirically given fact in human history and tries to describe the rules that have determined Christianity and the symbolic interpretation used to express the knowledge of God.

AUGUSTINE'S EXISTENTIAL APPROACH

Augustine's existential approach to theology shows the connections of faith, knowledge, and action. It reflects the experience of his conversion and a gradual interpretation of the experience, something that Augustine perceived as his lifetime duty. This developing and changing interpretation of faith lies at the roots of what Augustine sees as adequacy for the subject of theology, even if he uses a different terminology. We need not be confused by the fact that Augustine did not call himself a theologian because theologians, according to him, were those, such as Varro or Porphyrius, who dealt with polytheistic religious systems. He regarded himself as a philosopher, that is, a man seeking and "loving wisdom."[53] Secondly, for him, the understanding of faith was not connected to science (*scientia*) but to wisdom (*sapientia*). *things of this WORLD*

Scientia deals with temporal things. It helps us to understand the world and to find the right direction for our acting in the world. *Scientia* grants us knowledge on the basis of observation, in which our rational

Science or Knowledge

52. See Tracy, *The Analogical Imagination*, 5–6, 31.

53. See Augustine, *DeCiv* VIII:8. Augustine, glossing Plato, says that he never doubted that to philosophize means to love God.

faculties are used.[54] With their help we arrive at instances of what to avoid and what to follow. We could say that with regards to theology Augustine's *scientia* gives us tools to investigate the practical, moral, and social dimensions of faith, hope, and love. Although Augustine puts rational reflection in second place, it still plays an indispensable role and protects faith, hope, and love against escape to otherworldliness. Augustine's knowledge, *scientia*, comes from three sources: (i) experiences; (ii) authorities; (iii) signs. Thus we move from what can be grasped by the senses to what is hidden to the senses, from immanence to transcendence. According to Augustine, the whole of creation bears traces of the Trinity, and thus makes such a movement in knowing possible. The word, however, is seen as the most important sign. It leads to the fear of God, necessary for recognizing God's will, to humility without which there is no real devotion, to diligence in loving God and one's neighbor, in which mercy and justice meet, to the purification of heart, and to the wisdom of contemplation. Contemplation, finally, leads to the understanding of eternal things. "And what is there in eternal things more excellent than God, of whom alone the nature is unchangeable?", Augustine writes.

Sapientia, then, is concerned with worshipping and loving God: "And what is the worship of Him except the love of Him, by which we now desire to see Him, and we believe and hope that we shall see Him?"[55] For us, it presents the spiritual, mystic concept of faith, hope, and love, and will protect Christianity from being reduced to a social phenomenon. Wisdom in Augustine stands and falls with grace, an initiative from God's side. God is both giver of faith and of the inner understanding of the God in whom we believe. Wisdom entails understanding God, God's salvation, and bearing witness to it all continuously.[56]

Despite the fact that in Augustine's theology wisdom (*sapientia*) stands above science or knowledge (*scientia*), there is no division between the two, but rather a relationship of interdependence. This means not only that we move beyond the knowledge of temporary things to their goal, but also that knowing temporary things gives us a language to speak about eternal things. After having contemplated the mystery of God, if

---

54. See Augustine's distinction between *ratio* (natural reason, Spirit's gift oriented to temporary things) and *intellectus* (reason enlightened by the Spirit, given to observe eternal things). *DeTrin* XII:14.25.

55. Augustine, *DeTrin* XII:14.22.

56. See Augustine, *Conf* I:i.

we want to communicate the insights coming from this contemplation, which indeed is our duty, we have no other means than human words to witness to this mystery of God's otherness and closeness.

We can rightly criticize Augustine for the world/God, physical/ spiritual dualism that has caused much harm in Christian theology and practice down the centuries. Yet, in his emphasis on a lived human experience, this dualism is at least partly transcended. The more holistic understanding also flows through the experience to the outlines of his theological method, which in today's terminology we can call an existential one. In this method *scientia* presents a practical, moral, and social understanding of Christianity, originating in experience and authority (a reliable person's testified experience) and signs (uncovering the invisible through the visible). Thus orthopraxis prepares the way for orthodoxy. Then orthodoxy becomes a celebration of God through a person's practical life. Contemplation, which should be at the heart of orthodoxy, needs however a continuous catharsis and seeking of justice.

Aquinas's Dialectical Approach

While it is possible to say that Augustine's method with its focus on contemplation is largely indebted to the Platonic tradition of thought, with Thomas Aquinas we re-enter Aristotelian intellectual territory. The basic feature of Aquinas's approach is a willingness to discuss things. Following the examples of both Plato and Aristotle, Aquinas sees dialogue not only as a way to communicate information, but also as a way to seek the truth and to struggle for as precise a formulation of it as possible. His dialectic conception of theology finds its expression in the scholastic disputation. It is not based on an authoritatively given text, but on a collection of questions referring to premises that have provoked doubts. Each argument has the right to be heard, according to Aquinas, not because any one would be seen as *a priori* right, but because he is convinced that the truth has an inner strength to reveal itself. In this sense Aquinas is an intellectual optimist for whom faith and reason are related at their roots. Because of God's grace, given at creation, the truth can be known.[57] Moreover, we can demonstrate

57. Aquinas holds that "for the knowledge of any truth whatsoever man needs Divine help, that the intellect may be moved by God to its act." To know the truth is to use "intellectual light" that is not added to the natural light, "but only in some that surpass his natural knowledge . . . We always need God's help for every thought, inasmuch as He moves the understanding to act; for actually to understand anything is to think, as is clear

how we have arrived at the truth, and why what we have arrived at is the truth, although never the whole truth on any subject and least of all on God. In our life here and now the dialogue is never finished.

Like Augustine, Aquinas is interested in all that can be investigated and known. He is convinced that an empirical study of nature as well as rigorous rational reflection contribute to natural knowledge in which the works of God the creator are examined. Although these forms of knowledge have to follow their own principles and methods, they are relevant for theology. Likewise, theology has something to offer to them. Using its own methods, theology teaches them about the primary principles and causes they presuppose, and about the ultimate fulfillment of all things.

Aquinas's argument is structured according to the questions he wants to examine. Each question is divided into several articles, according to the specific issues involved. His consideration begins with the voices of the adversaries. Aquinas tries to introduce their positions as faithfully as possible, respecting their argument and their personal qualities. For example, in the *Summa Theologiae* he asks whether theology, in his terminology sacred doctrine, is a science. First, objections (theses) are raised: firstly, that it does not stem from generally acceptable principles but from the articles of faith; secondly, that a science does not deal with individual things, whilst theology discusses, e.g., the Acts of Abraham, Isaac, Jacob, and others. Thomas puts an antithesis against the thesis in which he quotes Augustine's treatise *On the Trinity*: "'to this science alone belongs that whereby saving faith is begotten, nourished, protected and strengthened.' But this can be said of no science except sacred doctrine. Therefore sacred doctrine is a science."[58]

Aquinas's own synthesis follows, after having cited some other figures of authority. He explains that there are two types of science, the first originating from the principle of common sense, such as arithmetic or geometry, the other from the principle of "a higher science." Here he means such things as perspective that builds on the base of geometry, or music that develops the principles of arithmetic. Theology is a science of the latter type because it builds on the base created by "God and the blessed."

---

from Augustine (*DeTrin.* XIV:7)." *Summa Theologiae* I.2.cix.

58. Thomas Aquinas, *Summa Theologiae* I.1.ii. He quotes Augustine, *DeTrin* XIV:1. Aquinas's argumentation is more precise than the modern identification of science with the natural sciences which we find in prestigious textbooks, dictionaries and encyclopedias, even nowadays. See *The New Encyclopaedia Britannica*, vol.27, 1991: 32.

So, theology as a "sacred science is established on principles revealed by God."[59] In the end, Aquinas responds to the objections that he mentioned at the beginning. To the first, he says that apart from the principles that are clear in themselves, sciences can also build on principles that are taken from other sciences and a higher science, such as theology, can build on them. To the latter objection, he responds that details are not the main subject of theology. They provide figurative examples for the inspiration of the faithful, or document the authority of those through whom divine revelation came.

Aquinas adopts Aristotle's conception of science, namely that science investigates the causes of the effects. Aquinas then defines theology as a science of faith. Thus, theology is a science as long as those who engage in it do so with faith. According to Aquinas, anyone who is not at home in faith, but defends what is of faith in another way than through faith, holds conclusions without being able to demonstrate how they reached them. It is apparent that such a person has no scientific knowledge in this area, but only holds an opinion. Theology as a science unites within itself research as well as practical orientation, and with that a whole variety of approaches, even if theology is one, inspired by God, based on revelation.[60]

In his defense of plurality, Aquinas goes beyond Augustine's Platonism. He does not, however, reject Augustine. Rather, he attempts a synthesis between Aristotle and Augustine. So it is that he claims that theology is not only a science, but also wisdom, and even the highest wisdom, because it organizes things according to their causes and orders them with regard to God, the highest uncaused cause that causes all true being.[61] In his "classification of sciences" Aquinas proceeds from those that are based on sense data to those founded in rational knowledge, and finally to theology rooted in revealed knowledge, and thus the highest ranking. The lower sciences, which rely on natural knowledge (whether of empirical or rational orientation) are not abrogated by theology, but perfected by it.[62] Although they are given the status of servants,[63] Aquinas

Abrogate - to Abolish by formal or official means; Repeal [handwritten annotation]

59. Aquinas, *Summa Theologiae* I.1.ii.

60. Ibid., I.1.iii.iv.

61. God does not cause evil, because evil is not a true being but a parasite on being, according to Aquinas.

62. See Aquinas, *Summa Theologiae* I.1.vi; I.2.iii, I.1.vi.viii.

63. "Other sciences are called the handmaidens of this one: "Wisdom sent her maids to invite to the tower" (Prov. 9:3)." Aquinas, *Summa Theologiae* I.1.v. In the symbolic

defends their freedom to do research and to use their own competence, which is to be respected by theology. Theology holds a privileged place not because theologians understand everything else, but because theology speaks of God and believes that God is present in its words, above all in the Scriptures.[64] Further, the goal of theology, according to Aquinas, is nothing less than "eternal bliss, to which as to an ultimate end the purposes of every practical science are directed. Hence it is clear that from every standpoint, it is nobler than other sciences."[65]

Aquinas's concept of theology as a science is clear and methodologically coherent. It links the sphere of natural reason and supernatural faith in such a way that each of them has its place and competence. Thus it provides a good basis not only for tolerance towards different approaches, but for an interest in them, for the art of dialogue. Aquinas, despite his inherent dualism, also has a more positive relationship to the world and the body than Augustine. On the other hand, Aquinas's theology is more hierarchically organized,[66] and his model of the church stems from this fact. He does not advocate a closed system in theology, but compared to Augustine, the truth of faith at which Aquinas arrives is perceived as less provisional, despite its plurality and despite his emphasis on ongoing dialogue. This has to do with the fact that he takes much less notice both of the context as a theme of his reflection and of the fact that the truth of faith develops as we arrive at more precise formulations while encountering new challenges in different historical or cultural situations.[67] Paradoxically, however, despite his low appreciation for the contextuality of theology, his own position echoes a struggle with Augustinianism that was predominant in the Paris Faculty of Arts of his time. Aquinas distances himself from the reduction of theology to pious images of spiritual things and shows the necessity of rational argument.[68] In subsequent

------

language of his time, Aquinas's expression *ancilla* (a maid) referred to the necessity to get help, to be served. See Davies, *Aquinas*, 181.

64. See Aquinas, *Summa Theologiae* I.1.x.

65. Ibid., I.1.v.

66. Here there is a discernable influence from Dionysius the Areopagite, from whose *The Celestial Hierarchy* and *The Ecclesial Hierarchy* Thomas quotes. In his time these writings carried great authority.

67. See, e.g., Aquinas's evaluation of the Inquisition in *Summa Theologiae* II.2. 11.iii; *De secreto* 3.

68. See Kerr, *After Aquinas*, 14.

cultural-historical conditions, his distinction between the lower and the higher realms of knowledge would, through his followers, become as problematic as was the Augustinian fundamentalism of his time.

The temptations to change Aquinas's distinction into a division between lower and higher reality, to abandon the dialectic space, and to define the indefinable accompanied Thomist and Neo-Thomist theologians of future generations.[69] When they gave in to these temptations, new problems arose. Natural reason was automatically considered to lead a person to believe in the existence of God, and any absence of this belief would be interpreted as an intellectual and moral defect.[70] Further, God's unchangeability was linked to the unchangeability of language forms conveying this knowledge and the unchangeability of the institution guarding it. Ultimately, the "unchangeable" was extracted and put above the changing history, society, culture, and even above the life of individuals as they became aware of the value of their subjectivity and came to reject a religion that seemed to deprive them of such value. However, just as Augustine cannot be held responsible for the Augustinianism of Aquinas's time, Aquinas cannot be held responsible for all the Thomist and Neo-Thomist theologians who quote him. Despite them, Aquinas and his concept of theology as science remained inspirational for subsequent generations and, interestingly enough, it greatly contributed to the Roman Catholic theological renewal that peaked at the Second Vatican Council.

SCHLEIERMACHER'S HISTORICAL APPROACH

In his introduction to the *Brief Outline on the Study of Theology* Friedrich Schleiermacher starts with historical and ecclesial plurality, declaring that various parts of Christian theology come together because of their connection with Christianity. Together they form theology, which he defines as a "*positive science*, the parts of which are connected into a whole, only by their *common relation* to a *determinate mode of faith*, that is, a deter-

---

69. Thomism has held a prominent position in Catholic theology and especially the period between 1850 and 1960 was rife with syntheses of the natural and revealed theology that do indeed reduce Thomas's method to a rationalistic-deistic system, easily taught in seminaries and theological faculties because it provided exact answers to particular questions and annihilated the space for the dialectics of fact that would make these answers relative. See Balthasar, "On the Tasks of Catholic Philosophy," 173; de Lubac, *Surnaturel*, 435–36; *Letters of Etienne Gilson to Henri de Lubac*, 23–24.

70. See the Encyclical of Leo XIII, *Aeterni Patris* (1879), and the Dogmatic Constitution of the First Vatican Council, *Dei Filius* (1870).

minate form of the God-consciousness."[71] Theology is a "positive" science because it does not have a primarily empirical, speculative. or theoretical character, but refers directly to historical experience in terms of given social interactions and serves a definite practical function, namely, to present in a concrete way the God who can be found in the historical experience of Christians. This practical purpose is to aid effective leadership in the Christian church. Theology is a "science" because, with the help of rational and systematic methods, it organizes a certain type of knowledge that can bear fruit in experience.

Theology has its own character, its own subject, and its own language. It is not a part of general science, because theology refers to God's action, and that exceeds the boundaries of natural knowledge common for general science. It is not a special science about religion, either, for the religious consciousness penetrates everything. It is present in every human being and, furthermore, it cannot be limited to one realm of life that would be called religion. Schleiermacher also distances himself from the concept of "natural religion," which he sees as unsatisfactory because opting for it would mean disqualifying any historically testified religious experience that failed to fit to this category. According to Schleiermacher, the science called theology takes place within the scope of all human ways of knowing, just as religion draws on the whole of human experience.[72]

Schleiermacher admits that every theologian must choose a scheme for their work. At the same time, though, he offers his own scheme in which he divides theology into three main disciplines: philosophical, historical, and practical theology. A theologian's freedom of choice does not, however, include whether he or she would care or not for the past, the present, and the future life of the Christian church.[73] All theology should relate its scientific rigor to addressing the actual needs of the church, which in the end is one of the determinants of an advancement of

---

71. Schleiermacher, *Brief Outline*, §1. T.N. Tice says that, in the first edition of the work (1850), Schleiermacher uses the expression "religion" instead of "faith". Later it came to seem insufficient, so he speaks either of faith or piety. This is reflected in the John Knox Press edition (1970) of the *Brief Outline*, 19, note 1. I quote from this edition.

72. Tice, "Editor's General Introduction," in Schleiermacher, *Brief Outline*, 15.

73. Schleiermacher always emphasizes the particular church in which one takes part. He is not that interested in denominational differences, but stresses the generic similarities while leaving space for the differences. See, e.g., Schleiermacher, *Brief Outline*, §3 or § 23.

theology as a whole.[74] For Schleiermacher, the church is the audience that obliges theologians to the greatest responsibility and gives their science meaning and direction. However, a focus on the church audience does not turn theology into doctrine. It remains first of all a historical reflection of devotion.[75]

Schleiermacher's concept of theology as a science is not universal. In its favor we can say that it concentrates on a critical, historically-based reflection of the human experience of God in the world in which given people live. On the other hand, this reflection does not engage in a dialogue or even argument with other concepts. His understanding of theology does not defend faith, or try to convert a non-believer. It seems that Schleiermacher would consider this inappropriate for theology, which for him should be content with an analysis of historically observable instances of faith (i.e. faith that is already present and the way it is present), and with conclusions aimed at improving the life of the church. Here Schleiermacher is consistent in rejecting a speculative approach to theology. He does not even address what in Augustine and especially in Aquinas would be the fundamental question: "What is true?" Instead he searches for "what is real," that is, what has some real representation. In this sense we can see in Schleiermacher a forerunner of phenomenology, with its advantages and its weaknesses. This is perhaps clearest in his stress on experience and on the fact that we do not arrive at a deeper understanding of our experience by rational abstraction but by diligent observation.

All the three concepts of theology as a science that we have investigated are rooted in divine revelation, granted to people by divine illumination. In a variety of historically, politically, culturally, or even psychologically conditioned situations, the three theologians searched for how all that is human can be integrated into the following of Christ, even if they did not always succeed in their undertaking. They observed

---

74. "*Whether* a man labors with a view to the perfecting of a *particular discipline*, and *what* discipline he selects for this purpose, are matters which are determined chiefly by the peculiar character of the *talent* possessed by the individual, but also, in part, by his views with regard to the prevailing *need* of the Church at the time. The prosperous advancement of Theology in general depends in a great measure upon the satisfaction of this condition." Schleiermacher, *Brief Outline*, §17.

75. Here we can see the apparent influence of the Pietism of Zinzendorf's renewed *Unitas Fratrum*. See chapter 5, 211–13. Tillich criticizes Schleiermacher for not dealing with the question of truth in his presentation of a scientific approach. See Tillich, *Perspectives*, 103.

and interpreted how the Holy Spirit was at work giving gifts to all that was created to the glory of the Father, even if their theology was not always explicitly Trinitarian. In this light, faith and experience belonged together, along with spiritual life and Christian involvement in the world. All these formed a historical-existential unity.

Augustine spoke of the goal of theology in terms of achieving the wisdom that is contemplation of God, and at the same time the God-given pursuit of inner purification and justice. Aquinas saw the goal of theology in eternal blessedness and Schleiermacher in the particular ways our consciousness becomes aware of God in our historical experience and thus inspires us to develop the church. In each case, the scientific character of theology rested on how adequately theology observed reality—including the reality of faith—and how adequately it communicated with its audiences, who were struggling for meaning and for truth in their actions, convictions, and hopes. In the following part I move to consider contemporary methods that help a theology to be fitting for its tasks as defined above.

CONTEMPORARY METHODS

Theologians must search for those methods that will enable them to solve the tasks they encounter. In addition they should try to present their theology as ecumenically oriented and enable Christians from different traditions to draw on their own resources, as well as on resources from other traditions. In doing so they would give them a better understanding of others, as much as of themselves. Theologians need three types of analysis for their work: (i) of the situation we find ourselves in today; (ii) of our experience of God and the symbolic language representations of that experience; (iii) of the tradition which gave us the symbolic language and transformed the experience of the previous generations into an intelligible text, picture, or sound that can be handed down further, allowed to speak, be well or badly interpreted, become a critique of where and who we are. The second and the third type of analysis will be elaborated in the following chapters. But now I am going shortly to consider the first.

An analysis of current European post–modern culture[76] discloses a number of tensions and conflicts. Three of them stand out. The first is

---

76. See, e.g., Lyotard, *The Postmodern Condition*. From an American perspective: Westphal et al., *Modernity and its Discontents*. I have dealt with this subject in more

between the global and the particular. We are more and more aware of the globalization that influences the economic, political, cultural, and religious life of people today. At the same time, there are strong, sometimes good, sometimes fanatic attempts to keep a national, religious, or cultural particularity alongside or against the others. There is also conflict between [2ND] the narrative and the historical. On the one hand, we have learnt that we can better understand a person, a family, a church, or a nation if we listen to their stories. On the other hand, there is skepticism towards stories that are called history. Giving a privileged place to one account of reality seems almost blasphemous today. And yet the emphasis on the story and refusal of history can lead to giving up on any distinction between truth and lie, even if both are recognized as plural in their expression. The third [3RD] conflict is between process and progress. We are aware that the world we live in is permanently changing. This process has become part of who we are. However, it becomes increasingly difficult to discern between what is progress and what is regress in this movement. Again, although in practice we implement many implicit criteria for justification of who we are and what we do, there is a reluctance to reflect on them critically.

With these conflicts in mind, we can now focus on three current methods: the phenomenological, hermeneutic, and epistemological.

The Phenomenological Method

In order to avoid an ungrounded understanding of theology, we can be helped by the feedback of experience. This was emphasized already by Schleiermacher, and it is further developed by the phenomenological method, stressing that we have to take phenomena seriously. Here, I will first concentrate on Husserl's notion of *epoche* and his principle of donation, as they present the cornerstones of this method. After that, I will examine Scheler's analysis of a religious act.

EPOCHE AND DONATION IN HUSSERL

In the article he wrote for *Encyclopedia Britannica* Husserl introduced phenomenology as follows:

> The term 'phenomenology' designates two things: a new kind of descriptive method which made a breakthrough in philosophy at the turn of the century, and an *a priori* science derived from

detail in Dolejšová (Noble), *Accounts of Hope*, 31–47.

it; a science which is intended to supply the basic instrument
(Organon) for a rigorously scientific philosophy and, in its con-
sequent application, to make possible a methodical reform of all
the sciences.[77]

Phenomenology begins with a tautological "principle of non-presup-
position," that is, with a strict exclusion of all statements that cannot be
phenomenologically documented.[78] According to Husserl, a phenomenon
is what appears in our consciousness when we experience something as
something. All that appears to us in one way or another has to be taken
into account. Everything else has to be disregarded at the beginning as
speculation. We do not arrive at understanding by reasoning, but by seeing. We do not even pass understanding on, but rather make others see.
Our speech has to be oriented towards this aim, otherwise it would lose
its meaning.[79] Husserl further elaborates the question of "how" a phenomenon meets the one to whom it appears, and "why" it is possible. The
phenomenon stands at the beginning and is foundational for our knowledge. It is encountered through the intuition. Here we encounter what
Husserl calls the principle of donation. Intuition makes the phenomenon
possible; it becomes phenomenon through the intuition.[80] For him it is
a gift that knowledge is possible, a gift that stands at the beginning, and
not in the middle, of causal relations operating with certainties arrived
at by means of reasoning. Knowledge is possible because the intuition
of phenomena is possible, and there we start. For us, being opens up in
phenomena alone, and each and every phenomenon has to be taken into
consideration, without exception.

Phenomenological method works with the help of *epoche*: in other
words, it has a tautological beginning. It presupposes a non-presupposi-
tion, a putting into brackets, and thus disregarding, of all previous ideas,
feelings, and judgments. However, *epoche* has more than one form. First,
for Husserl, there is the *eidetic epoche*,[81] a reduction of the world and the

tautological—defined in terms of itself

77. Husserl, "Phenomenology."

78. See Husserl, *Logische Untersuchungen,* II, 19.

79. See Marion, "Metaphysics and Phenomenology," 285.

80. Marion shows the resemblance of Husserl's approach to that of Plato, who automatically ascribes being to the idea of good (see *Republic,* VII.509 b9). According to
him, indeed, Husserl extends "being as a given" for all phenomena. See "Metaphysics and
Phenomenology," 287.

81. "In it, every self-enclosed field of possible experience permits *eo ipso* the

"I" to phenomena.[82] This means that we concentrate only on mental images, on what appears to us in some manifestation, to what we encounter and notice, without ambitions to describe the world as it is in itself or for someone else, and without seeking in these images proofs for our identity. The *eidetic epoche* allows description and classification of phenomena. Husserl emphasizes that as such it provides the means of access "to the invariant essential structures of the total sphere of pure mental process."[83]

Then there is the *transcendental epoche*. The phenomenological interpretation is not theoretical but it focuses on an interpretation of what is given. Philosophy does not create meaning but finds it in the world.

> Phenomenological philosophy regards itself in its whole method as a pure outcome of methodical intentions which already animated Greek philosophy from its beginnings; above all, however, [it continues] the still vital intentions which reach, in the two lines of rationalism and empiricism, from Descartes through Kant and German idealism into our confused present day. A pure outcome of methodical intentions means real method which allows the problems to be taken in hand and completed. In the way of true science this path is endless. Accordingly, phenomenology demands that the phenomenologist foreswear the ideal of a philosophic system and yet as a humble worker in community with others, live for a perennial philosophy [*philosophia perennis*].[84]

Husserl is aware of the fact that "'the' world in its varying sense, then its whole mode of being, acquires a dimension of unintelligibility, or rather of questionableness."[85] The *transcendental epoche* also attempts to put into brackets the assumption that the world is an end in itself. Our experience seems to show the contrary, since we can gain the sense and

---

all embracing transition from the factual to the essential form, the *eidos*." Husserl, "Phenomenology," §4.

82. "The universal epoche of the world as it becomes known in consciousness (the "putting it in brackets") shuts out from the phenomenological field the world as it exists for the subject in simple absoluteness; its place, however, is taken by the world as given in *consciousness* (perceived, remembered, judged, thought, valued, etc.)—the world as such, the "world in brackets," or in other words, the world, or rather individual things in the world as absolute, are replaced by the respective meaning of each in *consciousness* [*Bewusstseinssinn*] in its various modes (perceptual meaning, recollected meaning, and so on)." Husserl, "Phenomenology," §3.

83. Ibid., §4.

84. Ibid., §16.

85. Ibid., §7.

validity of the world (and of ourselves) in relation to its transcendence, with the "being-sense of the 'transcendent' relative to consciousness."[86] Jan Patočka stresses this cohesion as necessary for finding meaning. The phenomenological method stands and falls with the relation to the "original", but also to the totality of natural life:

> . . . we can understand science only if we grasp how it grows from the soil of natural life, whereas the natural life can never be fabricated from the world of science. We have to carry out an act of abstaining from all scientific theses if we want to grasp this pre-scientific world; we must not use such theses for the interpretation of natural life, but rather communicate with its own *a priori* givenness. If we really want to grasp this *a priori* givenness of the world, it is not enough to live a naive life in this world, to immerse ourselves in it; the primeval fact of practical life is that because of the trees we do not see the forest and because of the individual elements and their combinations we do not see the *a priori* whole, . . . [for] the world as a whole is anticipated and implied . . . in every perception[87] . . . that . . . allows the meaning . . . and access to real situations and interests of our daily life . . . Reduction, here has quite a clear meaning, it discloses a hidden, implied meaning, a key to understanding of what is known to us by experience and what we have a tendency in our naive non-reflectedness to take as an absolute, independent entity without context in which meaning penetrates all.[88]

SCHELER'S ANALYSIS OF A RELIGIOUS ACT

While Husserl's main interest lay in philosophy and psychology, he expected that the phenomenological method could also be consistently applied in other sciences. Thus, returning to the field of theology, and using as an example Max Scheler, we will study the methodological reform initiated by phenomenology there.

With the help of phenomenological analysis, Scheler investigated what he calls the "religious act." Combining the "principle of donation" (knowledge made possible by the intuition of phenomena) and both types

86. Husserl, "Phenomenology," §7.

87. Henry Duméry conveys this point in the third *henological epoche,* the reduction towards one, which enriches the phenomenological method. See Dupré, *Religious Mystery,* 12.

88. Patočka, "Husserlova fenomenologie," 161–90: 175–76.

of *epoche* led Scheler to the discovery that not only the natural world but also God is directly presented to us, though only through the act of faith, devotion and worship. A believer knows God through immediate, but also through negative and symbolic intuition:[89] "The God of religious consciousness 'is' and lives exclusively in the religious act, not in metaphysical thinking extraneous to religion . . . The God of religion is the God of the saints and the God of the people, not the cerebral god of the 'intellectuals'. The fount of all religious truth is not scientific utterance but *faith* in the words of the *homo religiosus,* the 'holy man'."[90] This application of phenomenology uncovers a believer's relationship to God as to one who is here as meaning before being encountered in an act of faith and worship. Transcendent presence is then seen in immanent experience.

Jacques Dupré comments: "*Because* [in Scheler] that act aims at a transcendent . . . *telos,* it requires a symbolic representation to exist concretely. Religion consecrates objects in space and time, in order, through them, to transcend the spatial and temporal order itself. It draws its symbols from the entire range of the finite: inanimate objects, plants, animals, and humans."[91] Because neither any one of these finite forms, nor all of them together, are able adequately to represent transcendent reality, religion seeks help from the strongest symbol, the word. The word is, in Dupré, a bearer of revelation and a fulfillment of the symbolic system. According to Christianity, even God-the-Word becomes the body. However, Dupré also shows the limits of the phenomenological method. For a believer, the transcendent God is not reducible to a phenomenon, not even a phenomenon endowed with meaning.[92]

Here further weaknesses of the phenomenological method are revealed: it is too radical in rejecting any understanding that comes before experience, even if phenomenology itself is what it refuses—*a priori* principle.[93] Therein lies its paradox. It is optimistic in its relation to intuition and in attaching meaning to things as they are encountered, and it refuses to look at things from the viewpoint of intellectual constructions. On the contrary, it always judges intellectual constructions from the viewpoint

89. See Dupré, *Religious Mystery*, 5.

90. Scheler, *He the Eternal in Man*, 134.

91. Dupré, *Religious Mystery*, 7–8.

92. Cf. Dupré, *Religious Mystery*, 6.10.

93. Cf. Patočka, "Husserlova fenomenologie," 170–71.

→ bAsed upon obseRvAtion

STudy of the obseRvAble

of experience. There is no space for transcendence, anything of which we could know or assume something legitimate outside our experience.

Phenomenology can do harm to theology when it overestimates its ability to pass judgment on "how things are" by stating: "they are how I see them." When it becomes isolated from other methods, phenomenology can lead to subjectivism, which does not allow for any understanding of someone else's viewpoint and which does not make use of mediated experience. Thus it becomes difficult, if not impossible, to take part in the tradition of a shared experience, and, through that, in the bodies that come in to being through the particular tradition; e.g., families, churches, or societies. Nevertheless, in combination with other methods, phenomenology can offer an invaluable service to ecumenical theology because it is in principle anti-ideological: it despises constructions and presses us to take phenomena seriously.

Furthermore, the phenomenological method turns our attention to practice. It shows the relation between what Christians proclaim, what they really think about the traditions they profess, and what experiences they inspire in those who meet them. By its permanent refusal of theoretical answers, it helps to distinguish the "treasure of faith" from the "treasure of prejudices," as it is not satisfied till it discovers what really makes people fully alive. It wants to see it. The emphasis of the phenomenological method holds that a phenomenon can exist without a theory, that intuition alone is enough, while theory cannot rightly exist without a phenomenon.

In this aspect phenomenology needs to be complemented by a much richer understanding of theory than as an intellectual game. It needs an understanding of theory that takes into account both contemplation and rational rigor, as we have seen in Augustine and Aquinas. It also needs an understanding of theory that has tools to work with its own contextual given. In the following pages I will look at two other contemporary methods that are corrective of some of the blind spots of phenomenology, while recognizing its undoubtedly good contribution. These are hermeneutics, which concentrates on the process of understanding and interpretation of the texts, and epistemology, which critically analyses the adequacy or inadequacy of the authorities on which our statements are based.

The Hermeneutical Method

While phenomenology examined the world, and relationships and values within it, as these imprinted themselves on human consciousness, hermeneutics concentrates on the material traces in which meaning, values, and relationships are witnessed to. Here knowledge means understanding and the ability to interpret. Records of human speech, music, painting, architecture are all primary sources of knowledge in hermeneutics. In the case of theology, the material traces include all different forms of texts, excavations, artwork, etc., in which a testimony to Christian faith, hope, and love can be found. However, first I am going to outline the main features of modern philosophical hermeneutics, which, like phenomenology, initiated a methodological reform of other sciences, including theology. I start with an analysis of the relationship between being and understanding in Heidegger, where the division of subject and object, which dominates the Cartesian and Kantian tradition, is overcome. Then I will focus on the process of interpretation in Gadamer and finally, on the concept of tradition in Tracy.

BEING AND UNDERSTANDING IN HEIDEGGER

Martin Heidegger was a pupil of Husserl and his own philosophy is largely indebted to phenomenology, perhaps most of all to its emphasis on the natural world that can be observed and understood from within rather than speculated about as if from outside. He wanted to understand the dynamic existential structure of that world. Here phenomenology became too narrow for him, for in its general ambition to reach to the essence of things it showed itself too similar to metaphysics. He became one of the strongest critics of metaphysics, a mode of thought that has dominated the Western philosophical and theological tradition since the time of Plato and Aristotle. He says that forgetting the ontological difference between being and entities, metaphysics hierarchically classified reality as higher and lower, falsely presuming that it had a key not only to all that is, but to the mystery of being as such.[94] This led to a deformed understanding of the world, and of ourselves in relation to the world. If we postulate being as entity, we can never understand its difference from the things that constitute it.

94. See Heidegger, *Was ist Metaphysik?*

Understanding runs a similar danger of confusion, according to Heidegger. We need to distinguish between understanding and the analysis of understanding. Understanding is not just a form of knowledge. It refers to our ability to live and find our way in the world we have been thrown into. Interpretation presupposes understanding our place in the world. Then because the world always changes, our understanding must change too, and we must be aware of the fact that our interpretation is also always partial and temporary. The fact we understand the world can be recognized, according to Heidegger, by our ability to change ourselves. A change of interpretation is not a manifestation of weakness and inability, but, on the contrary, stands at the centre of the dynamics of understanding as a continuous challenge. Being is according to Heidegger always a being in the world, being thrown into the world (*Dasein*—being-here).[95] It is taken as a given that neither requires nor allows further explanation, similarly to Husserl's principle of donation.

What needs an explanation, however, is a situation when our being is in disharmony with the being of the world. According to Heidegger, our "being-here" can get lost on the way, can get confused, but at the same time has the ability to find itself and its possibilities.[96] Heidegger stresses that it is possible because our "being-here" constitutively includes understanding, with its agenda-making character. This means that our being-here *is* what it is becoming or what it is not becoming. In our self-understanding we can say: "Become who you are!"[97] If we understand theology as a form of interpretation and at the same time ask questions about its truthfulness, we need to take into account the fact that understanding does not concern only particular things, but the entire world in its totality and our being thrown into it. Thus we are not dealing with pure facts, but with openness to possibilities that our being in the world brings into life. Heidegger points to a circular relationship: Every exposition that is to lead into understanding must already have some understanding of what is being interpreted.[98]

---

95. See Heidegger, *Being and Time*, §31.
96. Ibid., §31, 144.
97. Ibid., §31, 145.
98. Ibid., §32, 152–53.

The Process of Interpretation in Gadamer

Heidegger's insights into understanding and interpretation were further elaborated by Hans-Georg Gadamer. He demonstrates how meaning reveals its continuity through our encounters with texts. Thus, while Heidegger was primarily concerned with understanding our being in the world, Gadamer focuses on speech. According to him, speech is constitutive for the whole of reality. In other words, the way we speak, write, or otherwise communicate forms the beliefs, values, and truths that are shared in the culture and community in which we live. Gadamer writes that our relationship to the world happens through understanding, and is, from beginning to end, speech-based.

He combines Platonic and Aristotelian insights, intuition and conceptual clarification, the need to wonder and, when we meet something strange, provoking, disorienting, to go beyond organizing things into pre-determined categories, and the need to appropriate new insights and relate them to the rest of our life-context. In this process understanding arises as participation in the process of tradition, a process of giving and receiving, in which mediation between the past and the present is permanently required.[99] This does not mean that tradition ought to swallow up the present, or that the present ought to swallow up the tradition. The process of mediating between the two tries to take seriously both "horizons" and even the time between them. The journey from the author's or text's horizon to the reader's horizon leads through seeking the common features, and through the art of interpretation. Gadamer speaks of merging horizons,[100] when interpretation is successful.

Gadamer uses the example of reading classics, for him represented mainly by Greek literature and philosophy. When we experience catharsis in our own lives through reading Homer, the classics have penetrated our horizon with their keys to meaning. They have persuaded us with their authority, which has been exercised on generations and generations before us as well. In this sense, together with others we have participated in the process in which the classics make claims on people of all times—and people of each different time take these claims seriously in their own different ways. The classics are thus also an excellent example of the fact that

---

99. Gadamer, *Truth and Method,* 290.
100. Ibid., 369–79.

understanding has its history. The history of understanding forms in us a "pre-understanding," necessary for participating in the tradition.

Jürgen Habermas, more interested in praxis, criticized Gadamer's hermeneutics for its uncritical confirmation of tradition. He insisted that tradition also involves the sustaining of unjust relationships and the justification of unjust actions. According to him, Gadamer was too charmed by the aesthetic beauty of tradition without sufficient recognition of the social and political implication of its claims. Tradition is not innocent. It needs to be subjected to an ideology critique, according to Habermas.[101] For Gadamer, however, this critique as well as the orientation towards praxis is already present in the classical texts.[102]

The disclosive power of speech and of speech recorded in the texts has become inspirational for a number of Christian theologians, who have applied what Gadamer said about the Greek classics to Christian texts.[103] They have often found even more useful Paul Ricoeur's development of Gadamer's focus on speech, language, and text. Ricoeur's insistence on the narrative and metaphorical structure of speech opened a new space for working with the open but focused plurality of meaning in Christian symbols of faith, in the scriptural and liturgical texts, in doctrine and canonical texts, as well as in the tradition of theological interpretation. Gadamer's and Ricoeur's approaches gave new possibilities for a synoptic understanding of what previously seemed antithetical meaning. In ecumenical theology hermeneutics allows the validity of different traditions besides each other. This does not mean that any tradition or any interpretation of tradition is good, but that each has the right to be heard and that meaning emerges as plural, through a multitude of symbolic mediations.

THE ROLE OF TRADITION IN TRACY

David Tracy is one of the most prominent of the theologians who have made use of the hermeneutical method. He explains it in terms of the correlation of the Christian proclamation and a human situation.

---

101. See Habermas, *Hermeneutik und Ideologiekritik.*

102. See Gadamer, "Hermeneutics and Social Science," 308–19.

103. "Indeed, the same kind of rhetorical persuasiveness which Gadamer wishes to accomplish by means of his retrieval of classical Greek texts is what these systematic theologians effectively argue for by means of their hermeneutical and literary-critical of classical Christian texts." Tracy, *The Analogical Imagination*, 74.

According to Tracy, the main task of a theologian is "the reinter-pretation of the tradition for the present situation."[104] We can, however, faithfully interpret only what we participate in, and to participate in any Christian tradition means to be a practicing Christian. Without that it is not possible to interpret theology in an appropriate way. For Tracy, theology is primarily hermeneutics, but at the same time he emphasizes two things that reach beyond the boundaries of the hermeneutical meth-od: truth and practice. Tracy is aware that the "truth" can be handled very recklessly. It can be turned into an authoritarian, dogmatic, and fundamentalist ideology, and as such parasitic on the truth that theol-ogy operates with.[105] Tracy is, therefore, suspicious of all tendencies to create universalist conceptions. He writes: "All theological claims to the formulation of universal truth must be put under the strictly theological hermeneutics of suspicion of 'idolatry.'"[106]

A theologian's task must be largely hermeneutic. At the same time that does not mean he or she can afford not to deal with the truth. "'Truth' in systematics . . . ordinarily functions in some form of 'disclosure' model implied in all good interpretations."[107] Tracy thus develops Gadamer's position with the help of Habermas's critique, as he conditions the claims of the classics on our present time by their truth-disclosure. In addition he offers criteria for the adequate detection of truth: "If we desire to de-termine criteria of adequacy for meaning and truth, therefore, we must understand the foundational role of praxis in relationship to theory. We must, by theory's own internal imperatives, pay constant attention to the authenticity or inauthenticity (at the limit, the radical alienation) of the truth-teller's subjectivity."[108]

Tracy's hermeneutics offers to ecumenical theology not only ways of working simultaneously with different traditions, but also critical tools stemming from skepticism towards universalist approaches and the demands of unity between the content of the truth-teller's message and his or her existential situation. Tracy's method helps to articulate why any ecumenical "meta-theology" would be harmful, and what would be

104. Tracy, *The Analogical Imagination*, 64.
105. Ibid., 65.
106. Ibid., 66.
107. Ibid., 68.
108. Ibid., 69.

lost in doing away with the particular differences. At the same time, the differences are not sanctified. They include distinctions between what is authentic and what is inauthentic in each and every tradition, as well as in dialogues trying to bridge the traditions. Faithful interpretation of tradition requires not only standing within its streams, but also openness towards truth in the past as much as the present.

As we said previously, the attention Tracy pays to truth and practice exceeds the framework of the hermeneutical method. It links interpretation of the texts with an investigation of experience, more typical for phenomenology. Furthermore, it also includes the quest for truth and a critical analysis of authorities that claim the truth. Without these additions the hermeneutical method would be endangered by the emptying of meaning or its loss in a coherent sophisticated rhetoric. Tracy shows that everything could be defended by arguing that there is "some truth in everything," but not everything provides us with a meaning and truth on which we can build our lives. Ecumenical theology needs to complement hermeneutics by other methods for very much the same reasons. It needs tools for admitting errors, for distinguishing the just from the unjust, the devout from the ungodly, the real from the unreal, together with a deep awareness that our judgments, however necessary, are not final or free from the negative possibilities they try to identify and avoid. Tracy's two criteria for adequacy, practice and truth, however vulnerable and subject to error they are, thus represent an indispensable complement to a good interpretation.

The Epistemological Method

The epistemological method inquires into the character of our knowing, believing, and acting. It asks about the foundations underpinning the "certainty" they operate with, about the "truth" they presuppose or try to prove, and about the "authority" they refer to. In a negative definition one can also say that the epistemological method deals with doubt, error, and ideological reduction. Nevertheless, as we will see with Wittgenstein, even a positive certainty that we uphold may be acting outside of its limits, and as such harmful to the relationship between knowledge, belief, and action. Jaspers will help us to understand how his philosophical logic forms a space for a confrontation with reality, and with Habermas we will concentrate on the tension between knowledge and human interests, which may provide false motives for justifying human behavior.

METHODOLOGICAL DOUBT AND THE ADEQUACY OF CERTAINTY IN WITTGENSTEIN

In the epigram to this chapter Ludwig Wittgenstein reminded us of the positive role of doubt in the process of searching for truth. It can take us away from false certainty and help us to hear truth once again.[109] Wittgenstein's methodological doubt, however, differs from Descartes or Hume. It presupposes "certainty" and operates as its corrective.[110] Wittgenstein distinguishes among different types of certainty, and shows that a "certainty of knowing" follows different rules to a "certainty of believing," or a "certainty of acting."[111] We can say with certainty that we know that 2+2=4 or that Wittgenstein's name is Ludwig, not Ferdinand. If we want to verify this certainty, we can use another mathematical operation to provide a proof (4–2=2) or look up the name in a textbook. The certainty of knowing can be proved but it has a limited validity. At a certain moment we have to move to the certainty of believing on which our knowledge relies. We realize that we trust that a certain mathematical system is representative of reality, or that our textbooks are reliable. When we are dealing with a certainty of believing, verification no longer functions the same way. We cannot prove that our belief is true or false, but, instead, we can demonstrate how we have arrived at the belief we hold.

About the third type, the certainty on the basis of which we act, we often cannot say even that. It may not have a verbal expression necessary for the previous two certainties. The certainty of acting comes across through human behavior.[112] The hierarchy of certainties is thus reversed. The most foundational is what we can say so little about, the certainty of acting; then comes the certainty of belief, which backs up the certainty of knowledge, the only certainty we can prove, but in a way the most superficial. If we assumed that the certainty of knowledge was foundational or that an expressed belief was the bottom layer on which we built our lives, we

---

109. See Wittgenstein, *Remarks*, 1e.

110. See Dolejšová (Noble), "Wittgenstein's Account," 222.

111. For a more detailed analysis, see Dolejšová (Noble), *Accounts of Hope*, 250–61.

112. See Wittgenstein, *On Certainty*, §§ 174, 253, 284.

would be making a methodological error, according to Wittgenstein. He demonstrates this in his critique of Frazer's understanding of religion:

> Frazer's account of the magical and religious notions of men is unsatisfactory: it makes these notions appear as *mistakes*. Was Augustine mistaken, then, when he called on God on every page of the *Confessions*? Well—one might say—if he was not mistaken, then the Buddhist holy-man, or some other, whose religion expresses quite different notions, surely was. But *none* of them was making a mistake except where he was putting forward a theory.[113]

The epistemological method views truth as having to do with the adequacy of the certainty on which we rely. Wittgenstein warns that, besides the statement "I know," there is another statement: "I thought I knew."[114] In the realm of faith, this adequacy is given by what people practice: "we can see from their actions that they believe certain things definitely, whether they express this belief or not."[115] The truth as an adequately held certainty includes an adequate relation to an adequate authority. It includes simple things like the ability to choose a reliable book or an internet page when I need to find information. But here my knowledge always rests on basic trust that it is possible to get hold of reliable sources, a trust broken many times, and not only in totalitarian cultures. Aiming at the truth then presupposes learning how I arrived at the beliefs that I hold, and where I confused knowledge and belief. And it renews interest in the forms of life that different beliefs either initiated or failed to initiate in history as well as in our present day. Thus my relationship with God, my belonging to a particular tradition with its holy stories, rituals, teachings, ethics, institutions, and shared experience, is subjected to an investigation, without its being reduced to a single realm of knowledge. The epistemological method with its critical emphasis on certainty, and on the foundations of what we see as authoritative, can help to diagnose different ideologies than the previous methods, which revealed the absolutization of experience, or the twisting of interpretation.

---

113. Wittgenstein, *Remarks*, 1e.
114. See Wittgenstein, *On Certainty*, §12.
115. Wittgenstein, *On Certainty*, §284.

JASPERS'S PHILOSOPHICAL LOGIC

Karl Jaspers's emphasis on truth in philosophy introduces what we may call an existentially oriented epistemological method.[116] He is interested in the typology of worldviews, which is where he locates his main question: "how to live truthfully?" Thus, instead of Wittgenstein's emphasis on certainty and the diversity of its forms, Jaspers works with the notion of truth. The need to distinguish between truth and illusion forms the basis of his "philosophical logic."[117]

This can be summarized in the following five points.[118] First, truth does not appear as a totality, but as the fullness of historical plurality. The community of all people cannot be built on a universal truth, but on communication. Philosophical logic is helpful in the mediation of different views, to make them conscious, accessible, and reliable.[119] For this, one needs an unconditional good will to communicate and an awareness of the forms and consequences of distorted communication. Secondly, communication requires the self-awareness of reason. This means that we should understand the forms and methods by which we think, and the direction as well as the origins of our thought.[120] Thirdly, to reach as far as the origins we must make a seemingly impossible movement. This consists in holding together subject and object, and rejecting all understandings that treat them as independent of each other. Where the consciousness is a being, the object and subject are joined together in unity.

Fourthly, objective (rational) thinking does not own the objects of investigation. They are not a property of our consciousness, which expresses itself in being, not in having. Philosophical logic focuses on limit situations, where the limits of the rational are revealed. Instead of playing down the unsolvable problems, or twisting them into a systematic expla-

---

116. Jaspers himself does not use the expression "epistemology," but his emphasis on truth in philosophy contributes to the subject of the epistemological method. See Jaspers, "Philosophical Autobiography," 3–94.

117. Jaspers responds with his philosophical logic to the growth of totalitarianism in Germany. He formulates it as an antidote to the Nazi system with its claims to universal truth and validity. See Jaspers, "Philosophical Autobiography," 72–75.

118. Here I follow Inwood, "Jaspers," 428.

119. Jaspers insists that philosophical truth can be communicated only indirectly: it cannot be adequately captured by any verbal statement. Jaspers, "Philosophical Autobiography," 70.

120. See Jaspers, "Philosophical Autobiography," 85.

nation, philosophical logic opens up contact with infinity. In this way it uncovers the limits of closed approaches. In doing so, however, it needs to be methodologically transparent and not to force the systems it criticizes into tautologies. Only then will communication rest in encountering the existence of my neighbor. Only then will no single approach be favored at the expense of others, but all will be open to discernment between the meaningful and meaningless. This involves acknowledging that what is meaningful or meaningless for me may evoke different reactions from someone else in a different existential situation, or in a different culture. Good will here extends the realm of the meaningful: something can be meaningful, even if it is not meaningful for me.

#5 Finally, philosophical thinking breaks through rationality and its ambition to be the ultimate. It reaches beyond the intellect without losing it. In general, philosophical thinking represents completeness as ungraspable. It leads to openness and to a confrontation with being, which speaks to us through all that is included in it.[121]

Tension between Knowledge and Human Interests in Habermas

Jürgen Habermas concentrates on how ideology critique can help in healing social communication. In his method he combines epistemology and social theory, in order to analyze the relationship between knowledge and human interests.[122] He complements Wittgenstein's hierarchy of certainties with a critique of the supremacy of practice over theory, by which an unwillingness or inability to think is justified.[123] We need to name human interests in order to work towards being liberated from them. We know from experience that human interests often serve to provide the justifying motives of our acting instead of the real motives. In other words, we say what people (often including ourselves) should think about the reasons for our actions, and sometimes we project this way of reasoning even towards God. Habermas distinguishes between how an individual arrives at the justification of his or her interests, which he calls rationalization, and how a collective body such as a society or a church does so, which he calls

121. See Jaspers, "Philosophical Autobiography," 85.

122. Under the influence of Marx's critique of society, Habermas concludes that the radical critique of knowledge is only possible as a social theory. See Habermas, *Knowledge and Human Interests*, vii.

123. See Habermas, *Knowledge and Human Interests*, 301.

ideology. In both cases, however, the manifested contents of the statement in favor of the desired impression are falsified by the non-reflected ties of the consciousness to interests, despite its illusion of autonomy.[124] Ideology critique then gives a space to include transformative practice, and to be able to take responsibility for our own actions.[125]

The epistemological method requires theology to examine time and again the relationship between theory and practice. It allows neither to be downplayed or reduced. In its insistence on the adequacy of the authorities to which theology refers, epistemology purifies theological claims to known truth, and extends the meaning of truth-claims to belief and practice, provided they follow their own "grammar." It addresses also the problem of an adequate relationship to the authorities, and shows that both have to be in place if we are to discern between certainty and error, truth and illusion. Epistemology makes possible a critique of interpretation and even a critique of experience. It reveals that not every interpretation and not every experience are interpretations or experiences of what is claimed. Adequacy as a criterion of truth allows various statements to be valid side by side, and concentrates on their inner integrity and correspondence between the word and act. Yet this method cannot afford independence from other methods. Both previous methods bring the material that epistemology examines and organizes. Without them the epistemological method would be a closed world of thinking about thinking.

CONCLUSION

In this chapter I defined theology as a critical reflection on experiences of faith, hope, and love, in which traces of the revealing God, the Creator, Redeemer, and Sanctifier, are sought and found. Theology was seen as simultaneously a spiritual journey and a science. Its first characteristic rooted theology in a pre-reflective religious immediacy, in the spiritual, liturgical, and social practice of believers. The second characteristic subjected theological reflection to an on-going struggle for clarity, historical and conceptual accuracy, interpretative and systematic coherence. Although theology shares these requirements with other sciences, it has to fulfill them adequately to its own fields and methods of investigation.

---

124. See Habermas, *Knowledge and Human Interests*, 311.

125. The disadvantage of Habermas's approach is that it employs Hegelian totalitarian language to critique ideology. See *Knowledge and Human Interests*, 305.

Our next task was to examine how this could be done. Three illustrative examples ranged from Augustine's existential concept of theology as a journey from science to wisdom of contemplation, through Aquinas's dialectical concept within which the unity of faith and reason was postulated, to Schleiermacher's historical concept of theology as a "positive" science, rehabilitating its difference from other sciences and yet its relevance to all dealing with human experience.

Finally we followed three main methodological influences on contemporary theology, and asked what the phenomenological, hermeneutical, and epistemological methods contributed to it, and in particular to working simultaneously with different Christian traditions. Requirements to move as close as possible to a pre-ideological layer of experience were complemented by an analysis of the process of the understanding of tradition, and by the ideology critique of tradition, and of our relationship to what we perceive as reality. Thus methodological foundations were set in place for considering specific theological themes emerging from personal as well as inherited experiences of faith, hope, and love. Before we move to the following chapters, dedicated to such themes, it is important to repeat that none of the methods we use is self-sufficient, and none uncovers reality in other than partial ways. In each theme a different method will be used to serve our investigation, to reach the intended aim, but none of them is an aim in itself. We can methodologically grasp the experiences and attitudes of faith, hope, and love and work with them, but they cannot be replaced. Thus theology as a science, if it is truly adequate to its subject, always returns us in the end to where we started, to the spiritual journey, where communication with God, and in God with others, is lived before it is reflected on.

2

Revealing God

So the other disciples told him: 'We have seen the Lord.' But he said to
them: 'Unless I see the mark of the nails in his hands, and put my finger
in the mark of the nails and my hand in his side, I will not believe.' A
week later his disciples were again in the house, and Thomas was with
them. Although the door was shut, Jesus came and stood among them
and said: 'Peace be with you.' Then he said to Thomas: 'Put your finger
here and see my hands. Reach out your hand and put it in my side. Do
not doubt and believe.' Thomas answered him: 'My Lord and my God.'
Jesus said to him, 'Have you believed because you have seen me? Blessed
are those who have not seen and yet have come to believe.'

JOHN 20:25–29

If God wishes to make his love for the world known, it must be recogniz-
able—in spite of, and because of, its being totally other.

HANS URS VON BALTHASAR[1]

CHRISTIANITY, LIKE JUDAISM AND Islam, understands itself as a revealed religion. This means that it is based on the belief that at its
beginnings there were events that disclosed truths about human life and
its fulfillment, about the world in which we live. Moreover, all this is in
relationship to a personal God, who is the giver as well as the revealer
of such truths. Yet, as Balthasar points out in the opening quotation, for
the truths, such as that God loves the world, to be known, two sides are
necessary. There must also be someone who recognizes the revelation
as revelation, who receives it and understands it as revelation, i.e., as

1. Balthasar, *Love Alone*, 61.

something different, as that which fulfils as well as transcends our ordinary experience. The emphasis on divine revelation and on religion as a faith-response, whose more or less open structures became fixed in a tradition, is common to all three monotheistic religions. Here, however, I am not going to examine their differences or their relationship to other religions, which also interpret revelation in some way.[2] My task is confined to Christian theological reflection on revelation, and in particular to the types of relationship between events, experiences, and tradition in which God speaks and acts and provokes a relationship of mutual personal communication.

Here it is necessary to make two comments. First, revelation, as I understand it in this chapter, has a public character. This means that it is concerned with events that have had an impact far beyond the individuals who experienced them directly. Revelation includes the process of understanding and passing the understanding on, in which the primary experience becomes a part of the tradition of a particular community. The second comment concerns the fact that we are dealing with a personal communication that is free on both sides. God has chosen to reveal something of divine actions and being, not out of necessity, but because God wanted to do so. Witnesses to this revelation and the community to whom the revelation was addressed have also chosen their answer freely—they may or may not respond with faith; they may or may not change their ways in communication with God.[3]

In the first part of this chapter I am going to outline the main notions of revelation in the Scriptures. Then I concentrate on the basic categories and methods employed for interpretation of revelatory texts in the Church Fathers and in thinkers from the contemporary Orthodox, Protestant, and Catholic traditions. In conclusion I sketch how a theology of revelation rooted in the concepts discussed above can be beneficial both for ecumenical and for inter-religious dialogue.

2. On the question of revelation in other religions see *LG* 13–17, *Nostra Aetate*, Rahner, "Christianity and the Non-Christian Religions," 115–34; Dupuis, *Jesus Christ and the Encounter: Towards a Christian Theology*; "Interreligious Dialogue."

3. See Davis, "Revelation and Critical Theory," 88–89.

CASES OF REVELATION IN THE SCRIPTURES

As we are going to examine the scriptural notions of revelation on the basis of the narrative events in which the notions emerge, it is important not to lose track of their unique particularity, which can never fully pass on into the tradition. The biblical writers, as we will see, are aware of this problem, and offer to us as much of the flesh of the story as possible whilst reminding us that it was still other than we might think. The plurality of meaning of revelation-in-stories is underlined by the fact that the Old Testament does not even possess a single term for revelation events.[4] In the New Testament there is one main expression *apokalyptein*, from which *apokalypsis* (revelation) is derived. Nevertheless we will see that this expression has a multiple use.[5] We will not understand revelation by analyzing the terms, but by analyzing situations, their similarities, differences, and mutual cohesion.

The Old Testament Testimonies

The Old Testament typology follows on from the narrative history. However, it is important not to assume that we are ascending some kind of ladder, from a lesser to a greater perfection of understanding. Instead, tracking how God revealed himself to Abraham, and to Elijah, we will try to point out the symbolic wealth present in each narrative, and in particular to those aspects that have been long lost and with much effort rehabilitated in current theology.

GOD REVEALED TO THE ANCESTORS: PROMISE AND WORSHIP

The Israelite tradition dealing with the lives of the ancestors links revelation events with particular places where the Lord's holiness "was revealed." We can, then, speak of what is called a cultic-etiological understanding of revelation.[6] This means that the biblical authors tried to interpret the current state of affairs, in this case to explain the origin of the worship-

---

4. Hebrew uses here three different expressions: g-l-h (to uncover, appear, expose oneself); r-a-h (to show oneself); v-d-a (to be recognized).

5. In a minority of cases the New Testament also uses the expression *phanein* (to make apparent). There is only a small difference in meaning between *apokalyptein* and *phanein* and both expressions can be used interchangeably to a certain degree. The expression *apokalypsis* takes these new meanings: exposure, denudation, uncovering of unknown circumstances that can be related to people as well as to God.

6. See Rendtorff, "The Concept of Revelation," 28.

ping of the God Yahweh in those very cultic places where he had been worshipped. At the same time, they give accounts of the promises from this God connected to the places.

Yahweh appears to Abram on the way to Shechem: "Abram passed through the land to the place at Shechem, to the oak of Morech. At that time the Canaanites were in the land. Then the Lord appeared to Abram, and said, 'To your offspring I will give this land.' So he built there an altar to the Lord, who had appeared to him." (Gen 12:6–7) God appears, gives the promise, Abram in response to this event worships the Lord God who appeared by building him an altar. A similar sequence of events appears in Gen 17:1–27: "When Abram was ninety-nine years old, the Lord appeared to Abram, and said to him, 'I am God Almighty, walk before me, and be blameless. And I will make my covenant between me and you, and will make you exceedingly numerous.' Then Abram fell on his face, and God said to him . . ." (1–3) Yahweh appears and gives the promise, Abram falls on his face. The sequence repeats itself once more, and now with a clearer content of the promise. As Abraham lies on his face before the Lord, the Lord specifies the terms of his covenant, beginning with the change of Abram's name: "As for me, this is my covenant with you: You shall be the ancestor of a multitude of nations. No longer shall your name be Abram, but your name shall be Abraham, for I have made you the ancestor of a multitude of nations." (4–5) We discover that Abraham has been promised a multitude of offspring and land to live in. From him nations with kings will arise, his offspring will inherit the land of Canaan.[7] At the same time, the Lord requests circumcision as a sign of this covenant: "Every male among you shall be circumcised. You shall circumcise the flesh of your foreskins, and it shall be a sign of the covenant between me and you." (10–11) The Lord also changes the name of Abraham's wife Sarai and again reveals the particular way of fulfilling his promise, "your wife Sarah shall bear you a son [this time next year], and you shall name

7. We cannot ignore here the very questionable consequences of the interpretations of this promise concerning eternal and exclusive possession of the land of Canaan. Is this promise given to Jews only, so that they alone have the right to settle in the "promised land?" Or is it given to all nations who have arisen from Abraham and who keep the circumcision, thus to Arabs too? The text here is equivocal: 17:6–7 speaks about the covenant with all Abraham's offspring, the promise given to Sarah narrows the focus to Isaac's offspring (17:21). 17:26, however, stresses again that Abraham and Ishmael were circumcised on the same day. The application of Rendtorff's etiological interpretation is very relevant here.

him Isaac." (19) Abraham again falls on his face and worships God by fulfilling his covenant: "Then Abraham took his son Ishmael and all the slaves born in his house or bought with his money, every male among the men of Abraham's house, and he circumcised the flesh of their foreskins that very day, as God had said to him." (23)

The stories about Isaac and Jacob, too, contain similar references to the Lord's revelation to them. The Lord appeared to Isaac in Beer-sheba, where he made him the heir of Abraham's covenant,[8] and he then "built an altar and worshipped the Lord's name. He also built there his tent and his servants sank a well." (Gen 26:25) The Lord appeared to Jacob in a dream while he was on the way to Haran: "And he dreamed that there was a ladder set up on the earth, the top of it reaching to heaven, and the angels of God were ascending and descending on it. And the Lord stood beside him and said: 'I am the Lord, the God of Abraham your father and the God of Isaac.'" (Gen 28:12–13). A renewed promise of land and offspring follows through which "all the families of the earth shall be blessed" (14) and the promise of the Lord's everlasting guidance and protection is given and received. Jacob awakes from his sleep and comments on this event: "'Surely the Lord is in this place—and I did not know it!' And he was afraid and said, 'How awesome is this place! This is none other than the house of God, and this is the gate of heaven.' So Jacob rose early in the morning, and he took the stone that he had put under his head and set it up for a pillar and poured oil on top of it. He called that place Bethel." (16–19) Jacob's response culminates with his own promise: "If God will be with me, and will keep me in this way that I go, and will give me bread to eat and clothing to wear, so that I come again to my father's house in peace, then the Lord shall be my God, and this stone, which I have set up for a pillar, shall be God's house, and of all you give me I will surely give one tenth to you." (20–22)

The Lord also "appears" as the unknown, for example in Gen 32:25–32. Many years later when Jacob was preparing to meet his brother Esau whom he had once deprived of his birth–right, he waded across the stream Jabbok, with all he had, and stayed there alone. The scriptural narrative continues:

---

8. "And that very night the Lord appeared to him and said, 'I am the God of your father Abraham; do not be afraid, for I am with you and will bless you and make your offspring numerous for my servant Abraham's sake.'" (Gen 26:24).

. . . and a man wrestled with him until daybreak. When the man saw that he did not prevail against Jacob, he struck him on the hip socket, and Jacob's hip was put out of joint as he wrestled with him. The Unknown one said, 'Let me go, for the day is breaking.' Jacob said, 'I will not let you go, unless you bless me.' So he said to him, 'What is your name?' And he said, "Jacob." Then the man said, 'You shall no longer be called Jacob (*deceitful*) but Israel (*it is God who strives*), for you have striven with God and with humans, and have prevailed.' Then Jacob asked him, 'Please tell me your name.' But he said, 'Why is that you ask my name?' And there he blessed him." (24–30)

Here, too, a response follows, but this time it is mediated through creation: "The sun rose upon him as he passed Penuel" (32); through Jacob's body: "he was lame in his hip" (32); and through the community: "Therefore to this day the Israelites do not eat the thigh muscle that is on the hip socket, because he struck Jacob on the hip socket at the thigh muscle." (33)

The texts dealing with the lives of the ancestors connect God's revelation with two promises: that of land (Gen 12:2) and of offspring (Gen 26:24). Yahweh appears, he is present in a way that inspires awe and leads to worship, but at the same time these revelatory events do not reveal his essence, just his intentions for those to whom he appears (Gen 32:29).[9] Revelation also has its particular content. In the second part of this chapter I will concentrate on the questions of interpretation of the content, and especially on the changing aspects of the interpretation, required by different contexts, if the message of the revelation is not to be violated.

The texts we have introduced so far have a common structure. Yahweh appears and makes a promise, Yahweh is worshipped, the place or even some elements of it (e.g., stones) where he appeared are identified as holy, the promise is received by faith, and it is proclaimed that the one who made the promise will also fulfill it by acting upon it. At the same time, each of these stories is different. They reflect the uniqueness of the situation and the person with whom the Lord communicates, their position in the community, their personal history and character traits. It is possible to say that the Lord appears gradually. Each story introduces a new depth, and a new dimension of a person's own limits and tendencies

---

9. W. Pannenberg prefers to talk of these events not as revelation but as manifestations, by which he means "the revealing of God without revealing his essence." "Introduction," 9.

to exploit the Lord. Thus revelation also includes defense mechanisms against such abuse. While Abram meets God directly, deceitful Jacob and his successors are led to understand their injuries first: we are walking with the Lord, but we are limping. God appears either implicitly in a dream or as radically unrecognizable so that, when Jacob asks his name, he does not receive an answer. Abraham, Isaac, and Jacob may see the Lord God Almighty, but are not allowed to know God's name. Moses is told something radically new. God lets his name be known, lets himself be known as "the one who is."[10]

REVELATION OF THE DIVINE NAME AND THE DIVINE LAW TO MOSES

The cultic-etiological structure can still be traced in the calling of Moses, as recounted in Exodus 3. Moses, tending the flock of his Midian father-in-law Jethro, comes close to Horeb, "the mountain of God" (1) and sees a bush that is burning without being consumed by the fire. He is curious and moves closer to take a look. Then God calls him: "Moses, Moses! . . . Come no closer! Remove the sandals from your feet, for the place on which you are standing is holy ground." (4–5) Here the act of worship is even ordered. The Lord calls Moses to bring Israel out of Egypt. He promises that he will remain with Moses and his people, and that they will return to this mountain and worship God.[11] Moses is scared and asks for more guarantees in the same way Jacob did: "'If I come to the Israelites and say to them, 'The God of your ancestors has sent me to you,' and they ask me, 'What is his name?' what shall I say to them?'" (13) Moses receives the answer: "I AM WHO I AM" (14). Alongside this, the Lord repeats the command, "Thus you shall say to the Israelites: 'I AM has sent me to you.'" (14) Moses does not fall on his face like Abraham, but protests again: "'But suppose they do not believe me or listen to me, but say, 'The Lord did not appear to you.'"(4:1) This narrative shows that Moses' attempt to get to know who God really is through getting hold of the divine name still leaves him puzzled. Or more exactly, the name that the Lord reveals to him does not give him access to the essence of divinity other than a realization that here is and always will be a holy mystery. Still, the mysterious God gives him signs: the staff that becomes a snake when thrown down; the hand that, when put under the cloak, becomes

---

10. See Rentdorff, "The Concept of Revelation," 30.

11. Compare to the promise to Jacob in Gen 28:20–22.

leprous and when put there once more is healthy again; the water from the Nile that, if poured on dry land, turns to blood.[12] When Moses still protests, this time about not being eloquent, the Lord becomes angry: "Then the anger of God was kindled against Moses and he said, 'What of your brother Aaron . . . He shall speak for you to the people, he shall serve as a mouth for you and you shall serve as God for him.'" (14.16)

We could say the Lord reveals "more" of himself here than in the previous narratives. Yet at the same time, the Lord is more hidden. Moses, who was given the Lord's name, begins to penetrate what it means only as he goes and follows God's calling, only when he sees what his God does. On the way he comes to realize more and more his inadequacy: he has experience, but no words. He could only stutter face to face with God's people. Aaron has no experience, but has the gift of eloquence, so he can mediate; but his mediation carries the danger of self-centeredness. Aaron betrays Moses' experience.[13]

After Israel's exodus from Egypt, when Moses is in the cloud on the mountain where he abides with the Lord and receives the law from him to instruct the people, this experience remains closed to others in its depth, including to Aaron: "Go down and warn the people not to break through to the Lord to look, otherwise many of them will perish." (Exod 19:21) People are afraid of God's closeness[14] and ask Moses to mediate: "You speak to us and we will listen, but do not let God speak to us, or we will die." (20:19) Moses ascends the mountain of the Lord three times because of the covenant of the people with the Lord, just as three times he rebelled against his calling from the Lord.[15]

Aaron, seduced by the impatient people, is brought to believe that, as he has language, he surely can produce God with it, and replace Moses' inaccessible experience. The knowledge given by the Lord contrasts with

---

12. See Exod 4:1–9.

13. See lectures by M. Kirwan on hermeneutics, summer course of IES in Strašice, September 2000.

14. See Exod 24:1–2.

15. The Scripture says that Moses was in the cloud for forty days and forty nights (Exod 24:18). The same number symbolizing fullness appears for the flood in the days of Noah (Gen 8:6). Israel wandered in the wilderness for forty years (Exod 16:35; Josh 5:6), Elijah walked before the Lord for forty days and forty nights (1 Kgs 19:8), Jonah is sent to prophesy that Nineveh would be overthrown in forty days and instead it turned to the Lord in forty days (Jonah 3:4), Jesus fasted in the desert for forty days and forty nights (Matt 4:2; Mark 1:13; Luke 4:2).

the blindness of the people who want a god who would be close to them, who would not be so different, a god who would be the image of the people, not the other way round. Thus an idol is made.[16] Moses, ascending the mountain of the Lord for a third time, begs for forgiveness for his people's perverted ways. Again he writes the words of the covenant onto the tablets, for when he saw the "bull and dancing" in the Israelite camp, he had smashed them in anger.[17]

God's revelation on Sinai develops what had already begun with Moses' calling. Now Moses, accompanied by thunder and lightning, accepts the Decalogue[18] and the people are brought into a new covenant with the Lord.[19] The code of law itself is not the whole of revelation. Its tablets are breakable as the book of Exodus tells us and then it is necessary to go to receive them again. The law is a part of revelation, participating in the relationship between the Lord and his people. Its content is to serve this relationship, to guard the difference between friendship with God and with the people, and between the selfishness or hate that destroy this friendship.

God's Word Given to the Prophets

The next type of revelatory events focuses on the word. The word of God given to the prophets, as we will see, combines two meanings: it is the word revealed and the word of inspired interpretation of what is revealed. Both meanings feature in the prophetic tradition, where a prophet is seen as a mediator of God's word.[20] Unlike with the eloquent Aaron, who did not avoid idolatry, in the case of the prophets the word of God acts independently of people's wishes, and its freedom is one of the early criteria supporting its being genuine.

---

16. See Exod 32.1–6.

17. See Exod 32:19.

18. In Hebrew *debarim torah*, which the Septuagint translates as *deka logia*, hence Decalogue.

19. The covenant does not appear for the first time in connection with Moses. It is preceded by the covenant with Abraham (Gen 17:1–4), to which Judaism, Christianity, and Islam refer. This in turn is preceded by the covenant with Noah (Gen 6:18; 9:8–17), which is connected with all of creation and which has, of course, consequences for our deciding who the people of the covenant are. They are in a certain sense all living creatures (Gen 9:10), all Abraham's offspring (Gen 17:6–7), and all Israelite tribes (Gen 19–32).

20. See Dunn, "Biblical Concept of Divine Revelation," here especially 11–14.

Let us consider the story of Balaam (Num 22–24) who was hired by Balak, the king of Moab, to curse the people of Israel: "Come now, curse this people for me, since they are stronger than I, perhaps I shall be able to defeat them and drive them from the land, for I know that whomever you bless is blessed, and whomever you curse is cursed." (Num 22:6) Balak recognizes Balaam as a prophet but not the fact that a prophet cannot act as a prophet independently of God's word. The text shows this as follows: "God came to Balaam and said, 'Who are these men with you?'" (9) After he spoke to Balaam about where he was going and why, he ordered him: "You shall not go with them, you shall not curse the people, for they are blessed." (12) The Lord opposes Balak's plans for Balaam, who, however, disobeys and goes along with Balak's men to curse Israel. But when he opens his mouth, words of blessing come out instead. Balak confronts him and Balaam replies: "Must I not take care to say what the Lord puts into my mouth?" (23:12) and "If Balak should give me his house full of silver and gold, I would not be able to go beyond the word of the Lord, to do either good or bad of my own will. What the Lord says, that is what I will say."(24:13) The prophet does not reveal what he would want to do, but what he must do. His will is confronted with God's will, his words with God's word. This is clearly expressed in Amos: "The lion has roared, who will not fear? The Lord God has spoken, who can but prophesy?" (Amos 3:8) However, these stories also show that prophets do not act out of fear of a greater force, but most of them are in fact God's friends. God talks to them; sometimes they argue, but their words and actions are linked with the journey of their personal understanding.

The prophetic word shifts from ecstatic speech[21] to a conscious relationship with the Lord, in which the prophet experiences the ecstatic states of mind, but also freely and consciously responds to them, and in this way cooperates with God.[22] The prophet can be chosen for this task from within the structures of his community, as is shown in Num 11:16–30: "So the Lord said to Moses, 'Gather for me seventy of the elders of Israel, whom you know to be the elders of the people and officers over them, bring them to the tent of meeting, and have them take their place with you. I will come down and talk with you there, and I will take some of the spirit that is on you and put it on them, and they shall bear the

21. See, e.g., 1 Sam 10:5; 19:20–24.
22. See, e.g., the calling of Isaiah (Isa 6) or Jeremiah (Jer 1).

burden of the people along with you so that you will not bear it all by yourself.'" (16–17) The prophet can also be chosen independently of these structures, and even sent to prophesy against them, as we can see, for example, with the prophet Amos, who announces the judgment in Bethel and speaks of the resettlement of Israel: "Surely the Lord God does nothing, without revealing his secret to his servants, the prophets . . . I am no prophet nor a prophet's son, but I am a herdsman and a dresser of sycamore trees, and the Lord took me from following the flock, and the Lord said to me, 'Go, prophesy to my people Israel.'" (Amos 3:7; 7:14–15)

Biblical texts also speak about false prophecy. Jeremiah warns the people: "Do not listen to the words of the prophets who prophesy to you, they are deluding you. They speak visions of their own minds, not from the mouth of the Lord." (Jer 23:16) False prophecy is something that claims the authority of the Lord's word though it does not have it. False prophets manipulate people by their thoughts and give false promises that help them to maintain the *status quo*: "They keep saying to those who despise the word of the Lord, 'It shall be well with you,' and to all who stubbornly follow their own stubborn hearts, they say, 'No calamity shall come upon you.'" (Jer 23:17) False prophecy does not issue from a relationship with the Lord, but how can this be discerned from the outside? Deuteronomy asks this question: "You may say to yourself, 'How can we recognize a word that the Lord has not spoken?' If a prophet speaks in the name of the Lord but the thing does not take place or prove true, it is a word that the Lord has not spoken. The prophet has spoken it presumptuously." (Deut 18:21–22) This apparently straightforward answer is in fact complex because we were warned even before that false prophecy can be accompanied by signs: "If prophets or those who divine and promise you omens or the portents declared by them take place, and they say, 'Let us follow other gods (whom you have not known) and let us serve them,' you must not heed the words of those prophets or those who divine by dreams." (Deut 13: 2–4)[23] Signs and miracles are not always reliable evidence of the authenticity of God's words nor are they superior to God's word, for even the pharaoh's magicians in Egypt were able to do some of the signs and miracles Moses did.[24]

---

23. See Deut 13:4–6.
24. See Exod 7:22.

The conflict between true and false prophecy is also reflected in Elijah's confrontation with Baal's prophets on Mount Carmel (1 Kgs 18:1–46). They, unlike Elijah, are not able to make their god receive their sacrifice, and Elijah slaughters them for leading the people astray.[25] Then, however, he is confronted with his own actions. On the run from the king, Ahab, and queen, Jezebel, he makes his way into the wilderness, sits down under a thorn tree and wishes to die: "It is enough; I am no better than my ancestors."(1 Kgs 19:4) Elijah lies down and falls asleep and, as he had to his ancestors, the Lord appears to him through a messenger: "Suddenly an angel touched him and said to him, 'Get up and eat.' He looked, and there at his head was a cake baked on hot stones, and a jar of water. He ate and drank, and lay down again. The angel of the Lord came a second time, touched him and said, 'Get up and eat, otherwise the journey will be too much for you.' He got up, and ate and drank; then he went in the strength of that food forty days and forty nights to Horeb, the mount of God." (5–8)

So far, Elijah knew God only through his word and through his messengers. That, though, was enough for him to be capable of doing signs and miracles, even bringing the son of the widow of Zareptath back to life. He knew the Lord as the one who sent him, but who also heard his prayer, accepted his sacrifice. Yet until now, God had revealed himself always in a particular symbolic way, never simply as God "himself."[26] God's revelation to Elijah takes another form now. On Mount Horeb, Elijah first encounters the voice of the Lord that he has already known. The Lord says to him: "What are you doing here, Elijah?" and Elijah has to describe his situation: "I have been very zealous for the Lord, the God of hosts; for the Israelites have forsaken your covenant, thrown down your altars, and killed your prophets with the sword. I alone am left, and they are seeking my life, to take it away." (9–10)

Elijah is then encouraged to stand on the mountain before the Lord and here his knowledge is transformed. There was a great wind splitting mountains and breaking rocks, but the Lord was not in the wind, nor the

---

25. Any interpretation of this text must deal with the question of how the mass slaughtering of false prophets is connected with the God of life, and whether Elijah still has to experience the horror of the life and death conflict, as, for example, Shakespeare describes it in *Macbeth*: "I am in blood / Stepp'd in so far, that should I wade no more, / Returning were as tedious as go o'er." *Macbeth*, III.135.

26. See Pannenberg, "Introduction," 9.

earthquake, nor in fire. Elijah expected to find the Lord there, but it was not so. The Lord was not in any of the demonstrations of power. Instead we read: "and after the fire a sound of sheer silence . . . What are you doing here, Elijah?" (12–13) Elijah repeats again what he said before. The Lord replies that there were seven thousand people in Israel who were not led to idolatry and the Lord would save them. The Lord wants Elijah to return to appoint a successor. His weariness, however, is taken seriously by the Lord. Second Kings describes Elijah's assumption,[27] and in the tradition of Israel Elijah will come again at the end of days.[28]

The prophets show us not only the revelatory value of a personal relationship with God, when God speaks "directly" and sends his servants to pass judgment on and announce plans to his people, but also the struggle for understanding and passing on the message. Their lives are changed by this word, as is the life of the community that they belong to and for whom they mediate. God's word not only speaks but also has an effect. Revelation provokes understanding and acceptance in which people are transformed. The Old Testament understands revelation in a broad sense. There is indeed a revelation "face to face." At the same time, through ritual, through dreams, through the traces of God's holiness, God's word, and events, revelation emerges even through the struggle of interpretation. In the end, the whole of the Old Testament is a reflection on revelation—in creation, in history, in God's journey with Israel. This multilayered character of revelation is transferred to the New Testament, despite its focus on Christ.

Revelation in the New Testament

The New Testament proclaims the fulfillment of the promises announced in the Old Testament in Jesus Christ. The Kingdom of God has come near, in the incarnation, in the person of Jesus with his Spirit-filled attitudes, words, and actions, in his giving of his life for his friends and for the whole world, including the new people of God, the church. The revelation, often in narrative form, includes the process during which the primary experience becomes part of the tradition of a certain community. The relationship of the communication between people and God thus moves from the initiating events to become "embodied in a community and institutional-

---

27. See 2 Kgs 2:1–11.
28. Cf. Mal 4:5; Matt 11:14; 16:14; 17:3–4; Mark 9:11–13; Luke 9:7–8, etc.

ized, so that subsequent generations may join themselves to that communication, adding their response to the response of earlier generations."[29] In this process revelation gains its public character. Its results, however, have always to be measured against the events that initiated the process. Thus here I will concentrate on three moments testified in the Scriptures as foundational events. They come across through experiences of people who met Jesus of Nazareth in his earthly life, who encountered him as the Risen Lord, and who were filled by the Spirit and experienced the life of the early church.

ENCOUNTERS WITH JESUS OF NAZARETH

The gospels offer a testimony about what it was like to meet Jesus, what his presence radiated, how he acted. In narrating Jesus' life, the Gospel writers tried to lead their audience to the very immediacy of the events they presented. Nevertheless, it is necessary to bear in mind that we will not be able entirely to distinguish the Jesus who walked the earth with his disciples, preaching the Kingdom of God, and the Jesus remembered and proclaimed as the one who guaranteed the presence of the Kingdom. The gospels, as well as the other New Testament writings, integrate both, situating the life-story of Jesus into the message about his death and resurrection.[30]

The testimonies of the first encounters of the disciples concentrate on the unity between the teaching and actions of their new Master. Jesus proclaims the Kingdom, and in his presence the Kingdom is revealed. This raises questions concerning Jesus' authority and identity. The gospel narrators trace the process of the revelation of who Jesus was and why he came, reaching back to the time when the disciples did not know the answer. All the synoptics tell the story of how Peter answered Jesus' question: "And who do you say that I am?" by professing: "You are the Messiah."[31]

In Matthew's gospel Jesus responds to Peter: "Blessed are you, Simon son of Jonah! For flesh and blood has not revealed this to you, but my Father in heaven. And I tell you, you are Peter, and on this rock I will build my church, and the gates of Hades will not prevail against it. I will

---

29. Davis, "Revelation and Critical Theory," 88.

30. Compare Sobrino, *Jesus the Liberator* and *La fe en Jesucristo*.

31. In Matthew's version even "You are the Messiah, the Son of the living God." (16:16). Cf. Mark 8:27–30; Luke 9:18–22.

give you the keys of the kingdom of heaven, and whatever you bind on earth will be bound in heaven and whatever you loose on earth will be loosed in heaven." (Mt 16:17–19) Here Jesus contrasts two names, the old one referring to Peter's earthly father and the new one related to his heavenly Father, a name that promises Peter's transformation. The continuity with the Old Testament comes across in the similar structure of the event, here the structure of revelation—promise. However, worship does not follow: instead, Jesus warns the disciples not to tell anybody he is the Messiah, and for the first time he tries to share with them the intuition of his suffering. Mark and Matthew then reflect on the contrast between "divine" and "human" thinking.[32]

The statement about Jesus' journey towards death is accompanied by Peter's shift from the one to whom the truth is revealed by the heavenly Father to the one who is blind to the truth, unable to accept it. His new name is now in contrast with his old way of thinking. The promised rock of the church becomes a stumbling block. Jesus even says that through the same Peter, through whom the heavenly Father spoke a while back, Satan now speaks. Using Old Testament categories, Peter is thus a true and a false prophet. At times he mediates God's word, but at other times the word of his personal desires provides a negative influence, whether motivated by love or by fear.

The gospels link revelation to salvation and this connection culminates in Jesus' death and resurrection. Jesus enters Jerusalem like a king and is killed by its leading representatives like a criminal. The shouting of the crowds changes during one festival from "Hosanna to the son of David! Blessed is the one who comes in the name of the Lord!" to "Let him be crucified!"[33]

The reflection on revelation includes the understanding of why it had to happen. Matthew reminds us of the fulfillment of the Law, Luke of the contrast between the rule of this world and God's rule, John of the journey of rebirth. The word that has become flesh is neither recognized nor accepted. This word suffers and is crucified before it shines through the new birth, the resurrection. "He was in the world, and the world came into being through him; yet the world did not know him. He came to what was his own, and his own people did not accept him. But to all who

---

32. See Matt 16:21–23 and Mark 8:31–33.
33. See Matt 21:9 and 27:22–23.

received him, who believed in his name, he gave power to become children of God, who were born, not of blood or of the will of the flesh or of
the will of man, but of God." (John 1:10–13)

Jesus' trial and crucifixion are narrated with the emphasis on the disciples not being able to see God acting in these events. Jesus' prayer from
Psalm 22:2 "My God, my God, why have you forsaken me?" captures well
their own situation. At the same time, there is a contrast between their
inability to see and the revelation to the Roman soldiers standing under
the cross, who, with fear, recognize that he truly was the Son of God.[34]

The resurrection testimonies are recounted against the backdrop of
the hopelessness of the disciples. The evangelists point out that when Jesus
appeared after the resurrection, not even those closest to him recognized
him at first. Mary Magdalene mistook him for a gardener, the disciples
going to Emmaus for a pilgrim who had come from afar and did not know
what had happened in Jerusalem.[35] The risen Jesus does not appear to all
people, and yet neither the gospels nor Acts provide a clear answer to the
question whether only those who believed could meet the resurrected
one.[36] Instead, they emphasize the variety of inner dispositions and outer
circumstances of those who met the risen Lord. Let us return now to the
introductory text of this chapter, taken from John's gospel.[37]

Thomas is not able to believe on the basis of the experience of the
other disciples. John the Evangelist stresses the "materiality" Thomas
needs for his faith and that he was given. The risen Jesus is the same Jesus
who was crucified; he is not a ghost, he has a body, even the marks of
the nails in his hands and a wound in his side, which Thomas is encouraged to touch. He did not stop being human, so he eats with his disciples,
and yet he is different: he can go through the door, appear to them, and
disappear again from their sight. With all that, the disciples receive a new
understanding of what is "real." Before these encounters the death of their
Master was evident, now when his words about resurrection have "become flesh," his life becomes obvious. The first and second testimonies

34. See Matt 27:54.

35. See John 20:11–18; Luke 24:13–35. A very good analysis of the journey from
blindness to belief that can see is found in Chauvet, *Symbol and Sacrament*, 161–68.

36. See Saul's journey to Damascus in Acts 9:1–19; the difference between this and
the gospel texts is that this revelation of the risen Lord takes place after his ascension to
heaven and thus has a different form.

37. See John 20:25–29.

are not identical. The second cannot be proven. The disciples who saw their Master are not able to convince Thomas. The risen Lord himself can convince him through letting himself be recognized in the way that Thomas needs. But even Thomas has no other way to "prove" that the Lord has risen from the dead than by reference to his own experience and the transformation caused by this experience. And thus we have already moved to the second theme elaborated by the New Testament writings, namely revelation through the witness of the risen Lord, through the words and lives of his disciples, to whom God has granted his power.

PROCLAMATION OF THE RISEN LORD

According to the gospels, the first recipients of the message about the resurrection are the disciples themselves. This news and the events included in it becomes revelation for them. The women who found the empty tomb on the first day after the Sabbath are commanded by the angels:[38] "Go quickly and tell his disciples, 'He has been raised from the dead, and indeed he is going ahead of you to Galilee; there you will see him.'" (Mt 28:7) The disciples meet the risen Jesus on the way and worship him. "And they came to him, took hold of his feet, and worshipped him." (28:9) The command is repeated now by Jesus himself: "Do not be afraid; go and tell my brothers to go to Galilee; there they will see me." (28:10)[39]

The first chapters of Acts show the shift in understanding of what revelation is, as the Proclaimer becomes the Proclaimed. The one who revealed the mysteries of God's kingdom is transformed into the one in whom God's kingdom is revealed. With this shift the role of the disciples changes, too. They are now filled with the Holy Spirit, and become witnesses and at the same time mediators of God's revelation. The message about the risen Lord reaches out from the disciples, first to other Israelites, and soon beyond the borders of Israel. Philip baptizes an Ethiopian court official,[40] Peter baptizes Cornelius of Caesarea, his family, and friends.[41]

---

38. The Greek word *angelos* means not only an angel, but also a messenger, legate. In this meaning the mediation of God's revelation is entrusted to the women, who now also become God's messengers.

39. The evangelists differ on whether they include or exclude women among God's messengers. Mark's addition says: "So they went out and fled from the tomb, for terror and amazement had seized them; and they said nothing to anyone, for they were afraid."(16:8) According to Luke they told the others but nobody believed them (see 24:11).

40. See Acts 8:26–39.

41. See Acts 10:1–48.

The persecutor of the church, Saul, ultimately becomes "Apostle to the Gentiles" (Rom 11:13). We will now concentrate on his proclamation.

Paul shifts between the emphases on the cross and on the resurrection as basic *topoi* of revelation. On the one hand he wants to know "nothing among you except Jesus Christ, and him crucified" (1 Cor 2:2). And thus his testimony builds upon an antithesis between human visions of success and the revelations of God's power and wisdom in the powerlessness of the Savior. Paul proclaims that God revealed himself in Christ's radical self–giving, even to the hands of sinful people. Salvation comes to us not through their violence, but through Christ's faithfulness. The new life that is opened as we follow Christ is, then, a life of subverting violence, of overcoming suffering, not of worshipping either.[42]

The "old life" does not, however, disappear after the acceptance of the message, not even from the lives of those who are its messengers. Using Habermas's language, their human interests, personal or communal,[43] justify unjust relationships, whether it is Peter's unspoken preference for Judeo–Christians (or at least for not having trouble with the circle of James),[44] or Paul's assumption that women are inferior.[45] Yet both of these examples also include their own subversion. In Galatians Paul rebukes Peter for being hypocritical,[46] and in his own ministry encountering good examples teaches him to accept women in authority.[47] These are just a few examples of the struggle of the witnesses of Christ to participate fully in what they proclaim: that the "new life" comes through despite our

---

42. See Rom 8:17; 2 Cor 4:7–16; 13:4; Phil 3:9–11; Col 1:24.

43. See Habermas, *Knowledge and Human Interests*, 311.

44. See Gal 2:11–13.

45. This comes across in Paul's account of the witnesses of Christ's life, death, and resurrection, where, in contrast to in the gospels, which were written later, women do not figure. Compare the texts talking about the women at the empty tomb (Matt 28:1–10; Mark 16:1–8; Luke 24:1–11) and Mary Magdalene meeting the Resurrected One (Mark 16:9–11; John 20:1–2.11–18). Then there is the well–known and much abused passage about silencing women in the church and subjecting them to male authority. See 1 Cor 14:34; or 1 Cor 11:3; Eph 5:22.

46. See Gal 2:14. Paul calls such behavior "not acting consistently with the truth of the gospel."

47. See the texts where he accepts women in positions of authority without reservations or limits, such as Acts 18:2; Rom 16:1–12; Phil 4:2–3; Col 4:15. See on this Dunn, *The Theology of Paul*, 586–93.

weakness; that to us, caught in the struggle between the new and the old humanity, the full meaning of Christ's victory is gradually revealed.[48]

THE SPIRIT AS THE GIVER—THE CHURCH AS A MEDIATOR OF REVELATION

After Jesus' death, resurrection, and ascension, the position of the disciples changed. They were equipped with the power of the Spirit. This power would give their lives the shape and the direction that the Spirit had given to Jesus' life, whilst bringing into sharper relief their inclinations towards other powers, their fear, their search for short-term profit, and their old habits of mind.

Acts starts by narrating how the Spirit gathered the followers of Christ into the church, how the prophecy of Joel[49] was fulfilled, and how the church, as the special people of the end times moved from being an inward looking community to a worldwide missionary body. Pentecost, then, consists in two changes: the disciples are filled with the Spirit, and thus their inner world changes; the Spirit enables them to become witnesses, and thus their outer life is changed.[50]

Jesus established the church to act in history but its institution is fulfilled only when the Holy Spirit is sent. The Spirit helps the disciples to understand their experiences of God and his Christ, as well as their mission as a church now, which is to mediate Christ's salvation to the world in which they live. The Spirit is present in this mediation, but never confined by it. The Spirit would also reveal when something else than Christ is mediated and Christ's authority is exploited.[51] It is the Spirit who will reveal links between creation, salvation, and sanctification. By the Spirit we breathe and live, are renewed at our roots, brought into community, enabled to understand and change. The Protestant interpretation stresses the dynamism of the voluntary relationship. The church does not contain "God's pre-set form" in itself, but is open to a voluntary acceptance of the Spirit who leads.[52] The Roman Catholic interpretation does not deny this

48. See 2 Cor 5:16–18; Gal 3:28–29.

49. "I will pour out my spirit on all flesh; your sons and your daughters shall prophesy, your old men shall dream dreams, and your young men shall see visions. Even on the male and female slave, in those days, I will pour out my spirit." (Joel 3:1–2).

50. See Acts 2:1–4.14.37–38.41–47.

51. See Acts 5:1–11.

52. See Gunton, *The Promise of Trinitarian Theology*, 67.69.

freedom, but balances it with the presence of God's love for us in Christ as ever present and independent of our disposition to be able to receive it. The church, then, forms an inclusive community among people, one that can act upon the promise of the Spirit as it re-presents Christ.[53] In the Orthodox conception, the reality and permanency of God's gift is perhaps even more emphasized and embedded in God's economy of salvation. The church, too, enters this economy and mediates it in the power of the Holy Spirit and always will.[54]

THEOLOGIES OF REVELATION IN THE CHURCH FATHERS

The concept of God's self-revelation first emerges in Ignatius of Antioch. In the Letter to the Magnesians, Ignatius writes that prophets and those very close to God brought the following message to the unbelieving world, that the one God had revealed himself through Jesus Christ.[55] However, revelation is not approached as a specific theological theme in the way we have treated it since the Enlightenment. In patristic theology we find a reflection on the ways the church understood the events of revelation and on how such events, embedded in its self–understanding, were handed down to the next generation. Furthermore, it was necessary to reinterpret biblical narratives and symbols for new situations in which new questions arose. Sacramental practice and the need to defend Christian orthodoxy led the church to a binding interpretation of what represented the basic sources and events of revelation. Before and besides the need to formulate the canon of Scripture or to extend the baptismal Creed to include the dogmas about Christ and the Trinity, the Church Fathers examined the interpretation of revelation, its possibilities, and limits. Here I will concentrate on Justin Martyr, the theologians of the Alexandrian and Antiochian schools, and finally Gregory of Nyssa. In their own way, all explored the following questions: How does God appear? How can we recognize what is God's revelation? What consequences does it have for our relationship with God and the world?

---

53. Compare to Rahner, *Foundations*, 307–11.

54. See Zizioulas, *Being as Communion*, 197.

55 Ignatius of Antioch states that "there is one God, who has manifested Himself by Jesus Christ His Son, who is His eternal Word, not proceeding forth from silence, and who in all things pleased Him that sent Him." *Magn* VIII.

Divine Logos in Justin

The divine *Logos* as a bearer or revelation comes to patristic theology from biblical as well as philosophical sources.[56] Justin Martyr (c.110–165) distinguishes between *Logos spermatikos* (the Word sown like a seed in the whole world), and *Logos Christos* (the fullness of the Word). *Logos spermatikos*, found in the human "power of thought and of choosing the truth and doing right,"[57] can, according to Justin, lead, even after the Fall, to the intuition of God, as people are still born rational and contemplative.[58] It can be seen, for example, in the wisdom of prophets, philosophers, and poets. Each one of those who led to such awareness and to a just course of action was a bearer of God's revelation, but not yet fully. Justin says: "But since they did not know the whole of the Word, which is Christ, they often contradicted themselves."[59] The revelation in Christ is, according to Justin, a fulfillment of what has already been here in the seed. Christianity is then understood as a growth and coming to fruition of the Jewish religious tradition, as well as Greek philosophy, and all other traditions in which only fragments of the truth are visible.

We can criticize Justin for underestimating revelation in the Old Testament and Judaism. He cannot see any significant difference between Moses and Socrates, both of whom received a partially revealed truth. The difference, then, comes in Christ, in whom as Justin says, is revealed the fullness of the truth for Jews, Greeks, and everybody else.[60] We may not agree with this interpretation of the universality of Christianity nowadays but let us focus on a different point, one which is often overlooked.

Justin also claims that: "Whatever things were rightly said among all men are the property of us Christians."[61] That does not mean that we would be their exclusive owners, but that they can claim us. In other words, the revelation of the *Logos* scattered across the whole of creation is

---

56. The term *Logos* enters Christianity especially through Platonic and Stoic philosophy, but its roots stretch back as far as Heraclitus and Anaxagoras. The Church Fathers were further influenced by the synthesis of Hellenic and Jewish thought represented by e.g. Philo of Alexandria. See Price, "'Hellenization' and Logos Doctrine in Justin Martyr"; Dolejšová, *Accounts of Hope*, 75–80.

57. Justin, *1Apol* XXVIII.

58. See Justin, *1Apol* XXVIII; *2Apol* VIII.

59. Justin, *2Apol* X.

60. Ibid.

61. Justin, *2Apol* XIII.

not invalidated by the revelation in Christ. For us today, this could mean that people active in the field of human rights or ecology, although not Christians, are still able to mediate the revelation of God's truth that belongs to us—i.e., has a claim on us—Christians.

Justin's position had its opponents too, of course. The opposite stream was represented, for example, by the North African lawyer Tertullian, according to whom Jerusalem has nothing in common with Athens, so by this logic revelation is not present in the gentile world.[62] However, openness towards other traditions of the Hellenic world prevailed in patristic theology, despite Tertullian's skepticism concerning their coexistence.

Alexandrian and Antiochian Schools

The Alexandrian school was the oldest theological center of Christianity. Alexandria had a long tradition of education, with the world's biggest library, and had been a meeting point of the Egyptian, Hellenic, and Jewish cultures. Here the Hebrew Scripture was first translated into Greek, and a space provided for speculative thinking and the desire to understand faith and revelation. The Jewish thinker Philo (c.14BC–AD54), who applied the allegorical method to the reading of the Scripture, lived and worked in Alexandria.[63] This method was later adopted by Christian theologians, starting with Pantaenus,[64] then Clement of Alexandria, and Origen. Alexandria also produced the heresies of monophysitism and monotheletism.[65]

62. "What indeed has Athens to do with Jerusalem? What concord is there between the Academy and the Church? what between heretics and Christians? Our instruction comes from 'the porch of Solomon,' who had himself taught that 'the Lord should be sought in simplicity of heart.' Away with all attempts to produce a mottled Christianity of Stoic, Platonic, and dialectic composition! We want no curious disputation after possessing Christ Jesus, no inquisition after enjoying the gospel! With our faith, we desire no further belief. For this is our palmary faith, that there is nothing which we ought to believe besides." Tertullian, *DePraescr* VII.

63. The allegorical method had been used before him by the Stoic thinkers for the interpretation of myths. See Grant, *The Letter and the Spirit*.

64. Pantaenus is considered the founder of the Alexandrian school, which dates back approximately to 180.

65. Among the supporters of monophysitism can be numbered Dioscuros of Alexandria († 454) and Eutyches (c.378–454) who taught that Jesus has only one nature because his human nature dissolved in his divine nature. The Constantinopolitan patriarch Sergius († 638) tried to reconcile this teaching with the Chalcedonian teaching about the two natures of Christ, human and divine, by supporting the teaching about

What was the point of the allegorical method? The Greek *alla agurei* (to speak in public different things or different sense), from which "allegoric" comes, shows that the method deals with looking for a deeper meaning as the reader is led from the level of literal sense to another level. The text tells a story about one thing on the surface, but its deeper meaning is different.[66]

Clement of Alexandria (c.155–215), like Justin, defended the importance of a mutually enriching relationship between Christianity and other traditions of wisdom, especially Greek philosophy. According to him, the latter in fact took many of its insights from the Jewish prophets. However, philosophy could never replace revelation.[67] Clement distinguished between true knowledge, whose basis—actual or anticipated—is faith, and false knowledge, lacking this basis.[68] Scripture stood at the center of Clement's attention. He claimed that to understand what God reveals, it is necessary to take into account the symbolic character of the language.

Origen (c.185–c.254), who continued after Clement, shows that the language of the Scriptures is often poor. That is why his reader should not presume that he was holding the treasure of human wisdom, but instead he was to lift up his eyes to God's activity.[69] God's activity is present in the preaching of the Word, which breaks open the "spiritual sense" of the Old Testament and bears witness to what happened in the story of Jesus Christ.[70] In Origen it is difficult to distinguish between the allegorical method and the typological method, which interprets the characters of the Old Testament and events as "figures" or "types"—*typoi*—of the New Testament characters and events. His interpretation refers to Jesus' words: "You search

---

two natures but with only one divine will—monotheletism. The Lateran Council (649) and the Third Council of Constantinople (680–681) rejected this new attempt to restrict Christ's human nature.

66. See Šandera, "Alexandrijská a Antiochejská škola."

67. Clement here differs from Justin in that he sees *Logos spermatikos* in connection with the imitation of Judaism or Christianity. We would not find in Justin remarks, such as, for example, that Plato imitated Moses: see *Strom* 7,18,111,4. Nevertheless, he would want to praise philosophy for its criticism of the superstition, cruelty and eroticism of pagan cults and myths.

68. See Clement, *Strom* I:5,28. 2:2.8,4.

69. See Origen, *DePrinc* I:1.7.

70. See Origen, *DePrinc* IV:1.2, 6; Karfíková, "'Celé pole plné rozmanitých bylin,'" 14–15.

the Scriptures . . . and it is they that testify on my behalf . . . If you believed Moses, you would believe me, for he wrote about me." (John 5:39.46)[71]

Origen distinguishes between the physical, mental, and spiritual meaning of the Scriptures.[72] The physical, or literal, or historical sense (*historia*) of the Scriptures is intended for simple people who by following it would improve their lives. The depth of the Scriptures is in no way exhausted by this physical meaning. Some texts do not even have this meaning,[73] but their purpose is to draw the reader's or listener's attention to the mysteries hidden below the surface. Mental interpretation is the next step. It relates the physical (literal, historical) meaning to the situation of the human soul, its expectations, worries, and fears in the world in which the person lives.[74] The third spiritual interpretation (*theoria*) shows heavenly things and the future well–being that stems from God's redemptive action for humankind. Yet in order to arrive at a complex and holistic understanding of God's revelation as testified in the Scriptures, one must include all the meanings, including the physical and the mental, without resting on any single one. The journey from the simple to more nuanced and deeper understanding should be in accord with the apostolic tradition, according to Origen.[75]

The Antiochian school was founded by Lucian of Samosata in 312 as a counterpart to the Alexandrian school, with which it justly or unjustly

71. The distinguishing of allegory and typology earlier make it possible to reject the "allegoric frivolity" and at the same time to work with images. E.g., Abraham's sacrifice of Isaac was seen as an image of God the Father sacrificing Christ, etc. See de Lubac, "Typologie et allegorisme."

72. The teaching about the triple meaning of the Scripture was reworked by medieval hermeneutics into a teaching about the fourfold meaning of the Scripture: direct (physical or historical), allegorical, moral and anagogic (disclosing the mystery of the end of time). The basis of this teaching had already been formulated by John Cassian (c.360–430/35).

73. Origen mentions as examples the story of creation in seven days (Gen 1), or the story of the first people, Adam and Eve (Gen 2–3), or the devil's taking of Jesus to the high mountain (Matt 4:8). He says of each of these texts: "This metaphorical narration through an imaginary story that has never happened shows us a mystery." *DePrinc* IV:3.1; Karfíkova, "Celé pole plné rozmanitých bylin," 26–27.

74. Paul's interpretation that the one who works has to work in hope of reward (1 Cor 9:10) is an example of a spiritual interpretation.

75. This interpretation is represented by Paul's words about the sowing of spiritual goods (1 Cor 9:11). Its inner meaning, *dianoia*, must indeed be consistent with the "rules of *anagoge*." See Malherbe, "Introduction," 6.

found faults for its exaggerated use of imagination in allegory. This school concentrated on the text itself and taught their pupils to respect the literal meaning of the Scripture most of all, and to use historical context, grammar, and logic in its interpretations. Among the most important students of this school were Diodorus of Tarsus (†before 394), John Chrysostom (c.344/354–407), Theodore of Mopsuestia (c.350–428), as well as Arius († c.336) and Nestorius († c.451).[76] For the Antiochians, *theoria* meant a prophetic vision directed towards future fulfillment.[77] Their spiritual interpretation differentiated between typology, which they used, and allegory, which they avoided. Theodore, in his Commentary on Galatians 4:24,[78] writes:

> There are some people who make it their business to pervert the meaning of the divine Scriptures and to thwart whatever is to be found there. They invent foolish tales of their own and give to their nonsense the name of 'allegory'. By using the apostle's word, they imagine that they have found a way to undermine the meaning of everything in Scripture—they keep on using the apostle's expression 'allegorical'. They do not realize what a difference there is between their use of the term and the apostle's use of it here. For the apostle does not destroy history; he does not get rid of what has already happened . . . But they act in a totally opposite way . . . Adam, they say, is not Adam . . . paradise is not paradise and the serpent is not a serpent.[79]

Both the Alexandrian and Antiochian school stressed the Christ-centeredness of revelation. For the school of the allegorical interpretation, God's revelation in Christ was the deeper meaning of the Old Testament texts, but sometimes it forced such an interpretation on texts where the connection was difficult to trace. The Antiochian school, with its greater emphasis on historicity, assigned the Old Testament revelation a greater degree of independence. However, it also, when possible, searched for a Christ-type. At their most extreme, the Alexandrians ran the risk of underestimating Christ's human nature, whilst for the Antiochians it was his

76. Arius's teaching denying the divinity of Christ was condemned by the Council of Nicaea (325). The Nestorian teaching that Mary was the mother of the human Christ only was rejected by the Council of Chalcedon in 451. It is not certain, however, whether Nestorius really believed what was attributed to him.

77. See Malherbe, "Introduction," 7.

78. "Now this is an allegory: these women are two covenants . . ." (Gal 4:24).

79. Theodore of Mopsuestia, *Commentary*.

divinity that could be neglected. In their valuable contribution to theology both schools emphasized that in Christ the reader of the Old and the New Testament has to undergo a process of learning how to understand God's revelation more and more bountifully.

God's Infinity and the Infinite Human Journey
according to Gregory of Nyssa

In the middle of the fourth century the Christian understanding of revelation was endangered by the heretical teaching of Eunomius (†394/5), a radical Arian,[80] who proclaimed that if human reason grasps the right teaching, it is able to recognize God perfectly, and God ceases to be a mystery. Around that time the Cappadocian fathers, Basil (c.329–379), his friend Gregory of Nazianzen (330–389), and Basil's brother Gregory of Nyssa (c.330–c.395) formulated Trinitarian teaching and developed an approach to God's revelation that does not violate the divine mystery. Gregory of Nyssa, on whom I focus here,[81] states that revelation gives us neither the knowledge of God's ultimate name whether positively or negatively expressed, nor God's essence. In his works he produces a counter-position to Eunomius, arguing that the most important attribute of God is divine infinity.[82]

God can never be fully grasped and thus limited by our spatio–temporal categories. Our thinking and understanding is always particular, and always developing, insists Gregory. This process is situated not outside, but within our relationship with God, where we learn who God is by how God acts. There is an important difference between divine essence, which is hidden to us, and divine energies, such as love, mercy or kindness, which we are able to recognize in their effects.[83]

---

80. Eunomius also developed Arius's teaching, arguing that the expressions "unbegotten" or "not created," applicable only to God the Father, are not only his basic characteristic feature, but also directly capture his essence (*ousia*). Thus Eunomius introduced a type of negative theology that stemmed from the affirmative theology, for it believed that it had a privileged knowledge of God's negative name.

81. A more detailed analysis of Gregory's position is contained in my article "The Apophatic Way in Gregory of Nyssa."

82. Gregory of Nyssa, *ContrEun* I.673.

83. This differentiation between *ousia* and *energeiai* was further elaborated by Gregory Palamas (c.1296–1359) and accepted in 1351 at the Council of the Orthodox Church in Constantinople.

Gregory distinguishes between three types of infinity. The first is the absence of limits; the second deals with God's infinity, not mediated in time; the third type is related to us as people, existing in space and time, but bearing within ourselves God's image. Thus the divine infinity is imprinted into the human journey, leading always to a greater participation in God, but one that remains incomplete, even after death.

Here Gregory argues with Origen, whom he otherwise respects as an inspirational teacher of the Alexandrian tradition. Gregory himself took over the Alexandrian teaching about human freedom and eschatological hope, according to which everything will attain the goodness of God in the end.[84] However, Gregory disagrees with Origen's idea of the cyclic universe, where the human soul can become bored with the contemplation of God, turn away from him, and lapse back into embodied life, into time and space, where something is still struggled for, and where the return to God can start all over again.[85] According to Gregory, people can never be sated with contemplation of God, not even after the resurrection. The journey does not end even then, but enters a new phase. Here we can apply Paul's comment about "forgetting what lies behind and straining forward to what lies ahead," as a type of never-ending effort on the way to God.[86]

The theme of God's infinity and the never-ending human journey to God also appears in Gregory's interpretation of the Old Testament texts, especially in the *Life of Moses*.[87] The work is divided into four parts: (i) introduction; (ii) *historia*—a paraphrase of the biblical story; (iii) *theoria*—a contemplative reading, concentrating on the spiritual meaning of the story; (iv) conclusion. The Alexandrian method of interpretation can be identified behind these divisions. Gregory starts from the books of Exodus and Numbers and stresses that events recorded there must serve as a basis for every spiritual reading. *Theoria* cannot work without *histo-*

84. We can find in Gregory a similar position to Origen's teaching about *apokatastasis*. This held that everything will be included in God's goodness in the end, all will be converted and saved, even all the dark forces including Satan. Gregory's position, unlike Origen's, has never been condemned.

85. Gregory is aware that Origen here effectively opens up space for reincarnation. On this point he is in agreement with the anathemas of Constantinople, as we know them from the Justinian Code of 542.

86. Gregory employs here the term *epektasis*, which is taken from the Greek of Phil 3:13: "*epekteinomenos*". This can be literally translated as "he strives after what I am coming to."

87. Meyendorff, J., "Preface," xiii–xiv.

ria. Gregory shows the need to let the lives of honorable people speak, so they could become "patterns of virtue for those who come after them."[88] Contemplation of their lives enables a symbolic understanding of the journey of the soul to God.[89]

On this journey divine revelation breaks in both in its comprehensible and acceptable forms, but also as a darkness, in which the divine is beyond understanding, and at times even beyond our grasp. This is also what we can see in contemplating the lives of honorable men and women.[90] Gregory stays with the theme of darkness in God's revelation, and offers a distinction between the darkness of ignorance and the darkness of restoration. As to the first, more frequent according to him, he says: "the darkness of ignorance remains with the one who is obstinately disposed and does not permit his soul to behold the ray of truth." The other sort of darkness is a precursor to light, the ability "to perceive the final restoration which is expected to take place later in the kingdom of heaven of those who have suffered condemnation in Gehenna."[91] This darkness does not mean a stage where it is impossible to know God and God's plans for creation. Rather, it signifies the nature of such knowledge.

> For leaving behind everything that is observed, not only what sense comprehends, but also what intelligence think it sees, it [human mind] keeps on penetrating deeper until by the intelligence's yearning for understanding it gains access to the invisible and the incomprehensible, and there sees God. This is true knowledge of what it sought and transcends all knowledge, being separated on all sides by incomprehensibility as by a kind of darkness.[92]

The revelation of the darkness Gregory talks about is not the final stage of revelation, but it is an accompanying feature of it. The attempt to understand what God is not, and the nature of fellowship with God, which is different to the knowledge of anything and anyone else, links Gregory with the apophatic tradition. This is not Eunomius's negative

---

88. Gregory of Nyssa, *VMos* 65.

89. Danielou compares Gregory's approach to Jewish *haggada*, with both stressing the necessity of mystery, but the mystery itself, not its explanation in a naturalistic way. See Danielou, *Grégoire de Nysse*, xi–xiv.

90. See Gregory of Nyssa, *VMos* 79–80.

91. Ibid., 73.

92. Ibid., 95.

way, not the desire to find a higher "negative" knowledge, but the desire to continue infinitely on the way to the infinite God.

GOD'S REVELATION AND GOD'S MYSTERY IN CONTEMPORARY THEOLOGY

In this last section of the chapter I will deal with questions about the truth of revelation. This topic is not particular to modern and post-modern times. As we have seen, it was already present when Moses asked the Lord how the Israelites would recognize that God really appeared to him, and that he was not lying, or making things up, or offering them an illusion (Exod 4:1). Moses received God's name, but also the experience that those who want to know who God really is are sent back to the divine mystery, in whose light they have to fight with their own idolatrous tendencies and the idolatrous tendencies of others. Or, to use the example from John's gospel, Thomas was unable to believe in the Lord's resurrection until he could hold on to the invisible and untouchable reality, and when he could, he heard the Lord saying to him that they are blessed to whom this reality is available only through faith and the testimony of others.[93]

Justin believed that people are born "rational and contemplative," and that they are able to "choose the truth and do what is right" because *Logos spermatikos* has been "sown into every human generation."[94] Gregory stressed that genuine knowledge is at the same time a symbolic non-knowledge, "being separated on all sides by incomprehensibility as by a kind of darkness."[95]

The types of theology that came out of the Age of Enlightenment had the tendency to reduce the search for truth to a rational act and do away with contemplation. Faith in revelation then had to be based on obedience of will, as decreed, for example, by the First Vatican Council (1869–1870):[96] "If anyone says that the one true God, our Creator and Lord, cannot be known with certainty with the natural light of human reason

---

93. See John 20:29.

94. Justin, *1 Apol* 31 and 78.

95. Gregory of Nyssa, *VMos* 95.

96. The Constitution of the First Vatican Council "*Dei Filius*" *de fide catholica* had, for the first time, an individual chapter devoted to revelation. Various forms and ways of revelation are listed here and its timelessness and static form are stressed. See Fries, *Fundamental Theology*, 367–89.

by means of the things that have been made: let him be anathema."[97] Here
the certainty of knowledge is based on the authority of the church that the
faithful are obliged to believe. This point is even more emphasized by the
dogma of papal infallibility (1870) that concluded the Council.

Another example of post-Enlightenment reductionism is found in
Protestant liberalism. This claimed that the pure essence of Christianity
can be isolated by rational means alone. This task, necessary according to
them for modern people if they were to remain believers, was undertaken
by means of removing the layers of dirt stuck to the essence, where faith
in revelation is substituted by faith in what is rational and human.[98] These
positions were overcome in the middle of the twentieth century, even if
they have not entirely disappeared.

The Second Vatican Council in its constitution *Dei verbum*, dedicated to divine revelation, includes both an emphasis on the economy
of salvation and the historical dimension in its understanding of revelation. It also renews respect for the mystery of God[99] and concentrates on
the sources that testify God's revelation, and on their interpretation.[100]
Theology on the Protestant side returned to the sources as well, whether
Barth's theology of the sovereignty of God's word,[101] or Tillich's endeavor
to renew the traditional Christian understanding of symbol, on the one

---

97. DS 3026 (1806). The translation is taken from Clarkson, *The Church Teaches*, 28.
Knowledge of God in this text is treated as ordinary knowledge, which, however, according to Wittgenstein, is the least grounded certainty. See chapter 1, 39–40.

98. See, e.g., Harnack, *What is Christianity?*

99. The Constitution begins with a chapter entitled "Revelation Itself," which affirms:
"In His goodness and wisdom God chose to reveal Himself and to make known to us the
hidden purpose of His will (see Eph 1:9) by which through Christ, the Word made flesh,
humanity might in the Holy Spirit have access to the Father and come to share in the
divine nature (see Eph 2:18; 2 Peter 1:4) . . . This plan of revelation is realized by deeds
and words having in inner unity: the deeds wrought by God in the history of salvation
manifest and confirm the teaching and realities signified by the words, while the words
proclaim the deeds and clarify the mystery contained in them." (DV 1.2).

100. The major part of the Constitution is devoted to the Holy Scripture, which is not
isolated but rather connected with tradition, so that both "flowing from the same divine
wellspring, in a certain way merge into a unity and tend toward the same end." (DV 2.9)
Both are equated to a mirror in "which the pilgrim Church on earth looks at God, from
whom she has received everything, until she is brought finally to see Him as He is, face
to face." (DV 2.7).

101. See Barth, *The Word of God*.

hand, and God's infinity mirrored in the abyss of being on the other.[102] Orthodox theology has gone its own way, without the reductionism of the Enlightenment, but also without an emphasis on history, and often without any appreciation of the innovation of the tradition down the centuries.[103]

My intention here is not to examine this historical development in detail, but to focus on the contemporary problems. To demonstrate this I have chosen topics and authors from the Orthodox, Protestant, and Catholic tradition. I will deal here with the apophatic and kataphatic way as Vladimir Lossky understands them, then with the issue of how to connect the immediacy of the relationship with God with human critical thinking, as treated by Paul Ricoeur, and, lastly, with the sacramental mediation of revelation and the question of God's presence and absence in Louis-Marie Chauvet.

The Apophatic and Kataphatic Way according to Lossky

Gregory of Nyssa pointed out the God is revealed as a mystery and that non-knowing necessarily belongs to the knowing of this mystery. Orthodox theology builds on this paradoxical understanding[104] and develops it further by identifying the apophatic and the kataphatic ways of knowing God.

The Greek word *apophatike* (or its root *apophasis*) has two basic meanings, revelation and negation. The apophatic way includes both of these meanings. It is a complement and criticism of the kataphatic way (*katafatike*), meaning the "positive" symbolic content of theological statements. Vladimir Lossky puts the distinction as follows:

> Apophaticism consists in negating that which God is not; one eliminates firstly all creation, even the cosmic glory of the starry heavens and the intelligible light of the angels in the sky. Then one excludes the most lofty attributes, goodness, love, wisdom. One finally excludes being itself. God is none of all this; in His own nature He is unknowable. He 'is not.' But here is the Christian

102. See Tillich, *Biblical Religion* and *Dynamics of Faith*.

103. For Orthodox theology the return to the sources is a permanent topic. Nevertheless, even here we can find the movement of Neopatristic theology, represented by, among others, V. Lossky, G. Florovsky, J. Meyendorff or A. Schmemann. Its novelty lies in the fact that these authors work critically with patristic sources and use other disciplines.

104. See Meyendorff, *Byzantine Theology*, 11–12.

paradox; He is the God to whom I say 'Thou,' Who calls me, Who reveals Himself as personal, as living.[105]

Meyendorff stresses that the apophatic way does not include only an intellectual process of negation, but also the process of spiritual *katharsis*.[106] Using the example of the Liturgy of St. John Chrysostom, Lossky develops this point. He shows that the apophatic way consists of all we are and take on the way to the personal God: "In the liturgy of St. John Chrysostom, before the Lord's Supper, one prays: 'And grant us, O Lord, to dare to invoke Thee with confidence and without fear, by calling Thee Father.'"[107] The negative moment of the meeting with God's hiddenness can be found in the Scriptures too: when Jacob struggles with God as someone Unknown;[108] when Moses meets the Lord in the midst of the burning bush and asks his name;[109] when Elijah recognizes on Mount Horeb that God is not in the wind, or earthquake, or fire, or in any other phenomena where Elijah expected to meet him.[110] In the New Testament, the Apostle Paul says: "For now we see as in a mirror, dimly, but then we will see face to face." (1 Cor 13:12) Knowledge of the hiddenness of God, or better, meeting the hidden God, has a personal character now, as Lossky stresses and the Scriptures and patristic tradition acknowledge.

Alongside the apophatic way of knowing God, there is the positive, kataphatic way, in which the hidden God, dwelling beyond all that he reveals, grants us the narratives and symbols in which the revelation has taken place. Lossky characterizes the kataphatic way as follows: "God, Who is the hidden God, beyond all that reveals Him, is also He that reveals Himself. He is wisdom, love, goodness. But His nature remains

---

105. Lossky, *Orthodox Theology*, 32.

106. See Meyendorff, *Byzantine Theology*, 12. The expression *katharsis* originates in Platonic philosophy. Plato ascribes the method of catharsis to Socrates. (*Sophist* 231.e). As the body can be cleansed from diseases or ugliness by means of medicine and gymnastics, the soul can be cleansed from evil and ignorance by means of a virtuous life and education (see *Sophist* 229.d). The Church fathers emphasized in connection with the need of catharsis (*katharsis*) the need of cleansing from the evil of sin. See Gregory of Nyssa, *Treat* I.8.

107. Lossky, *Orthodox Theology*, 32. He goes on to comment that the Greek text says precisely: "God on high Whom one cannot name, the apophatic God." (*ibid.*)

108. See Gen 32:25–32.

109. See Exod 3:1–14.

110. See 1 Kgs 19:4–13.

unknowable in its depths, and that is exactly why He reveals Himself."[111] The kataphatic way gives us necessary content for our faith, and yet, if this content is not to become idolatrous, the kataphatic way has to be continually complemented by the apophatic way.

The positive way of knowing God is not a rival to the negative one. It is not a question of following one or the other, in each case arriving at God's self-revelation. Lossky stresses their interdependence, and in particular, the dependence of kataphaticism on apophaticism: "The permanent memory of apophaticism must rectify the kataphatic way. It must purify our concepts by contact with the inaccessible, and prevent them being enclosed within their limited meanings."[112]

In avoiding agnosticism, as well as the trivialization and idolization of the content of God's revelation, Lossky is reminiscent of Gregory's distinction of God's essence that remains hidden and God's actions through which we understand what God is like. He refers the kataphatic way, subjected as it is to continuous criticism and the need of catharsis, to the historical memory of how God dealt with his people. In this sense it is the way of reminiscence, *anamnesis*.[113] Both the catharsis of our whole being and the remembering of salvation history are only possible because of *methexis*,[114] participation in God. We are included in the communion of the Holy Trinity, but our participation does not nullify the difference between God and creation. On the way towards God, people (and with them the created world) do not merge with the Holy Trinity, but are brought

---

111. Lossky, *Orthodox Theology*, 32–33.

112. Ibid.

113. The term *anamnesis* comes from Plato. In the dialogue *Meno* Plato states that knowledge of the ideas is always latently present in the soul. We can access this knowledge by recollection of realities that the soul saw before its incarnation. See *Meno* 81. The Church Fathers applied his method of recollection not to the world of ideas but to the history of salvation. See e.g. Gregory, *V Mos*, 65; Lossky supports this point: see *Orthodox Theology*, 30.

114. The Platonic conception of *methexis* comes from his dialogue *Parmenides*. Its meaning is shown through a conflict. If the ideas are limitless, how can they be known to us, who are limited? Plato answers, because we participate in them. We participate in the ideal world that is far beyond our human knowledge. See *Parmenides* 129.a–ff. For the Church Fathers participation in God does not cancel out the fact that our knowledge of God includes the knowledge of our limits of this knowledge and of the infinity of who and how God is. See Gregory, *VMos* 93.

into radical communion with God and in God. It is this for which they were created.[115]

Western theology also knows negative and affirmative theology. The terms do not, however, completely overlap with the Eastern apophatic and kataphatic way. In Western theology until recently the *via affirmativa* has dominated, concentrating more on teaching than on the remembering of the history of salvation, and on the symbolic and sacramental language by which our participation in God is expressed. The Western *via negativa* was more embedded in speculative thinking and concentrated especially on what we cannot say about God.[116] There are indeed exceptions, represented mainly by the Western mystical tradition that, like Orthodox theology, relates the negative way to the whole of our being in relationship to God.[117] Mystical writers stress that God's self-revelation leads to our transformed knowledge of God and of the world in God and that it comes from silence. There God touches the depth of our being, and changes our understanding of what we know by leading us through the darkness of not knowing towards the intimate communion of all things in God.

Ricoeur's Critical Immediacy

A child, if it is allowed to be a child, has the certainty of his/her convictions—"This is mummy"; "this is home." This, we may also be tempted to say, is God who knows about us, who looks after us and allows himself to be recognized by us, even if we cannot see God the same way we can see other things. Belief in divine revelation is here understood in terms of trusting our interpretation of experience, in which God appears through all things. But trusting such experience and being convinced that, as we have such experience, our grasp of reality is divinized is quite another thing.

The latter notion is criticized by Rowan Williams, who argues that, if belief in divine revelation is separated from an experience-based knowledge of our fallibility, it forms non-critical convictions that our knowl-

---

115. In Orthodox theology this is called the journey of deification. It was developed by Athanasius, Gregory of Nazianzus, Dionysius, Maximus the Confessor, John Damascene, and from there it passed into the Byzantine tradition. See Russell, *Doctrine of Deification*.

116. In the theology of Thomas Aquinas, the negative moment refers to the fact that our knowledge is subject to error and to the difference between knowing physical and spiritual things (see *Summa Theologiae* I.84.vi).

117. See Macquarrie, *Two Worlds Are Ours*.

edge, if referring to the divine revelation, cannot seduce us. Williams criticizes the impact of such non-critical convictions on the theology of divine revelation, where, by accepting the statement that "God reveals himself," we participate in "this ultimate epistemological security" with regards to the contents of what the divinely imparted truth is.[118] This approach to revelation has no tools to work with personal development, with the development of our societies, cultures, and churches, in which errors belong to the process of growth. This process was so dear to Gregory of Nyssa, who emphasized that infinite possibilities of growth belonged to our being created in the image of God.

Likewise, the dynamics of the apophatic and kataphatic journey reflected this process of development, not only from the bad to the good, but also within the good, within our relationship with God, which starts with the divine self-revelation. From there, we can learn that our knowledge of God changes, and the recognition of partiality and error is a part of our life with God. As we grow, we need a humbler understanding of divine revelation, which differentiates between our temporal convictions (even those shared by a community of believers), and the knowledge of God and of all things in God. This, though, is not knowledge as we normally understand it,[119] but rather an intimate relationship, including insights and symbolic mediations of meaning, as much as the awareness of how different God is, and of how what we do not know might still change what we know.

Revelation, both "fitting" and "extending" human circumstance, has "nothing to do with absolute knowledge," insists Williams.[120] We might be aware of this while learning about the past: for example, the relationship of Christians to the institution of slavery or a woman's position in society. However, a recognition that our convictions are not divinely imparted truths, the results of God's revelation, is needed at all times, even today. For example, we still struggle with views that hold that the equality of women and men is not something relevant to the church, as we are faced with complicated issues concerning social justice or the possibilities of science applied to medicine and sexuality, and with the limits of where and how human life is allowed to be and to flourish.

118. See Williams, *On Christian Theology*, 142.

119. Compare to Wittgenstein's understanding of knowledge in chapter 1, 39–40.

120. Williams, *On Christian Theology*, 142.

Our openness to people of other religions, to homosexuals, to heterosexuals, to transsexuals, or even to terminally ill people who refuse further treatment, or who are refused treatment when they need it, because of their economic conditions, still divides Christians today, to such an extent that the representatives of these antagonistic positions doubt whether their adversaries do not offend the order revealed by God or the infinite love required by God's revelation. And unless we subject our convictional beliefs, rooted in the "epistemological security" that Williams criticizes, to a hermeneutics of suspicion, not only is dialogue with others hardly possible, neither is our growth on the journey with and towards the living God.

The French Protestant philosopher Paul Ricoeur offers an interesting alternative. In his early work, *The Symbolism of Evil*, he asks how it is possible to reconcile the human hunger for immediacy in the relationship with God with critical thinking that loses this immediacy. Ricoeur returns to the basic symbols of our conscience[121] and shows that these symbols are present in our natural language. They enable us to convey feelings or be in silence. They give us words to profess our faith and our love, or to confess our sins.[122] They lead us to the world of immediacy, to the immediacy that has become a stumbling block for modern thinking, because it was presented as something where critical thinking was not allowed to enter. Thus the critical mind reduced immediacy in order to gain space for itself. Ricoeur follows this process and sees himself as participating in the stage where the "children of criticism . . . seek to go beyond criticism by means of criticism, by a criticism which is no longer reductive but restorative."[123]

The process of understanding the impact of divine revelation on our convictions about God and about the world and about ourselves in it could, with the help of Ricoeur's hermeneutics, be divided into three stages. The first is the "first naivety" or the "primitive naivety", the precritical stage, which is dominated by the immediacy of belief. To exist as a Christian at this stage seems to be easy, as the world is full of nonproblematic meaning. God is in everything, God speaks to us, acts in our lives, and through our lives. We have a language to speak about this

---

121. Ricoeur, *Symbolism of Evil*, 351.

122. Ibid., 350.

123. Ibid., 350.

and to invite others to participate in this world of faith, immediacy, and meaning. Perhaps this stage is well-known to people who had a strong conversion experience as adults.

Yet this paradise of childhood, this oriented space, where we know where things are, is not permanent, as we experience tensions and conflicts, doubts arise, and we have to reevaluate the identity of our image of reality and distance ourselves from non-problematic faith, immediacy, and meaning, as we find ourselves disoriented. This stage is called by Ricoeur "a loss of naivety" or a "hermeneutics of suspicion." It is the time of critical thinking. Ricoeur's main interest, however, lies in how to pass from this stage of adolescence to the third stage, which, according to him, completes the hermeneutical circle: "We must understand in order to believe, but we must believe in order to understand."[124] This stage is called a "second naivety" and "aims to be a post-critical equivalent of the pre-critical hierophany."[125] This is the stage of regaining the immediacy of the first naivety without abandoning critical thinking. Both previous stages are integrated and challenged, as one enters a re-oriented space, though no longer in a non-problematic way. It is a space where aporias are present, and yet do not distance us from contact with reality, from belief, immediacy, and the endless plenitude of meaning.[126]

This extension of meaning, however, does not lead Ricoeur to claim that every interpretation of God's revelation or any grasping of the plenitude of meaning of the world is good. In his work *The Conflict of Interpretations: Essays in Hermeneutics* Ricoeur deals with the difference between an interpretation that reflects on and symbolically represents reality and a false interpretation that constructs reality, and thus relates to reality in an idolatrous manner. Using as an example the word "Father," he shows that if we allow our image to become a description of a supposed reality, we destroy it.

> Biblical faith represents God, the God of the prophets and the God of the Christian Trinity, as a father; atheism[127] teaches us to re-

124. Ricoeur, *Symbolism of Evil*, 351.

125. Ibid., 352.

126. Ricoeur says that "the second *naïveté* would be a second Copernican revolution: being which posits itself in the *Cogito* has still to discover that the very act by which it abstracts itself from the whole does not cease to share in being that challenges it in every symbol." Ricoeur, *Symbolism of Evil*, 356.

127. Atheism, according to Ricoeur, has a religious meaning and is thus worth ex-

nounce the image of the father. Once overcome as idol, the image of the father can be recovered as symbol. This symbol is a parable of the foundation of love; it is the counterpart, within a theology of love, of the progression that leads us from simple resignation to poetic life. I believe that such is the religious meaning of atheism. An idol must die so that a symbol of being may begin to speak.[128]

We relate to the world and to God idolatrously when we allow our images to stand as an objective description of reality, one that determines what God is like and how God acts and the sense of God's actions; in other words, when we reduce the multitude of meaning to one absolutized interpretation. When we elevate discourse about reality to reality itself and disregard the fact that our speech only refers to but does not create the world in which we live, we become idol-makers. This is true in ethical life,[129] as much as in spiritual and intellectual life, or in social or political life. All our attempts to fabricate reality, whether deliberate or subconscious, are ultimately self-defeating, however much influence they exercise.[130]

Returning to our symbolic discourse about God's revelation in a non-idolatrous manner, Ricoeur points out that we need to keep in balance both the semantic and the non-semantic elements of such speech,[131] both what can and what cannot pass into words or other representation, be it a painted image, the sound of music, or even a gesture. The semantic moment in symbol bears literal as well as figurative meaning. For example, a lamb in the New Testament refers both to the actual animal and to Christ. The non-semantic moment precisely cannot be put into words. It represents a power that does not pass over into the articulation of meaning except as a blank space—but a necessary blank space. It signifies and refers to the divine transcendence on the one hand, and, on the other hand, to the sacred, attested by everything that is. Ricoeur speaks both of

---

amining. For him it is represented by Nietzsche and Freud. Ricoeur states: "atheism is not limited in meaning to the mere negation and destruction of religion, but . . . rather, it opens up the horizon for something else, for a type of faith that might be called . . . a postreligious faith or a faith for a postreligious age . . . it looks back toward what it denies and forward toward what it makes possible." (Ricoeur, *The Conflict of Interpretations*, 440).

128. Ricoeur, *The Conflict of Interpretations*, 467.

129. Compare to Jas 2:14–26.

130. See Ricoeur, *Interpretation Theory*, 19–22.

131. Ricoeur, *Interpretation Theory*, 45–46.

God's transcending every attempt at our grasping him, of the numinous, the other (the non-figurative, non-semantic element) and of a religious person's vision of the world, where the sacred is present in the fertility of the soil, the vegetative exuberance, the flourishing of the flock, or fertility of the mother's womb (the figurative, non-semantic element). He goes on to show that symbols come into language to the extent that the elements of the world themselves become transparent. They have roots in the power of being, as well as in tradition.[132]

Ricoeur's distinctions, and his insistence that all elements must be guarded, if symbolic speech is to avoid idolization or emptiness, resemble the apophatic and the kataphatic way discussed earlier. The difference is that in Ricoeur's approach critical thinking is more accentuated and its integration more necessary. Critical thinking must, according to Ricoeur, transcend its own limitations and rediscover its place in our participation in a reality we have not created ourselves and that springs from both the direct relationship with the transcendent God and from the tradition in which the forms of life of previous generations formed an environment that gives meaning to our own narrative.[133] Williams sums it up as follows:

> If, then, we follow something like Ricoeur's analysis of revelation, a statement like 'God reveals himself' will mean that God invites us into his 'world': new life is manifested historically, in event, speech, and memory, restoring to us a 'participation—in or belonging—to an order of things which precedes our capacity to oppose ourselves to things taken as objects opposed to a subject.'[134] In this case, the 'order of things' in question is the primary order of all things, the creative liberty of God . . . 'God reveals himself' means that the meaning of the word 'God' establishes itself among us as the loving and nurturing advent of *newness* in human life—grace, forgiveness, empowerment to be the agents of forgiveness and liberation. This advent has its center, its normative focus, in the records of Jesus; it occurs among us now as the re-presentation of Jesus through the Spirit; and it rests upon and gives content to the fundamental regulative notion of initiative, creative or generative power, potentiality, that is not circumscribed by the conditions of the empirical world – but *arché* of the Father, the ultimate source.[135]

132. Ricoeur talks of the religious person's vision of the world rooted in the power of being, in tradition, and in God's transcendence. See Ricoeur, *Time and Narrative*, 70.

133. Compare Levi, "Suffering and Post-Modern Consciousness," 327.

134. The reference is to Ricoeur, *Gravity and Grace*, 101.

135. Williams, *On Christian Theology*, 145.

Sacramental Mediation in Chauvet

Finally, in considering current Roman Catholic theology of divine revelation, we can ask how divine revelation is related to the sacramental life of the church. Here we touch on issues that historically divided the churches, such as how God reveals himself in the Eucharist, in baptism, in the sacrament of reconciliation, and whether, and if so how, we can talk about God's revealing presence, and whether such presence is conditioned from our side. Instead of engaging with the historical-confessional debate, we will concentrate on the present situation, where some of the questions have reappeared with a new urgency, even in traditions that had well-developed notions of sacramental mediation. If people treat sacraments violently and devalue them, if, for example, they celebrate reconciliation and are not reconciled, if they celebrate baptism and are not willing to give up their evil ways, if they celebrate Eucharist and do not live together in unity, one is forced to ask whether and if so how God still reveals himself in the sacraments. Instead of dealing with these questions in terms of the validity of the sacraments, we will follow the debate with reference to the presence and the absence of God.

William Cavanaugh, in discussing the situation in Chile when Christians were confronted by the violence of General Pinochet's dictatorship, examines the underlying ecclesiology and sacramental theology that either paralyzed or enabled the church's resistance to violence and action in favor of the tortured.

> In a well-intentioned effort to extricate itself from coercive politics, the church had embraced 'social Catholicism', an attempt to confine the church's activities to a putative 'social' sphere while vacating the 'political' sphere. This attempt to stake a position as the 'soul' of civil society amounted to a handing over of bodies to the state.[136]

In the extreme conditions of the dictatorship the church bought into the state ideology by "acknowledging the state's monopoly on coercion, handing over the bodies of Christians to the armed forces, and agreeing to stay out of the fabricated realm of the 'political.'"[137] Parts of the church that were able to break free of this ecclesiological bond and draw on a more holistic understanding of the Eucharist found in their liturgical celebra-

136. Cavanaugh, *Torture and Eucharist*, 2.
137. Cavanaugh, *Torture and Eucharist*, 9.

tion sources to resist the anti-liturgy of fear, torture, and fragmentation of the physical, the ecclesial, and the social body.[138] Their sacramental understanding did not operate on a division of reality into graced and ungraced, but rather rescued the Eucharist as relevant to all realms of life in which God reveals himself. The nature of this revelation stopped being seen as otherworldly, but as "deeply involved in the suffering of this world—but . . . in sharp discontinuity with the politics of the world which killed its savior."[139]

Cavanaugh does not speak about God's absence in a world where violence is present, but about the presence of the Son of God, tortured to death. Those who actively participate in violence, according to him, participate in a certain anti-liturgy of the destruction of life. Human activity is not downplayed, for it influences the kind of world we live in, but the God who time after time offers his life and wants it to be celebrated is not restricted by it.[140] Discourse about God's presence and absence is not conditioned by people's actions. We do not make God present or absent in the sacraments by our being good or bad people, a good or bad church.[141] However, the discussion about God's presence and absence does not end there.

The French sacramental theologian Louis-Marie Chauvet approaches this subject from a different angle and shows that Western theology has imprisoned God into its schemes by speaking of God's presence with the help of its metaphysics: it has reduced God to being and being to a thing we can comprehend and describe.[142] Chauvet criticizes metaphysics for its

---

138. Ibid., 21–71.

139. Ibid., 13–14.

140. Ibid., 17–18.

141. Catholic theology follows the view it reached during the struggles with Donatism. Donatism arose as a charismatic movement in northern Africa after the great persecution under Diocletian (303–305). Donatus and his followers claimed that sacraments administered by bishops and priests who had collaborated in the time of persecution were invalid. They re-baptized and re-ordained and believed that God was present among them alone and acted in the sacraments administered by them alone because they did not fail morally. Catholic theology argued against the Donatists that God's presence in sacraments is not dependent on the moral qualities of the person administering them.

142. Metaphysics or onto-theology (theology of being) is understood negatively by Chauvet. He distinguishes various types of metaphysics and is aware that his critique is directed to a generally widespread understanding of these traditions rather than to their leading representatives, who were aware of the limited possibilities to capture being as such conceptually and describe it with the help of a meta-theory. See Chauvet, *Symbol and Sacrament*, 8.

one-sidedness, failing to take into account the tension between conceptual knowledge (without which there would be no scientific discourse)
and symbolic non-knowledge (without which the mystery of God will
no longer be respected).[143] His attention is directed to the neglected pole
of this tension, to the symbolic non-knowledge, and to what this non-
knowledge represents, namely God's grace aiming at the renewal of faith
and attitudes of gratitude and generosity.[144] Grace, according to Chauvet,
is an irreducible gift. It always comes first and is not caused by anything or
explained by anything; it is impossible to be reduced to "value", whether
in the conceptual, physical, or moral sense of the word. The journey to accepting grace is always a way characterized by "a gracious attitude of 'letting be' and 'allowing oneself to be spoken' which requires us to renounce
all ambition for mastery."[145]

Chauvet stresses the "materiality" of faith and he contrasts it with
"nostalgia for an ideal and immediate presence to oneself, to others, and
to God."[146] God's revelation cannot, then, be confused with an ideal non-
mediated presence of God. In this light Chauvet interprets the story of
the disciples going to Emmaus.[147] He begins with a key question: "How
does one pass from non-faith to faith?"[148] His answer comes through the
analysis of the transformation that this story addresses:

> In the first section of the story (vv.13–17, up until their first stop-
> ping on the road), the two disciples have in effect abandoned their
> mission; in turning away from Jerusalem, they are also in effect
> turning their backs on their previous experience with Jesus. They
> talk between themselves, each a sort of mirror image of the other,
> tossing back and forth the same expression of a definite postmor-
> tem on the failed mission of their Master. Consequently, their
> eyes are 'kept from recognizing him'; their spirits, like their eyes,
> are shut. For that matter, everything is shut. They have allowed
> themselves to be sealed up together with the dead body of Jesus
> in the constricted place of his death, the sepulcher, whose mouth

143. See Chauvet, "The Liturgy in its Symbolic Space," 36–37.

144. See Chauvet, Symbol and Sacrament, 139–40.

145. Ibid., 446.

146. Ibid., 154.

147. See Luke 24:13–35.

148. Chauvet, Symbol and Sacrament, 161.

has been blocked with a huge stone. Their past is dead; and in any case, it has no future.[149]

Chauvet further points out the shift when their closed circle is broken by the talk with a "stranger." He enters their conversation and lets them name their situation; he wants them to tell him their story. First he leads them to their memories, then he links their memories with the Scriptures: "Remember . . . how foolish you are and how slow of heart to believe what the prophets have declared . . . everything . . . must be fulfilled":[150] and then he opened their minds to understand the Scriptures.[151] Chauvet says: "Instead of holding forth with self-assured pronouncements *on* God, one must begin by listening to a word as the word *of* God . . . In allowing Jesus to open the Scriptures for them, the two disciples begin to enter into an understanding of the 'real' different from what they previously thought evident."[152] They urge the stranger to stay, and in his breaking of bread, when his word becomes flesh, their eyes begin to open, and they recognize the stranger in his radical strangeness. At the same time we can see that their eyes are now open to emptiness as he has vanished from their sight. This emptiness, though, is full of presence. The disciples recognize the Risen Lord. They receive this recognition as a gift of good news and in return they become Christian witnesses. It is their gift, their response to the initial gift of God. Chauvet stresses that one is not possible without the other.[153]

Chauvet's symbolic mediation works with the paradoxical notion of an emptiness full of presence. The emptiness does not mean the unreality of God's presence, but rather the fact that there is no place here that could contain and keep God the way God is. Chauvet's sacramental theology elaborates the consequences of the symbolic (and as such paradoxical) meaning of the place of the body in its materiality. We could say that the *topos* (place), where the sacramental presence is, is at the same time a *utopia* (non-place). The reality of God's presence is not abandoned—so, for example, we can still meaningfully speak about God's presence in the

149. Chauvet, *Symbol and Sacrament*, 167.

150. See Luke 24:6.25–27.

151. See Luke 24:44–45.

152. Chauvet, *Symbol and Sacrament*, 168.

153. "In the last analysis, faith can exist only if it expresses itself in a life of *witness*." (Chauvet, *Symbol and Sacrament*, 164).

Eucharist or in baptism—but the otherness of this presence is underlined, the otherness that includes and exceeds anything we mean by presence and absence, the otherness that is ultimately indescribable in language, but can be passed on by symbols. In this context Chauvet asks how God is present in the church:

> Those who reject the Church in order to find Christ by themselves misunderstand [in what sense Christ has departed] . . . But those who live too comfortably in the Church also misunderstand it: they are then in danger of forgetting that the Church is not Christ and that if, in faith, it is recognized as the privileged place of his presence, it is also, in this same faith, the most radical mediation of his absence . . . The church radicalizes the vacancy of the place of God.[154]

The church, as the body in which Christ is witnessed, is both rooted in and permanently de-established by Christ's *kenosis*, Christ's self-giving, which in turn asks for the church's *kenosis*. This is not expressed primarily in the zeal of its members to sacrifice themselves for others (which despite our best convictions can go in the wrong direction), but in a radical recognition that God is the sovereign Master and that the church is to follow where the Spirit of God blows. Chauvet even calls the blank space of God "the anti-name of God, the Spirit . . . which, while fully of God's very self, works to subvert in us every idolatrous attempt at manipulating God (whether at the conceptual, ethical or ritual level)."[155] At the same time Chauvet stresses that the church is where we are given a share in faith, and where we learn attitudes of gratitude and generosity, as God is revealed in the faith that marks our physical existence. There God's absence full of presence is mediated by the community of disciples, as "the Spirit inscribes it in the *body* of the community."[156]

Chauvet's emphasis on the sacramental dimension of our communication with God and with one another, his tracking of the transformation from blindness to a faith that can see but whose vision is at the same time subject to emptiness, the radical otherness of what can be seen, shows that revelation is neither the revelation of an abstract principle, nor of the unambiguous meaning of things. Revelation does not pull anyone out of

154. Chauvet, *Symbol and Sacrament*, 177–78.

155. Ibid., 517.

156. Ibid., 531.

their physical existence, or fellowship with other people, but it uncovers their foundation. It allows us to grasp again this foundation with the help of God's word, and with the help of sacraments to learn how to live a life of witness to the good news, and to mediate God with the awareness that we are continually on the way to God.[157]

CONCLUSION: THE RELATIONAL NATURE OF REVELATION

The attitude to revelation as illustrated through selected passages from Scripture and the tradition of the Church Fathers and as it appears in some significant current movements of Orthodox, Protestant, and Catholic theology is very varied. Now, at the end of the chapter, I will sum up the main insights that came out of our examination and conclude by asking what role theology of revelation plays and might play in ecumenical and inter-religious dialogue.

Summary

What do we know about the revealing God? The biblical stories that capture the experience of God's revelation show that we always ask questions about God when we are already in a relationship with God. Whether it is a relationship of faith or unbelief, hope or doubt, or even indifference, we do not approach revelation as a kind of neutral observer. Thus the situations that we are in and the traditions that we have accepted as our own or rejected—even if they still influence us—feature in our non-neutrality. Sometimes the question of God comes through the circumstances, even without us articulating it, as the examples we saw from the Old and New Testaments indicated. We could say that the limit situations speaking to us through the Scriptures have nothing to do with our ordinary lives. But then, which life really is ordinary? Which life lacks at least in some of its moments the urgency of spoken or unspoken questions concerning the ultimate?

The stories of Balaam or of Saul show that communication with God is not a reflection of some theoretical possibility of God's existence. Rather, it is a meeting with the practical necessity of changing one's ways. For, in these stories, encounters with the living God are not a question at all, but a basic certainty that gives meaning to everything else, even if this

---

157. Cf. the concept of Gregory's infinite journey to the infinite God examined above.

remains incomprehensible to those who have never had such an experience. Balak, king of Moab, who hired Balaam to curse Israel, could not understand what was happening with him.[158] Those who accompanied Saul to Damascus "stood speechless because they heard the voice but saw no one." (Acts 9:7) However, neither in the case of Balaam nor in that of Saul can we speak of what Williams criticizes as an "epistemological security", of the conviction that our knowledge cannot ultimately deceive us, because it comes with God's revelation.[159]

Instead in both cases we see a loss of epistemological security. This loss does not allow people to continue in their previous convictions and practices. It re-orients faith and human behavior. By challenging the established "certainties," it leads to a much more basic certainty. Now, we are no longer the center of gravity, but our lives and our understanding are included into the mystery of God. In this mystery a continual negotiation between conceptual knowledge and symbolic non-knowledge takes place, as people struggle to put into practice what the experience of revelation has uncovered for them.

Biblical narratives also reflect how the experience of God who appears is captured, so that the primary personal experience receives a public character and becomes a part of tradition. This tradition allows various experiences to exist side by side, without being reduced to one pattern. This plurality was noticed by the Church Fathers as they dealt with how to interpret God's revelation and how to hand down the experience of it without reducing the aspects they did not understand. The three examples of patristic approach to revelation that I explored put a different emphasis on tradition as a living memory in which God has sown seeds of his words, knowledge that people gifted with the Holy Spirit are learning to understand.

Justin stressed the need to be open to all traditions because each of them can mediate for us Christians the revelation of God's truth, and a deeper understanding of our Lord Jesus Christ, whom we believe is the ultimate truth. In Christ we need to grow and anything that helps us to grow is, according to Justin, good.

Theologians of the Alexandrian and Antiochian schools pointed out that we always interpret the tradition that has been handed down to us

---

158. See Num 23:11 and Num 24:3–4.15–16.
159. See Williams, *On Christian Theology*, 142.

with some pre–understanding. Whether we practice the allegorical inter-pretation of the Old Testament as the Alexandrian school did, or whether we search for a Christ-type in the fashion of the Antiochian school, we enter into a relationship with the understanding that previous generations had, and, in allowing ourselves to enter into dialogue with it, we allow the recorded events to become a living word speaking into our situation.

Gregory emphasized God's infinity and the never-ending human journey towards God, stressing not only that attempts to pin God down are futile, but also that we can never be bored with God, never reach the stage when nothing would surprise us any longer, nothing would give us the delight of a beauty or love newly discovered. A living relationship with God, which comes across when we contemplate the lives of people of faith, such as Moses, involves both closeness and continuous change. In this sense they are examples for us. Furthermore, in their lives we see not only the comprehensible side of God's revelation, but also the dark side, where human understanding fails, and, encircled as if by a fog or by darkness, these men and women become transformed into friends of God. The certainty of their faith, or even a certainty beyond faith, a cer-tainty on which they act, combines, at this new higher stage, knowledge and non-knowledge, suggesting that both of them are necessary for going still further.[160]

We could also see a common interest in the three current approach-es to revelation that I explored, namely the rehabilitation of God's tran-scendence as reaching beyond what can be captured by our explanation, and at the same time being a source of our conversion. The experience of conversion is something we know from tradition, but also from our own lives. In it we receive a new way of speaking about God as the one whom we have witnessed as acting in our lives and in our world. In this experience the transcendent God becomes an immanently present God, without God's transcendence and otherness ceasing to be transcendent, and thus radically different to anything we know. Lossky grasped these two aspects of transcendence by distinguishing two correlated ways of knowing God, the apophatic and kataphatic. Ricoeur pointed out that our symbolic discourse about God has a figurative and non-figurative side, and he showed each semantic and non-semantic element in it. Thus he was able to appreciate both imagination, in which we are able to see God

160. Gregory of Nyssa, *VMos* 65.78–80.95.

in everything around us, and the experiential knowledge that God always exceeds every attempt of ours to contain God and that God is always different. Chauvet pointed out that even at the heart of the sacramental mediation of God, there is an interplay between God's presence and absence. It belongs to faith that sees God in the Spirit without ever substituting God for a theory, to a faith that is born in the body of Christ's witnesses.

Theology of Revelation in Ecumenical and Inter-Religious Dialogue

The variety of approaches to revelation, to a certain extent subject to denominational belonging, has already been referred to in the section "The Spirit as giver and church as mediator of revelation." There is an agreement among the traditions that the same Spirit that gave shape to Jesus' earthly life now gives a Christ-like shape to the church. And yet there are differences with regards to what shape this is, how permanently it can be grasped, and to what degree human cooperation is needed. Here each of the traditions accentuates different aspects. The family of Protestant traditions tends to emphasize God's transcendence, and the freedom of the Spirit to act or not freely, independently of human affairs.[161] This emphasis can be a source of great humility and freedom. At times, however, the small flock of the faithful would be seen as privileged, with a robust certainty that having the Word of God sets them apart from the world, and makes them a graced exception, those who because of the Word know what to believe and how to live. Evangelical and Pentecostal theologies, which were not analyzed in the chapter, could be seen both as a radicalization and a reaction to such biblical positivism. The Catholic and Orthodox traditions elaborate the theme of God's faithfulness with regard to the church's privileged place in mediating God's revelation differently. For both groups of traditions grace usually comes already with creation, and as such it is not restricted to the elect. All are loved by God, even if some might have forgotten it. Catholic theologies struggle to keep this openness together with the emphasis on the church in its cultural, historical, and traditional particularity as the privileged place of God's revelation.[162] The Orthodox traditions stress the anchorage of the church

---

161. See Gunton, *The Promise of Trinitarian Theology*, 67–69; Williams, *On Christian Theology*, 142–45.

162. See Chauvet, *Symbol and Sacrament*, 509–31.

in God's economy of salvation in which, after Jesus' ascension, the Spirit takes over the role of mediator of the meaning of Jesus' words and acts, and leads the church, which was in God's plan from the very beginning, to the truth.[163] Again, one ecumenically very sensitive question is who is and who is not the church. We can say that the different approaches complement each other. Such complementarity, however, is not free of conflicting claims, sometimes rooted in different understandings of the relationship between the world and God, different ecclesiologies, different priorities of church practice, or different political, national, or cultural priorities.

In this chapter I have approached revelation from a Christian theological point of view. I have not dealt with inter-religious themes. These lead to an even more varied terrain, where the question whether talk about revelation refers to the same or a different reality or to the same or a different God is still more radically present. Yet I hope that the insights listed above might be useful even in this debate. There is the emphasis that we never approach revelation from a neutral position, but always include the situations we find ourselves in and the traditions we have adopted or against which we define ourselves. Also I believe that in the inter-religious setting Ricoeur's approach can be used, differentiating an interpretation that reflects the reality and an interpretation that twists it by not relating to it in the right way. His distinction between symbolic and idolatrous relations to reality[164] stemmed from the fact that an idolatrous relationship to the world and God gives our conceptions an inadequate authority. It turns them into a matter-of-fact description of reality that determines what God is like, how God acts, what God wants from us, what sense it makes. Even if we do not understand claims to revelation in other religions from within, the claim on us and our open hearts, in relationship to the God we profess, remains. In that relationship we are led away from false superiority to an ongoing conversion, allowing us to remain who we are called to be, people of the Spirit, trusting that, as Jesus Christ enabled us to see and to live, in God all things will be well.

---

163. Zizioulas, *Being and Communion*, 130.
164. Ricoeur, *The Conflict of Interpretations*, 467.

3

The Problem of Authority

*When he entered the temple, the chief priests and the elders of the
people came to him as he was teaching, and said, 'By what authority are
you doing these things, and who gave you this authority?' Jesus said to
them, 'I will also ask you one question; if you tell me the answer, then
I will also tell you by what authority I do these things. Did the baptism
of John come from heaven, or was it of human origin?' And they argued
with one another, 'If we say, 'From heaven', he will say to us, 'Why then
did you not believe him?' But if we say, 'Of human origin', we are afraid
of the crowd; for all regard John as a prophet.' So they answered to Jesus,
'We do not know.' And he said to them, 'Neither will I tell you by what
authority I am doing these things.'*

MATT 21:23–27

*Certainly, I have always contended that obedience even to an erring
conscience was the way to gain light, and that it mattered not where a
man began, so that he began on what came to hand, and in faith; and
that anything might become a divine method of Truth; that to the pure all
things are pure, and have self-correcting virtue and power of germinating.*

JOHN HENRY NEWMAN[1]

WHAT MAKES A PERSON or a community of people think, believe,
and act in a certain way? That is the question I will address in this
chapter. In the chapter on theological method we saw that Wittgenstein
differentiated between three types of certainty: the certainty of knowing,
the certainty of believing, and the certainty of acting. This latter certainty

---

1. Newman, *Apologia pro vita sua*, 192.

was considered the most difficult to communicate in words, but at the same time the most reliable criterion of what is really authoritative for us. This certainty is sometimes expressed in terms of belief, sometimes not,[2] but it has nothing to do with a conviction that our knowledge cannot ultimately deceive us because it is embedded in God's revelation.[3] The revelatory narratives mentioned in the previous chapter demonstrated that encounters with the living God always include elements of risk, of losing previous certainties, of challenge. With characters such as Balaam or Saul we could see that a more accurate way of naming the experience of God would be as an "epistemological danger" that is part of the deeper security in God.

It may be objected that it is easy to accept this danger if one is sure of being on God's side. But, as we also saw in the previous chapter, the difficulty is that even with faith and with the experience of God, we do not read life from God's point of view. Our experience of God, and the traditions that convey this experience, have given rise to various understandings of who God is and what he wants from us in our lives. I used Ricoeur's approach to show that the effort to extricate ourselves from the open-ended multitude of meanings can distort reality. By narrowing the meanings down and controlling their use, we begin to relate to images, to our creation of reality and of God, as if they were reality, as if they were God. Thus idols take the place of authority, of what influences our ways of acting, believing, thinking, and speaking, and we find ourselves in a place where the security provided by our idols must be disrupted, so that we can discover a fresh relationship with God and with each other in the world in which we live.[4] We have to learn to risk and to change again and again, in order to grow, and to respond more maturely to God's calling. This process does not, though, happen in isolation, but always in relationships, including the various different bodies we belong to, starting with family, through school, friends, church, working place, to society at large. There, if not together, then at least always with regard to others and their best interests, what is authoritative needs to be discerned and embraced.

This chapter will deal with questions connected with the understanding of authority in Christianity. This includes both references to the

2. See Wittgenstein, *On Certainty*, §§ 11, 12, 189, 284, 550.

3. See Williams, *On Christian Theology*, 142.

4. See Ricoeur, *The Conflict of Interpretations*, 467.

supreme authority of God as well as a web of authorities that mediate this divine authority. First, I will explore the meaning of the word "authority" and its roots in the Scriptures and tradition. Then I will deal with what happens when authorities come into conflict and how to solve such conflict, before turning at the end to the way in which authority is ideologized, so that reference to "authority" serves as a way to remain in power.

THE CONCEPT OF AUTHORITY IN THE SCRIPTURES

Where does the concept of authority come from? Can we find it in the Hebrew and Greek Scriptures? How is what makes people act in certain ways depicted there? On what basis do people share a common faith and belong to a community that follows certain rules? The choice of texts in this section of the chapter searches for possible answers to these questions.

The Language Roots

"Authority" comes from the Latin *auctoritas*. It was introduced into Roman culture through the law, where it meant to arrange a transaction, to have responsibility for subordinates, or the weight of opinion. From here another meaning was derived, namely reverence and respect for and the importance of a person who is the bearer of *auctoritas*. Then it is possible to talk about personal authority, based on personal charisma, traditional authority, given by the trustworthy transmission of insights and rules seen as valid from generations back, and institutional authority, founded on administrative structures and their practices, based on the validity of normative regulations.[5]

Neither Greek nor Hebrew has an exact equivalent, in spite of the scriptural usage of the meaning attributed to the term "authority" in both languages. In Hebrew we can find about thirty expressions carrying a similar meaning. Among these are, for example, *sh-l-t* which translates as "to be someone's master," "to rule over somebody," whether it refers to a political power, to a legal claim of a certain institution or to God's claims on his people.[6] In addition, we find the expression *r-b-t*, which appears, for example, in the book of Proverbs;[7] or *t-q-p*, which appears,

---

5. For a more nuanced understanding of authority, see Weber, *The Theory of Social and Economic Organization*, 152.328; O'Collins, *Fundamental Theology*, 180–81.

6. See Neh 5:15; Esth 9:1; Eccl 8:9; 2 Kgs 20:13; Ps 114:2; Dan 4:34–35.

7. See Prov 29:2.

for example, in the book of Esther.[8] Another expression *r-s-t* appears in rabbinic literature.

This is an equivalent of the Greek *exousia*, which translates as authority, power, freedom of choice, the right to act or make a decision or to dispose of one's own possessions according to one's personal discretion, as well as to the bearer of authority, as establishment, or as ruler. In the New Testament *exousia* is used to refer to divine authority, originating from who God is and how God appears to us. *Exousia* is also granted to God's creation: to the world of spiritual powers, people, society, and church. The concept of authority has an inbuilt tension because any delegated authority carries the possibility of its perversion. Thus the expression *exousia* is used for the realm of evil as well, even if this is always seen as temporary. We read, for example, that the authority of evil takes its power from the law, for it shows, according to the Scriptures, the discrepancy between justice and sin.[9] Besides *exousia*, the New Testament also employs the expression *dynamis*, which translates as power, influence, strength, or ability and means something similar to *exousia*.[10]

Divine and Human Authority in the Old Testament

After the short terminological excursion, we come to explore how both divine and human authority are represented in the Scriptures. Here, as in the previous chapter, it is not the usage of particular words and their context that we are looking for, but rather narratives that embody some of the meanings highlighted above and, more, what has not yet been expressed, and what resists verbal expression. In what ways is divine authority recognized and respected, what content does it have, in which sense is it direct, in which mediated through a whole web of fallible human authorities, and how could the people of God resist the temptation to put their pre-ultimate views in the place of the ultimate importance? These are our questions as we examine a selection of Old Testament texts.

8. See Esth 9:29.

9. See Acts 1:7; Rom 9:21; Rev 14:18; Matt 8:9; Luke 20:20; 22:25; John 19:10; John 1:12; Rev 13:5–8.

10. See 1 Cor 15:56; Rev 13:12.

SUPREMACY OF THE LORD GOD

In the Old Testament, God's supremacy and sovereignty were connected with the fact that God alone and no other acted in the way he did. Let us start with the story of how God brought Israel out of Egypt, a foundational etiological narrative for Israel's belief. Stepping into the narrative, we can move within the immediacy of meaning the text operates with, without reduction of the meaning from open plurality to idolizing singularity. In the story Moses and Aaron first asked the pharaoh to let the Hebrews go out of Egypt and celebrate with their God in the wilderness: "The God of the Hebrews has revealed himself to us; let us go a three days' journey into the wilderness to sacrifice to the Lord our God, or he will fall upon us with pestilence or sword." (Exod 5:3) During the first meeting with the pharaoh they spoke about God whose power had been recognized over a certain community of people, namely the Hebrews, but not yet over all nations. When the pharaoh's heart had been hardened, we read of a comparison of the power of this God and that of the deities of the Egyptians: "Aaron threw down his staff before the Pharaoh and his officials, and it became a snake. Then Pharaoh summoned the wise men and the sorcerers; and they also, the magicians of Egypt, did the same by their secret arts. Each one threw down his staff and they became snakes; but Aaron's staff swallowed up theirs." (Exod 7:10–12)

This moment was elaborated in the story of the ten plagues of Egypt.[11] When Moses and Aaron, following the Lord's command, turned the waters of the Nile into blood, when they let the Egyptian land be covered with frogs, then we find that the Egyptian magicians did the same. But they could not imitate the third plague, making gnats of the dust of the earth. During the next plague, the infestation of Egypt with flies, the pharaoh recognized the power of the Lord God as one of the gods whose cult could be introduced to the Egyptian land and wanted the Hebrews to sacrifice there. When Moses and Aaron refused this, he asked them to pray for him at least.

There is another key moment. While the pharaoh was willing to recognize the authority of the Lord God, this willingness did not change his course of action. The Bible says that "Pharaoh hardened his heart this time also." (Exod 8:28) The next three plagues of the deadly pestilence of livestock, boils, and hail came closer and closer to the announcement of

---

11. See Exod 7:14—13:16.

a deeper claim on the pharaoh: "For this time I will send all my plagues upon you yourself, and upon your officials, and upon your people, so that you may know that there is no one like me on all the earth." (9:14) The story of sending the hail also includes advice for the Egyptians on how to come under the Lord's protection. The pharaoh, however, did not follow this advice. This led him to a bitter discovery: "This time I have sinned; the Lord is in the right, and I and my people are in the wrong." (9:27) He requests the Hebrews to pray for him and he promises not to put any more obstacles in their way to freedom. But shortly after the next plague had dissipated, the pharaoh was again unable to use his insight from the time of need and follow it. We read that then he did not want to let the children of the Hebrews go, to grant them a free future. The grasshoppers came and ate all the green produce: the provision of life through crops had disappeared and then the darkness came. The pharaoh attempted another compromise: "Go, worship the Lord. Only your flocks and your herds shall remain behind." (10:24)

When Moses rejected this option, the pharaoh threatened him with death. In the last plague, the death of all the Egyptian first-born, the roles of the slaves and of the free were reversed. The slaves obtained the possessions of their masters, unpaid wages for their work, whilst the first-born of the cattle and offspring of those who were to murder the Hebrew boys disappeared, and together with them also the provision of the Egyptian future. The Passover celebrated by the Israelites that night was at the same time recognized as a verdict over the Egyptian gods. We are told, however, that the Israelites, although the external obstacles to freedom had been removed, were not wholly victorious. They had to witness to the transition in which they themselves would be confronted with their inner lack of freedom, the inner obstacles they faced if they wanted to be the people of God. Returning to the symbolic moment of the crossing of the Red Sea, they confess: "With his unyielding hand the Lord God brought us out of Egypt." In the text, this chorus accompanies the description of the other events and Moses' hymn praising God's power:

> Who is like you, O Lord, among the gods?
> Who is like you, majestic holiness,
> awesome in splendor,
> doing wonders?
> In your steadfast love you led the people

whom you redeemed;
you guided them by your strength
to your holy abode.[12]

The exodus narrative testifies the supreme authority of the Lord God: "So the people feared the Lord and believed in the Lord and in his servant Moses." (Exod 14:31) At the same time, as the journey towards freedom continues, we read that in times of need and danger, even those who had been depicted as the direct witnesses of the event of exodus began to doubt God's power and Moses' motives for mediating it.[13] In this way they faced a similar tension to the Egyptian pharaoh, between having the experiential knowledge of God's power and being unable to subject themselves to it, if it was going to cost them what they were not willing to give.[14]

PROPHETS, PRIESTS, AND KINGS

The prophet, *nabi'* in Hebrew, represented, as we saw with Moses, a person who mediated and interpreted God's intentions. The Septuagint translates this word into Greek as *prophetes*, which stresses the public role of the prophet.[15] The prophet represented a charismatic authority among his people, although final and unique authority was reserved to God alone. Not only Moses but also his brother Aaron and sister Miriam were regarded as prophets.[16] God sometimes speaks through them, but not always. He did not do so, for example, when Aaron, urged by the people "to make a god," cast an image of a calf for them to replace the Lord God who had brought Israel out of Egypt, or when he and Miriam grumbled against Moses. Moses has a special position among prophets because of his closeness to God and his humility.[17] But even in his case, the authority is based on the mediation of God's intention and not in himself. Even he

---

12. Exod 15:1–21; 11–13; compare Ps 118.

13. See Exod 16:3; 17:3; Exod 32:1–6.

14. The Israelites are also subject to a similar judgment to that passed on the Pharaoh. See Num 14:26–45; 26:65; 32:13–15; Deut 1:34–35; 2:14.

15. Bruce Vawter shows that the awarding of the status of an inspired person to the prophet was usually connected with intelligent speech and interpretation. Vawter, "Introduction to Prophetic Literature," 187.

16. See Exod 7:1; 15:20; Num 12:2–8.

17. See Num 12:3.

is rebuked and chastened when he does not believe the Lord and does not testify to the Lord's holiness.[18]

Israel knew the ecstatic prophesying common in the Ancient Near East and had room for it, but it was not accepted automatically as the authoritative word of God simply because it was linked to the experience of trance.[19] The lasting and conscious relationship with the Lord was valued more, for it was through this that the prophet was called and given special experiences and tasks. Both divinely inspired insights and the prophets' conscious voluntary cooperation with God established their authority among his people, whether in their own lifetime or in succeeding generations.[20]

When we come to the authority of priests, there are several interesting terminological nuances. The word priest, *kōhēn* in Hebrew, had primarily a positive meaning among Israelites. However, in talking, for example, of the priests of Baal or other cults connected with idolatry, the Old Testament texts use another pejorative expression, *kēmārîm*. However, the positive expression *kōhēn* is not restricted only to the Israelite priests. There is the Salemite king Melchizedek, described as the "priest of God the Most High" (Gen 14:18) who met Abraham halfway when he was returning from victory over the four kings and blessed him,[21] or Moses' father-in-law, Jethro, who is described as a Midian priest.[22]

In the time of the Judges and the early monarchy the authority of priests was not granted by the family,[23] for the priest was established by another authority—either individual or communal—in order to mediate God's grace and seek God's will for his people. From this period there

---

18. See the story about the quarrelling of the Israelites and how Moses brought water out of a rock, Num 20:1–13; cf. Num 23:14; Deut 1:37; 3:26; 4:21; 32:51; Ezek 36:23.

19. See Vawter, "Introduction to Prophetic Literature," 188; cf. 1 Sam 10:5–7.10–13; 19:18–24; 1 Kgs 18:19–40; Zech 13:4–6.

20. See 1 Sam 7:2–17; 12:1–25; 1 Kgs 17:1—18:44; Jer 11:16—12:17; 15:1–21; 20:1–18; 26:1–19, etc.

21. See Heb 7:1; Ps 110:4, which even talks about a priesthood that lasts for ever and is "according to the order of Melchizedek," something which Heb 5:6.10; 6:20; 7:11.15.17.21 takes over.

22. See Exod 3:1.

23. This is a result of a genealogical construction whose purpose was to show how the Levites gained their priestly rights; see Exod 29 and Lev 8. These texts are either of late pre-exilic or post-exilic origin. See Castelot and Cody, "Religious Institutions," 1256–57.

are both positive and negative examples of priests.[24] In the middle of the monarchy the priesthood was established as an "office" permanently connected with the house of Levi by birth. Their duty was defined as follows: "You are to distinguish between the holy and the common, and between the unclean and the clean; and you are to teach the people of Israel all the statutes that the Lord has spoken to them through Moses." (Lev 10:10–11) The priest's and prophet's authority came into conflict if the duty of the priest was reduced to ritual matters only, but antagonism between the prophet and the priest was not automatic.

The priests were concerned with oracles and sanctuary maintenance. Later they became responsible for offering sacrifices for the people, for looking after the temple, and for teaching the law. The order that the priestly authority was to guarantee was to mirror the permanency of God's faithfulness and of God's will for God's people, while the prophets more often spoke to a momentary situation. Priestly authority, often criticized by prophets for being corrupt, included positive examples. Thus, for example, at the time of decline of the northern kingdom of Israel when Ahaziah's mother, Athaliah, decided, after his death, to exterminate all the royal offspring, the priest Jehoiada hid Joash, a legitimate heir to the throne, in the house of the Lord for six years. After this he anointed him and made him king and put Athaliah to death. Jehoiada then removed the cult of Baal from the land and strove for the renewal of the covenant between the Lord and the king and the people.[25]

The king, *melech* in Hebrew, represents the other pole of institutional authority, one that, after the anointment of David as king, is given by family.[26] The king is regarded as the Lord's chosen one and as such is anointed by the prophet. Through this symbolic action the king is given the Lord's Spirit, but he still needs to be recognized and accepted by the representatives of the people over whom he rules.[27] The king exerts his

24. Saul had a priest Achaziah, who looked after the shrine (1 Sam 14:18–19.36–42) and David had his priests whom he asked about the future (1 Sam 23:9–12; 30:7–8); even David's sons are known as priests (2 Sam 20:26). Negative descriptions can be seen, for example, in Micah's installation of priests (Judg 17–18).

25. See 2 Kings 11:1—12:4.

26. The Book of Judges talks with contempt about the reign of Abimelech (see 9:1–57). The kingdom was taken away from Saul's family for his disobedience (see 1 Sam 13:1–14).

27. See 1 Sam 9:1—10:27; 16:1–13; 2 Sam 2:4; 5:4.

authority by being in command of an army in the times of war, and ruling the land in times of peace. The Book of Deuteronomy introduces in retrospect the picture of a king who will be capable of judging the people according to the Lord's law, distinguishing between good and evil, and whose authority will bring order to the land.[28]

This vision, however, is completely absent in the strong anti-monarchical tradition, which sees the later corrupt state of the actual kingdom as predicted by the prophets. This etiological criticism of royal authority can be found in the story of when the Israelites urged Samuel to appoint a king to judge them, as was the case for other nations. Such desire is seen here as a falling away from the Lord, as a rejection of God's supreme authority. The king's ways are then defined from a negative point of view, as dominating and subjecting the children of Israel, as taking away not only their best property, but also their freedom, all because they have given up the supremacy of the Lord God and traded it for having the temporary thrill of a kingdom like the other nations.[29]

The anti-monarchic tradition is supported by the fact that in the history of, first, Israel and then Judea, only three kings are described positively: David, though with reservations, then Hezekiah and Josiah.[30] Solomon, who, on the one hand, represents the period of the greatest prosperity of the kingdom, and whose royal wisdom was proverbial and respected even in the neighboring nations, is nevertheless ultimately referred to as one who was lead astray by idolatry.[31] In the Old Testament the authority of kings, like the authority of prophets and priests, stems from the respect for, and mediating of, the Lord's authority. As in the case of priests, here it is an institutionalized authority that is oriented to the law, but that needs "the king's heart to be in the Lord's hands." (Prov 21:1) Royal authority was severely criticized when it began to understand itself as supreme, and began to present itself as the last resort of decision-making. The period of Babylonian exile and the post-exilic period describe the Messianic character of royal authority that is, in contrast, ascribed to

---

28. See Deut 17:14–20.

29. See Sam 8:11–18.

30. See, e.g., David's affair with Bathsheba, leading to the death of Uriah the Hittite (1 Kgs 11:1—12:25). Hezekiah and Josiah were kings of Judea at a time when the independence of Judea could no longer be salvaged. See 2 Kgs 18:1—20:21; 22:1—23:30.

31. See 1 Kgs 11:4–6; 2 Kgs11:11–13.

the Lord and his initiative, and that would eventually lead to the setting of a Messianic figure on David's throne.[32]

THE LAW AND THE PROMISES

Previous authorities were personal, including the highest supreme authority of the Lord God. Apart from these, we can gradually trace a kind of material authority, exemplified by the law. Law, *tôrâ* in Hebrew, has several meanings in the Old Testament. In Exodus 19:1—23:33 it refers to the law code, laying out the covenant between the Lord and his people. The law here reflects the practice of the community and settles the relations with God and common ways of getting along by defining what is unacceptable. Those who obediently accept the authority of the law are promised: "I will be an enemy to your enemies and a foe to your foes . . . [I will bless] your bread and your water; and I will take sickness away from among you. No one shall miscarry or be barren in your land; I will fulfill the number of your days." (Exod 23:22.25–26) This authority, though, is not for its own sake, but to help the people to serve the Lord. The sovereignty of the Lord constitutes the authority of the law, but at the same time it relativizes it. The law makes sense in the relationship with the Lord, but cannot replace it. The promises included in the law have a utopian character, epitomizing the pattern of a world that is utterly under the reign of God.

This emphasis is even stronger in Deuteronomy, where the book of the law contains a warning against falling away, instructions for cleanliness, regulations for various positions, and rules for the protection of life, together with detailed ritual orders, and also promises of the type "there will be no one in need among you."[33] The promises—as well as the curses intended for those who do not fulfill the law—are then directed, in the closing words, to the day "that you cross over the Jordan into the land that the Lord your God is giving you . . . a land flowing with milk and honey." (27:2.3) Two types of eschatology meet here, one of present waiting for a concrete fulfillment of these words in the land of Canaan, which the Israelites defeated under Joshua's leadership, and the other directed towards the future in God, including and transcending earthly history.

In the prophet Isaiah we find a more general understanding of the law, as God's instructions under which people would cease to do evil.

32. See Isa 9:5–6; 11:1–5.
33. Deut 15:4.

Isaiah summarizes the meaning of such instructions as follows: "Learn to do good; seek justice, rescue the oppressed, defend the orphan, plead for the widow." (Isa 1:17) This more general understanding of the law is at least partly motivated by an interest in other nations and in their acceptance of the law. Isaiah explains such a change by reference to the "last days," when "many peoples" shall come to the mountain of the Lord to be taught the Lord's ways of justice and peace, and to walk in them.[34]

The origin of the Lord's universal authority is, however, still connected to the law, which will emerge from Zion with a new power. This time, however, the law does not speak about a single cult, or about ritual conformity. The previous cultic regulations seem to remain a duty for Israel, which now has the following missionary obligations to others: "Make known his [the Lord's] deeds among the nations; proclaim that his name is exalted." (12:4) And again the promises are repeated, though they no longer have a utopian character: "Shout aloud and sing for joy, O royal Zion, for great in your midst is the Holy One of Israel." (12:6)

Deutero-canonical and rabbinic literature[35] interpret the law in terms of wisdom:

> The law that Moses commanded us
> as an inheritance for the congregation of Jacob,
> it overflows, like the Pishon, with wisdom
> and like the Tygris at the time of the first fruits.
> It runs over like the Euphrates, with understanding
> and like the Jordan at harvest time . . .
> The first man did not know wisdom fully,
> nor will the last one fathom her.
> For her thoughts are more abundant than the sea,
> and her counsel deeper than the great abyss.
> (Sir 24:23–26.28–29)

The authority of the law here consists in offering wise advice that it would be foolish to turn down. Furthermore, wisdom is personified, and learning to live with it is seen in terms of a relationship. This personified wisdom is characterized as inexhaustible, always other, always at least partly removed from our attempts to internalize her. Apart from the passage quoted from Sirach, such wisdom is referred to in the book of

---

34. See Isa 2:3–4.

35. See Trakatellis, *The Pre-existence of Christ*, 53–92.

Wisdom,[36] as well as in the canonical book of Proverbs. There Wisdom calls people as her children to listen to her and be wise, to walk the way of righteousness, along the paths of justice, and thus obtain favor from the Lord. Wisdom is described as the one who was created at the beginning of the Lord's work, brought forth before the waters and the hills, rejoicing always before the Lord, and finding delight in the human race.[37] The relationship with wisdom is not a rival relationship in regard to the Lord, because God "is the guide even of wisdom and the corrector of the wise. For both we and our words are in his hand." (Wis 7:15–16) Wisdom does not lead away from the Lord God, but teaches the understanding of God's deeds, for wisdom was there when God did them.

We could say that the law here is fulfilled in a life of wisdom. At the same time, however, we are confronted by the impossibility of ever fully realizing such a position. One cannot be wise by one's own effort. Learning takes place in a relationship. One cannot fulfill the law through one's own effort, only with divine aid, and in a broken world such aid is more and more needed. When God's blessing becomes something inaccessible, a messianic hope begins to arise, and from the exile to the intertestamental period it grows into one of the most urgent needs, placing the authority of the law and its promises into a new light.

Authority as Power in the New Testament

In the introductory quotation to this chapter I cited Matthew 21:23–27, speaking of Jesus' authority as the power to act, to heal, and to transform human lives. This provoked gratitude among the needy, but fear and anger among those who, claiming to be the leaders of Israel, lacked such power. Thus they questioned the origin of Jesus' authority to which they did not seem to have access.

In this part we are going to examine the sources and forms of authority of Jesus, of the Spirit, and of the church. We will ask what kind of relationship to the Father such authorities presuppose, how they overlap, and what is irreducible and unchangeable in each of them.

---

36. "Therefore I determined to take her to live with me, knowing that she would give me a good counsel and encouragement in cares and grief . . . " (Wis 8:9).

37. See Prov 8:20–36.

Jesus—Power of the Relationship with the Father

We could say that the gospels take their reader through a process of transformation with regard to the question of who Jesus is and what power stands behind his works. Instead of speculations their attention is directed to what Jesus does. His teaching is full of power, unlike the teaching of the scribes,[38] because his word, his look, his touch changes the lives of people. The blind see, the lame walk, lepers are cleansed, the deaf hear, the dead are raised to life and the gospel is announced to the poor.[39] Jesus even had the authority to override natural disasters and to forgive sins.[40] At least in the synoptics, we are led to understand his authority through this economy of salvation, not through ontology. And even in John, after the Prologue, when we watch how the first disciples emerged round Jesus, the invitation to "come and see" (1:39) plays a vital role. The disciples in their closeness to Jesus could glimpse who he was, so different from anyone else they knew. But they began to understand fully only after Jesus' crucifixion, resurrection, ascension, and the sending of the Holy Spirit. These events revealed the source of Jesus' authority, and placed at the center Jesus' relationship with the Father: "All things have been handed over to me by my Father; and no one knows who the Son is except the Father, or who the Father is except the Son and anyone to whom the Son chooses to reveal him." (Luke 10:22)

This new understanding opens up a new way of participation in the unity between the Father and the Son. John expresses it in terms of re-rooting our humanity in God, so that our lives may bear fruits as did Jesus' life. And yet, as the disciples walk in this way, they discover a still deeper kenotic dimension of statements like: "The Father is in me and I am in the Father" (John 10:38) or "The Father and I are one." (John 10:30) Only with this dimension does the distant eschatological hope of God's reign receive a concrete meaning: "The kingdom of God is not coming with things that can be observed; nor will they say, 'Look, here it is!' or 'There it is!' For, in fact, the kingdom of God is among you." (Luke 17:20–21) Jesus is the prophet of God's kingdom and, at the same time, its presence. Where Jesus is, the kingdom of God has come into being. John summarizes this reality in the Prologue: "He came to what was his

38. See Matt 7:28–29.
39. See Matt 11:5.
40. See Matt 8:23–27; 9:6.

own, and his own people did not accept him." (1:11) This motif is present in the passion story, too. Jesus comes to Jerusalem on a donkey and is welcomed as a king, but when he starts to practice his authority, he becomes unwanted. [41]

The role of priest, prophet, and king blend in the passion story, and together they give meaning to the unique authority of Jesus, which is a mediating authority, but in a different sense than we saw, for example in Melchizedek, Moses, or David. Jesus' relationship with the Father is depicted as an equal relationship in the New Testament.[42] This paradoxically becomes apparent not in Jesus' power, but in his powerlessness on the cross.

The same crowd that greeted Jesus as a king called out a few days later "Crucify him!"[43] Both the traditional authorities of Israel and the Roman institutional authorities oppose Jesus and this conflict of authorities ends with Jesus' death. Jesus' personal authority reveals the "emptiness full of presence"[44] that we spoke of in the previous chapter. The authority of the Father, which is indeed much more than any attempt to mediate it, whether traditional or institutional, seems here like an emptiness made visible by Jesus' self-giving. Those who were present at Jesus' cross, or those who heard the testimony of the last events of Jesus' life, were not able to see the "otherness" of God's authority any other way than as its defeat. Jesus' words "My God, my God, why have you forsaken me?" recorded in Matthew and Mark[45] show this "defeat" most radically. Luke and John concentrate on the otherness of his kingdom, which is not of this world and therefore seems to be fatally vulnerable to the violence that rules in this world. At the same time, its vulnerability is its strength. Through Jesus' commending his spirit into the Father's hands,[46] a new time of renouncing evil can start. Jesus' forgiveness gives rise to the repentance of many, and to the new responsibility that these people take for their lives.

41. See, e.g., Mark 11:8–10.15–19.27–33; Matt 21:10–14.

42. See, e.g., Luke 10:22; John 10:30–38.

43. See Matt 27:22–23; Mark 15:13–14; Luke 23:21–23; John 19:6.

44. See Chauvet, *Symbol and Sacrament*, 164.

45. See Ps 69:22; Matt 27:46; Mark 15:34.

46. See Luke 23:44–48; John 18:36; 19:28–30.

The testimonies of encounters with the risen Lord show that Jesus' authority, in which powerlessness is changed into power, continues to be present and active in the world, and in it, Jesus' relationship to the Father and the life-giving Spirit's relationship to Jesus and to those who would form the body of his followers. The Father took the side of the victim and by the Spirit brought Jesus from death to life. The glorified Jesus becomes the professed Christ: "My Lord and my God," the one who has defeated death, the one who has been given authority to execute judgment. He is accepted as the Lord of the Universe, the Lord of the church, the Lord of human life.[47] The first Christians even expected that Christ's power over all the cosmos would become apparent during their lifetime, as they believed they lived in the final days. Jesus' powerlessness that became power remains, however, a different kind of power. There is no powerful *parousia* yet, but once again, in the Spirit, and through his ecclesial body spread gradually through the world, he returns sight to the blind, hearing to the deaf, and the good news of God's kingdom to the poor. At the same time, both in and through this same ecclesial body, Jesus' authority is subjected also to misunderstanding, manipulation, and rejection. This is because it remains always radically different to the power of those forces who seek to organize society for the profit of some and to the disadvantage of others.

THE POWER OF THE SPIRIT AND THE AUTHORITY OF THE CHURCH

The New Testament word *pneuma* integrates two traditions of talking about the Spirit. The first is the Hebrew tradition, where *ruach* (spirit, breath, wind), a personalized feminine force, gives and takes life, and in general intervenes in human lives, at times powerfully, at times extremely gently. The second is the pre-Christian Greek philosophical tradition, especially Stoicism, where *pneuma*, a word in the neuter gender, signified a universal power moving the Universe.[48] The New Testament adds an adjective to the Spirit, speaking of *pneuma hagion*, the Holy Spirit, first from the position of an experience of its power.[49] Mark and Matthew say

47. See John 20:28; 1 Cor 15:54–57; John 5:27; John 1:1–5; Rev 1:4–8; Eph 5:25b–27; Rom 14:7–9.

48. The Stoics developed Heraclitus's understanding of fire (*pyr*) as an interchangeable expression for *logos* and *pneuma*, and employed this triple expression as a figure for how the divine intervenes in our world. While the Platonic tradition divided the material and spiritual world, the Stoics, like Heraclitus, presumed a unity of the material and spiritual. See Williams, *Arius*, 203–4.

49. The word *pneuma* at an anthropological level designates the human spirit-soul as

that the power of the Holy Spirit is stronger than the power of demons because it alone can initiate the presence of God's kingdom: "But if it is by the Spirit of God that I cast out demons, then the kingdom of God has come to you." (Matt 12:28)

Jesus' life is depicted as lived in the power of the Spirit, from his miraculous conception, through his baptism in the river Jordan, his struggle with the temptations, his deeds and teaching, to his death, resurrection, and ascension.[50] The synoptics already indicated, and John elaborated further, that Jesus' self-giving brought the sending of the Spirit upon his disciples. Only then would they be "clothed with power from on high."(Luke 24:49) John has a long speech about the coming of the Paraclete, the Spirit of truth that will introduce the disciples into all truth.[51] In Jesus' prayer for his disciples we read: "Sanctify them in truth; your word is truth. As you have sent me into the world, so I have sent them into the world. And for their sakes I sanctify myself, so that they also may be sanctified in truth." (John 17:17–19)

The power of the Spirit is then illustrated by the event of Pentecost: "And suddenly from heaven there came a sound like the rush of a violent wind, and it filled the entire house where they were sitting. Divided tongues, as of fire, appeared among them, and a tongue rested on each of them. All of them were filled with the Holy Spirit and began to speak in other languages, as the Spirit gave them ability." (Acts 2:2–4) The power of the Spirit will from now on be joined with the power of the church. But how? This passage from Acts, it seems, offers a short answer: as the Spirit provides. In other words, this connection of the power of the Spirit and the authority of the church will always be directed by God. There is another level of the story, though. What is narrated refers also to God's faithfulness, revealed as God fulfils the promises given to his people.[52] There is here a source of trust for the church that God will also remain

---

an abode of sensation and feelings, a vitality which sometimes even stands as antithesis to the weak body (see Matt 27:50; Mark 2:8; 5:30; 8:12; 14:38). Mark also uses the expression *pneuma* for the unclean spirits, demons (*pneuma akatharton; daimonion*), which Jesus and his followers exorcised (see, e.g., Mark 1:34).

50. The Spirit of God, the Holy Spirit and Jesus' spirit are at times perceived as synonyms, but not always, as we can see in the warning concerning the blasphemy against the Holy Spirit or in the baptismal formula. See Matt 12:31–32; Luke 12:11–12; Matt 28:19.

51. See John 16:4–33.

52. Compare Isa 32:15; 44:3; Ezek 39:29; Joel 3:1–2; Zech 12:10; Matt 3:11; Luke 12:49.

faithful in fulfilling the promise that the Holy Spirit will always be present in the church as gift. There is, however, also a permanent challenge, as the story of the Pentecost is not the only fulfillment of God's promise of the Spirit announced in the Old Testament texts. The lasting presence of the Spirit in the church does not restrict the Spirit to the church only. There is not a symmetrical relationship here: the church is dependent on the Spirit, but the Spirit is not dependent on the church. It is still true that the Spirit, like the wind, "blows where it chooses, and you hear the sound of it, but you do not know where it comes from or where it goes." So it is "with everyone who is born from the Spirit." (John 3:8) And yet, as Acts and Paul stress, the Spirit builds the church, makes it its home, the body of Christ, by guaranteeing the continuity of the mission of Jesus' disciples and equipping them for it. The Spirit is present and active in the church's proclamation of the good news, in the celebration of sacraments, in those who serve and in those who gather in Christ's name. It is a presence that is both collective and individual, disrupting what is false, and building up what is right.[53]

The authority of the church is conditioned by the unity with Christ and the mutual unity of its members. It is an organic unity, with inner differentiations and the dynamism of various agreements and disagreements. Each member has been given a special gift (*charisma*) for the common good.[54] Personal (charismatic) authority is right from the beginning complemented by the traditional (sacramental) and institutional (disciplinary) authority of the church, the plural nature of which represents a certain analogy to the prophetic, priestly, and kingly authority attributed to Christ. The Apostolic Council as Acts describes it, Paul's instructions for the Lord's Supper, or the rules of church administration and pastoral service[55] reflect the need for structured acting in the Spirit, a need that became ever more pressing with the growth of the church. At the same time, however, such structured authority, combining the traditional (sacramental) and institutional (disciplinary) elements, would be permanently challenged by the non-structured, charismatic presence both inside and outside the church structures, and it would face similar dangers

---

53. See, e.g., Acts 5:1–10; 8:4–25; 1 Cor 12–14.

54. See 1 Cor 12:7–31.

55. See Acts 15; 1 Cor 11:17–34; 1 Tim 3–5.

of perversion as did the traditional and institutional authority in Judaism of Jesus' time.

CONTINUITY OF THE APOSTOLIC TEACHING
AND WAY OF LIFE IN THE CHURCH FATHERS

The New Testament understands the authority of the apostles as a guarantee of continuity between Jesus' life and mission and the life and mission of the church. Apostolic authority stands and falls with the relationship to Christ and the Spirit, and as such it is given support, direction, and to a degree even content by the authorities of the Scriptures and tradition. Yet even they had to be understood anew in the first centuries, as the church struggled to differentiate between who is and who is not a legitimate successor of the apostles, and what constitutes legitimate succession in the church. The discernment involved reflecting on the degree of continuity with both the apostolic teaching and the apostolic way of life. The Church Fathers, faced with such a task, realized that they had to start with what is and what is not a reliable support for the positions in question. Thus they were led first to look at what they understood by the authority of the Scripture and of tradition, and from there to the problem of how to recognize a "genuine" church, and "genuinely" Christian life, that is, to the criteria for Christian orthodoxy and orthopraxis.

Authority of the Scriptures and Tradition

The sense in which the Scriptures and tradition are authoritative, and the proper relationship between the two, are questions that re-emerged whenever the church needed to re-define its place in a new religious, political, cultural, or intellectual setting. Gradually, different answers to these questions were formulated. The Orthodox recognized one source of inspiration present in both the Scriptures and tradition. The Protestants used the Scriptures as the sole basis for Christian faith and life, and the Catholics, at least after Vatican II, accepted the common source whilst maintaining the supremacy of the Scriptures against which tradition should be measured. This is of course a largely generalized typology and we must bear in mind that the actual theological terrain is more complex and that differences often do not emerge only according to ecclesial belonging. Our task now is to turn our attention to the time before the challenge of the Reformation and before the schism of the East and West, and trace the relationship between the Scriptures and tradition in the early church, our common heritage.

CRITERIA FOR CANONICITY

The first followers of Christ relied on the authority of the Scriptures, even if they understood by the Scriptures something slightly different than we do today. Neither the New nor the Old Testament canons existed.[56] Christians took over the Hebrew Scripture of their day, mainly the Law and the Prophets and Psalms.[57] At the same time the church, which now included Gentiles as well as Jews, sought a new relationship to the Hebrew Scriptures, and interpreted them through the event of Jesus Christ and the development of the new people of God initiated by him.[58] The Apostolic Council decided that Gentile Christians were not subject to Jewish law,[59] finding support for this decision in the words of the Prophets.[60] The new situation needed a new solution and the Scriptures were in this context understood as an authority that enabled the discovery of such solutions in continuity with the past and inspired by the Spirit.[61]

When the generation of the apostles had died out, the need arose to keep the memory of Jesus' words and works, his life, death, and resurrection. It was necessary to write down the oral tradition and collect available documents about the life of the early church. New writings were

56. The Greek *kanon*, originally meaning "measuring rod," resembles the Hebrew *kaneh*, meaning "reed." This expression, as a transferred meaning, started to be used also for standard or norm (e.g. 2 Cor 10:13–16; Gal 6:16). Only much later was it applied as a standard for measuring which books are truly the Holy Scriptures.

57. In the second century BC the Pentateuch had already appeared in its final form. Alongside, the entire collection of the Prophets was gaining in authority as part of the Holy Scriptures. The Law and Prophets and some parts of the Writings, e.g., the book of Psalms, appear as the "Scripture" to which the evangelists refer (see Luke 24:44), even if the Writings as a whole were settled only in the first century AD, and even then Christians frequently used the Septuagint, which included, besides the "first canon," additional books that we call today deutero-canonical. See Brown, "Canonicity," 1026–27 (=66:24–29).

58. See 1 Thess 4:15; 1 Cor 7:10; 9:14 (cf. Luke 10:7); 11:23–25.

59. See Acts 15:28–29.

60. See Acts 15:13–19.

61. We can also read of the authority of the Scripture in Paul and in the Pastoral Epistles (see e.g. 2 Tim 3:15–17). The concentration on the Scripture without Spirit, without the relationship to who it comes from, is, however, also criticized (2 Cor 3:6b). See, too, John: "You search the scriptures because you think that you have eternal life in them; and it is they that testify on my behalf. Yet you refuse to come to me to have life." (John 5:39–40).

created but also new problems—would all these writings be a part of the extended Scriptures? Retrospectively, it became apparent that, when the apostles, as the direct witnesses of Jesus' earthly life[62] and the subsequent rise of the church, had been present, they had been seen as the direct visible instance of interpretation of Jesus' intentions.

After their departure a similar authority was even more necessary, characterized as "apostolicity." Thus when we say that apostolicity was a criterion for accepting writings into the New Testament canon, we have to understand it in this broad sense, that the writings represented the teaching and practices of the apostles, and came from the setting where such continuity could be guaranteed. The combination of requirements, however, still does not give a full answer to why some of the writings of the Apostolic Fathers, especially those of Clement of Rome, Ignatius of Antioch, and Polycarp of Smyrna, were not included in the New Testament canon. Here one more aspect was at play, namely how widely and commonly the writings were used in liturgy.[63]

The actual need to formulate a Christian canon was strengthened in the second century by the controversies with Marcion and with the Gnostics. Marcion in fact created his own canon, much smaller, as he intended to purify it of all Jewish elements,[64] while various Gnostic groups tended to make a synthesis between the Christian scriptural writings and the esoteric knowledge they represented.[65] The church's agreement as to what was to be included among the canonical writings took two more centuries. The Council of Laodicea (363) dealt with the question of the exact number

---

62. With the exception of Paul as he explains in 1 Cor 15:3–11.

63. See Haag, "Die Buchwerdung," 382.

64. Marcion appeared in Rome about 140, proclaiming that Christianity had a totally different character to Judaism, and thus should abandon the Old Testament God. This God, according to him, was not identical with the Father of Jesus Christ. Marcion argued for a new canon that would include Luke and ten of Paul's letters, all cleansed of any connection with Judaism. His teaching has been preserved only in quotations from his opponents, especially Tertullian.

65. The Gnostics—from Greek *gnosis*, knowledge—originated in the period around the beginning of the Christian era in the Eastern Mediterranean. Their doctrines were often handed down in the form of secret teaching. The various forms of Gnosticism have in common that they presented an independent non-Christian stream, originating at the same time, and offering a similarly holistic interpretation of the world, and seeking a way of salvation.

of canonical writings, but the struggle for the canonicity of the Book of Revelation and the letter to Hebrews lasted until the fifth century.[66]

THE ANAMNETIC-EPICLETIC CHARACTER OF TRADITION

The formulation of the scriptural canon presupposed a living tradition, both oral and written,[67] whose role would not be finished by the constitution of the canon and the subsequent authoritative decision of the church. The canonical writings were selected from the stream of the living tradition as separate, holy, but the living tradition continued to interpret them and to appropriate their meaning in the developing life of the church. Thus, the living tradition contributed to keeping the Scriptures alive by the Spirit, and the church in fact relied on both, even if there were always implicit decisions concerning what was and what was not to be followed in the tradition.

Furthermore, tradition did not refer only to the past but, as Irenaeus of Lyon (+202) stressed, it held a moment of eschatological hope. It represented the living memory of the church (*anamnesis*), the history of its salvation, a continuing flow of events that reflects the work of the Spirit invoked by the church's *epiclesis*. In the coming of the Spirit, the past and the present are transformed by the Kingdom coming from the future.[68] Irenaeus writes:

> But . . . the preaching of the Church . . . continues in an even course, and receives testimony from the prophets, the apostles, and all the disciples—as I have proved—through [those in] the beginning, the middle, and the end, and through the entire dispensation of God, and that well-grounded system which tends to . . . [human] salvation, namely, our faith; which, having been received from the Church, we do preserve, and which always, by the Spirit of God, renewing its youth, as if it were some precious deposit in an excellent vessel, causes the vessel itself containing it to renew its youth also. For this gift of God has been entrusted to the Church, as breath was to the first created man, for this purpose, that all the members

66. See Brown, "Canonicity," 1033 (=66:67–69).

67. The Latin *traditio* translates the Greek *paradosis*, meaning "delivery," "tradition," "story." The verb *paradidonai, tradere* in Latin, also includes the meaning "to give into custody," "surrender," and in the negative sense "give up" or "betray."

68. Irenaeus ties this anamnetic-epicletic approach to his teaching on recapitulation. See Irenaeus, *AdvHaer* V:1.3; Meyendorff, *Catholicity of the Church*, 26–27; Meyendorff, "Apostolic Continuity and Orthodox Theology," 83.

receiving it may be vivified; and the [means of] communion with
Christ has been distributed throughout it, that is, the Holy Spirit,
the earnest of incorruption, the means of confirming our faith, and
the ladder of ascent to God . . . For where the Church is, there is the
Spirit of God; and where the Spirit of God is, there is the Church,
and every kind of grace; but the Spirit is truth.[69]

In this way the Spirit guarantees all aspects of church life, including
the tradition and institution, but the church does not supervise the way
the Spirit can or cannot communicate. As John Zizioulas puts it: "'The
Spirit blows where he wills', but we know that He wills to blow towards
Christ."[70] The truth Irenaeus speaks about can be revealed by the Spirit in
various ways, but not all that is claimed to come from the Spirit does. We
find in the Church Fathers warnings against those sectarian charismatic
movements that often overestimated prophetic leadership and used it to
legitimize separation from the tradition and the institution of the wider
church. The early church does not denounce charismatic authority, but
it conditions it by unity with other manifestations of the Spirit in the
church, which have a more institutional character.[71]

The anti-Gnostic debate stresses that the church tradition is public,
visible, and expressible by a general formulation of faith or profession
(*symbolon* in Greek, *credo* in Latin), a basic set of order, liturgy, and
apologetics. According to Irenaeus, Clement of Alexandria, Tertullian,
Hippolytus, Origen, and others, the rule of faith stated the basic articles
of what Christians believed, as this had been preserved and handed down
by the church. This understanding of tradition was gradually extended
to the whole teaching and practice of the church, which, together with
the Scriptures, represented the authority for the authentic communication of Christianity.[72] This way the tradition included its own history,
cultural plurality, and diversity. It is important to note, however, that in
such an understanding of tradition, renewed in the church by the Spirit,

69. Irenaeus, *AdvHaer* III:24.1.

70. Zizioulas, *Being as Communion*, 186; he refers to John 3:8 and 16:14.

71. See the concept of apostolic succession below, 119–23.

72. Concerning the faith and way of life handed down by the apostles, we find in
Greek, besides the expression *paradosis* (tradition), also *didaskalia* (teaching), which
particularly concerns the church teaching about faith and the way of life handed down
from the apostles, liturgical practice, and the interpretation of the Scripture. The Church
Fathers did not normally use these two expressions interchangeably. Both, however, coincide with what is understood by tradition.

the church is primarily seen as a eucharistic community of witnesses of Christ. And we have to reclaim such a primacy against every attempt to move to a situation where the eucharistic community is replaced by administrative and territorial control, the church taking upon itself political and economic power for which it is not suited. The history of such deviations also belongs to the tradition of the church, but as a negative possibility of where not to go in order not to lose the truth that leads to human salvation, which comes from of old, and is always new.[73]

RELATIONS BETWEEN THE SCRIPTURES AND TRADITION TODAY

In the nineteenth century the churches found themselves losing the status that they had previously enjoyed. This, among other things, led to their rejection of modernity. For the Roman Catholic Church, the Second Vatican Council was regarded by many as a balm for the hurts of the past. However, it also offered a new understanding of the relation between the authority of the Scriptures and that of tradition. In doing so, it tried to reconcile the opposing poles of the previous debate. Thus, in the encyclical *Dei Verbum* we read:

> Hence there exists a close connection and communication between sacred tradition and Sacred Scripture. For both of them, flowing from the same divine wellspring, in a certain way merge into a unity and tend toward the same end. For Sacred Scripture is the word of God inasmuch as it is consigned to writing under the inspiration of the divine Spirit, while sacred tradition takes the word of God entrusted by Christ the Lord and the Holy Spirit to the Apostles, and hands it on to their successors in its full purity, so that led by the light of the Spirit of truth, they may in proclaiming it preserve this word of God faithfully, explain it, and make it more widely known. Consequently it is not from Sacred Scripture alone that the Church draws her certainty about everything which has been revealed. Therefore both sacred tradition and Sacred Scripture are to be accepted and venerated with the same sense of loyalty and reverence.[74]

The Reformation churches likewise arrived at more nuanced positions with regard to their insistence on the sufficiency of the Scriptures, and their sharp distinction between what was seen as the apostolic tradi-

---

73. Compare to Meyendorff, *Catholicity of the Church*, 93.
74. DV 2.9.

tion (identified with God's revelation) and the post-apostolic tradition (characterized as human invention). Due to the reception of historical criticism and of the insights from modern hermeneutics, they concluded that the apostolic teaching needs to be informed and interpreted in the light of Christian thinking as it developed over the centuries. Thus they moved beyond the long-lasting conviction that the apostolic tradition as recorded in the Scriptures represented the entire and unchanging truth about all things regarding our life and eternity.

The renewed emphases, one on a living personal relationship with God instead of on a set of rules, and the other on the interdependence between the two material authorities, Scriptures and tradition, though the supremacy of the Scriptures remained, opened up new ecumenical possibilities. Protestant theology, as well as Catholic theology influenced by Vatican II, at least in its major representatives, rediscovered the interdependence of the interpretation of the Scriptures and tradition. They also recognized that both need the presence of the Holy Spirit—on the side of the one who handed down the experience of God's self-revelation as well as on the side of the one who received and accepted it. Thus, for example, Paul Tillich talks about the living tradition, part of which is not only the Scriptures and church teaching, but also our lives.[75]

Orthodox theology seemingly underwent less development in this issue than other theologies. And yet the theme of the innovation of tradition or its transposition to a new key is as pressing as *aggiornamento* was for the Western churches in their struggle with modernity. What remains is a belief that both the tradition of the Scripture and the tradition of the church teaching belong to the treasure of God's revelation given by the Holy Spirit to the church. But Orthodox theologians have different opinions on whether it is a static or a dynamic treasure. Alexei Men writes: "The Holy Trinity and Holy Scripture are mutually bound and stem from the same source—God's Word."[76] And further, there is the church that God leads with the one and same Spirit that God breathed on the authors of the Scriptures and tradition. This same church, imbued with the Spirit, can help people in present times, as always, to find direction in their searching and in the new challenges they face. The church has the

75. See Tillich, *A History of Christian Thought*, 137–40.
76. Men, A. *Zamysel Božij*, 20.

power of the keys to unlock the understanding of the Word, for its head—Christ—endowed it with this power.[77]

Two Notions of Apostolic Succession

Now we need to return to the concept of apostolicity and touch upon another issue, ecumenically controversial up till now, namely the understanding of apostolic succession. The church's continuity with the teaching, faith, and practice of the apostles, one that appeared with urgency in the second century, did not concern only the process of formation and acceptance of the Scripture and Tradition, but also the church authorities. Drawing on different understandings of the catholicity of the church, the concepts of apostolic succession developed the ways in which and by whom this catholicity is preserved and allowed to continue.

The expression "apostolic succession" was mentioned for the first time by Irenaeus (+202) in his polemics with the Gnostics.[78] Irenaeus refers to an older tradition dealing with the meaning of catholicity, represented on the one hand by the historical understanding of Clement of Rome (c.96) and on the other hand by the eschatological understanding of Ignatius of Antioch (+107). Clement's notion of catholicity as a successive line through time back to the apostles, from the apostles to Christ and from Christ to God,[79] is thus from very early on complemented by Ignatius's understanding of catholicity as a community gathering around Christ's Eucharist.[80] The historical understanding of the apostolic succession as derived from Clement is, though, in a certain tension and contrast with Ignatius's eschatological concept.

CLEMENT'S HISTORICAL APPROACH

Writings ascribed to Clement show the reaction to the chaotic situation in the Corinthian community and, together with practical advice and orders, offer one of the first theological reflections on ordained ministry. Clement declares: "The apostles have announced to us the good news from Jesus Christ. Jesus Christ was sent by God. Thus Christ comes from God and the apostles from Christ. This double mission, therefore, with its

---

77. Ibid., 27.
78. See Irenaeus, *AdvHaer* III:3.1.
79. See 1 Clement 42–44.
80. See Ignatius, *Smyr* VIII.

order comes from the will of God."[81] The chain of mission is then further extended when the apostles, filled by the Holy Spirit, appointed bishops and deacons in the towns and villages where they proclaimed the good news of the Kingdom, and then instituted offices that could be handed over to those fit to fill them.[82]

Clement concentrates on the mission of individuals scattered throughout the world. His approach influenced Irenaeus's concept of "catholicity in time," and grounded the teaching about "historical succession." As we will see later, Ignatius's concept of "eucharistic catholicity," on the other hand, supported the teaching on "eschatological succession."[83] While both of the understandings come from the early church, different Christian traditions have tended to choose one of them as a key for understanding the other. Proponents of historical succession trace retrospectively whether the individual ministers had been appointed by those who were appointed by the apostles in the historical succession. The uninterrupted line of the tradition of the office, leading to Christ and from Christ to God, is of primary importance for them.

For advocates of historical succession there are several ecumenically relevant questions: (i) How to cope with the blank spaces in history? Should they be left blank and the line of succession followed where it is possible to be traced? Would this not mean, though, that none of the churches can document an entirely uninterrupted line of ministers leading all the way to the apostles? Would the attitudes of one church to another not be re-figured if the comparisons were humbler, concerning only a longer or shorter line, a more or less uninterrupted one? Or should the blank spaces simply be ignored? (ii) Who is the bearer of apostolic succession? Bishops? Or bishops and deacons, as Clement says? Or can we also talk about a presbyteral succession?[84] Answers to these questions will influence the willingness or unwillingness for mutual recognition of ministries among churches, or at least how ready they are to head towards this recognition.[85]

---

81. 1 Clement 42:1–2.

82. See 1 Clement 42:2–4; 44:1–2.

83. See Zizioulas, *Being as Communion*, 176.

84. See Jorissen, "Behindert die Amtsfrage die Einheit der Kirche?," 85–97.

85. See *Baptism, Eucharist and Ministry* and *Churches Responses to BEM*.

IGNATIUS'S ESCHATOLOGICAL APPROACH

While Clement's concept of the church comes from an emphasis on the mission of individuals scattered in the world, Ignatius concentrates on the corporate character of the apostolate. The church, for him, is primarily the gathering of people around Christ. Its continuity is not guaranteed by individuals succeeding one another from generation to generation, but by the succession of communities, of the churches in particular places gathered round a common celebration of the Eucharist presided by a bishop or somebody appointed by him. Bishops are important, but not as an isolated authority, not as a single stream guaranteeing catholicity in time, as in Clement. Ignatius sees an analogy between the college of the apostles round Christ and the college of presbyters round the bishop. In his view the body of presbyters takes on the communal character of continuity.[86] He is not interested so much in the hierarchy of ministries but rather in the guarantee of unity as a wall against quarrels and divisions, which Ignatius perceived as the "beginning of evil."[87] These deprive people of the bread of God. The church, in order to live what it has been instituted for, needs to be united.[88]

The continuity of the church according to Ignatius is not retrospective. It does not come from the past, but from the future, from where the Father raised his Son by the Spirit. The church gathered round the risen Lord is the memory of the future, which is invoked when the church in each particular place and time in history gathers round the eucharistic table to celebrate the fulfilled aim of all creation.[89] Expressed in the language of later days, apostolic succession is perceived as the work of the Spirit that gives the church its future form.

The advocates of the eschatological approach must, however, deal with these questions: (i) What role does history play? What value is ascribed to the earthly life, if our past experiences do not make us who we are? (ii) What role does an individual play? Is one always bound to go along with the community, even when one is convinced that the community is taking the wrong direction? What place is there for responsible

---

86. See Ignatius, *Smyr* VIII; Zizioulas, *Being as Communion*, 177.

87. Ignatius, *Smyr* VII.

88. Ignatius, *Eph* V.2. An emphasis on the eucharistic gathering appears also in the same work (13:1) and also, for example, in Polyc 4:2; Magn 7:12.

89. See Pannenberg, «La signification de l'eschatologie.»

dissent? Answers to these questions are vitally important especially for those churches where the eschatological understanding of their identity and continuity dominates. For, as Zizioulas summarizes, "if the Church is to be truly apostolic, she must be both historically and eschatologically oriented: she must both transmit history and judge history by placing it in the light of the *eschata*."[90]

IRENAEUS'S ATTEMPT AT A SYNTHESIS

As already mentioned, the term "apostolic succession" originated with Irenaeus,[91] who tried to integrate Clement's and Ignatius's insights. The concept of apostolic succession emerges in Irenaeus's polemics with the Gnostics and the need to correct their claims that their secret mysteries passed from mouth to mouth are the true and faithful teaching of the apostles. Irenaeus needed to underline that the church preserved the tradition publicly, through preaching and the celebration of sacraments. Thus, if we were to interpret the concept of apostolic succession against the background in which it emerged, we would avoid reducing it to questions of mechanical validity of ordained ministry. Faithfulness in preservation of the apostolic truth would then, as in Irenaeus, bring into relationship "eucharistic catholicity" and "catholicity in time." It interprets both of them from the point of view of the church's apostolic identity, as it emerged in its public witness:[92]

> It is within the power of all, therefore, in every Church, who may wish to see the truth, to contemplate clearly the tradition of the apostles manifested throughout the whole world; and we are in position to reckon up those who were by the apostles instituted bishops in the Churches, and [to demonstrate] the succession of these men to our times; those who were neither taught nor knew of anything like what these [heretics] rave about.[93]

The emphasis on the public ministry of the apostles and of those who follow faithfully in their footsteps is a further development of Clement. In Irenaeus it has a kind of objectified binding function to repudiate what are seen as false claims to such ministry. However, the reasons why one

---

90. Zizioulas, *Being as Communion*, 181.
91. See Irenaeus, *AdvHaer* III:3.1.
92. See Meyendorff, *Catholicity of the Church*, 91–92.
93. Irenaeus, *AdvHaer* III:3:1.

ministry is apostolic and the other is not are not purely historical. Irenaeus points to the centrality of the Holy Spirit, who renews the relevance of the apostolic proclamation in each generation.[94] Thus the eschatological perspective of Ignatius is included. The communal focus also finds its place in Irenaeus's argument, as he brings together right proclamation and the right celebration of the Eucharist.[95]

His correlation of "eucharistic catholicity" and "catholicity in time" enabled the historical and eschatological approach to apostolic succession to be mutually corrective, provided both kept the public character of ministry. The epicletic emphasis on the future church summoned now by the Spirit in the Eucharist prevented the reduction of apostolic succession to the norm of the handing over of the office to individuals. The anamnetic emphasis on God's having entered history and carrying his salvation in it preserved the value of the symbolic memory of the earthly Christ, and of the particular people who carried and handed down his good news and his healing power, who gave their bodies for him. Yet even in the anamnesis of their lives, the epicletic nature of who they were and what they did comes across. In the power of the Spirit they followed Christ, and in the power of the Spirit they sought and decided who would be their successor in the service.

How to Recognize the True Church

When the divisions of the church run even deeper, references to eucharistic catholicity, to catholicity in time, or even to the Irenaean synthesis of both are insufficient, since all sides claim to meet these conditions, just as all claim to be faithful and public followers of the Scriptures and tradition. Questions of who represents the genuine church, and how it can be recognized, surface with a new urgency. Or is the true church divided and a part of it and its authority to be found on each side?

CYPRIAN'S REQUIREMENT OF UNITY

In the middle of the third century, when the church was beginning to recover from the persecution of Decius, the Carthaginian bishop Cyprian (c.210–258) wrote a book now called *On the Unity of the Catholic Church*. It is more a pastoral manual than a theological treatise. Cyprian was con-

---

94. See Irenaeus, *AdvHaer* III:24:1.
95. See Irenaeus *AdvHaer* IV:18:5.

cerned with the fact that the church was divided in regard to the practice of repentance and the reception back of the lapsed. In his view the division was caused by the fact that the faith in God of one of the groups was false. From this, all other false convictions and attitudes followed. "Who has not the Church for mother can no longer have God for father,"[96] he declared. Cyprian was convinced that the more demanding position that he represented was the only one truly to represent the faith of the church. From here, it follows for him that others must have lost their salvation, since "He will not arrive at the rewards promised by Christ who deserts the Church of Christ."[97]

Those in opposition to him formed a group that appointed its own bishops. This, in turn, led to schism. Cyprian was thus forced to address the question of the validity of the sacraments and again chose the stricter solution: sacraments celebrated by the schismatic group were not valid, according to him. It is not possible to live in division and celebrate unity with Christ and his church: "He that holds not to this Unity, does not hold the Law of God, does not hold the Faith of the Father and the Son, holds not Life and Salvation."[98] For Cyprian the church of Christ is distinguishable by its adherence to unity, in which the divine law and faith in the Father and Son, in life, and salvation are preserved. Cyprian himself died as a martyr during Valerian's persecution. His approach to the question of how to recognize the true church, however, raised more problems than it solved.

DONATIST INTERPRETATION OF CYPRIAN

Half a century later, after several other waves of persecution and after the church's ongoing controversies over how to deal with those who, under threat, retracted their faith or handed over the holy books, Cyprian's position was reclaimed by a more extreme group in North Africa, the Donatists. They argued that the fact that they had not failed during Diocletian's persecution must have been because they, and they alone, formed the true Catholic Church. The Donatists further presumed that bishops who failed had not only lost all their spiritual power as a result, but that they had never had it in the first place. Thus even the sacraments

96. Cyprian, *The Unity of the Catholic Church* VI.
97. Ibid.
98. Ibid.

they had celebrated before the persecution proved invalid by this act of betrayal. The Council of Arles in 314 rejected their teaching and practice. It concluded that if the blame of the bishops was adequately proven, they should be removed from their offices, but those ordained by them, if all procedures of their ordination were rightly followed, should keep their positions.[99] The Donatists refused to accept the decision, and so their bishops were exiled. In 361 the emperor Julian the Apostate, who supported the Donatists, called their bishops back from the exile. Their return was accompanied by brutal violence and mass slaughter.[100] When Augustine became bishop in Hippo in 396, the African church was divided almost in half. He strove to reconcile both sides, but in the end he was unable to avoid violent coercion himself.[101] After this pastoral failure, Augustine engaged with the Donatist position theologically, arguing against their attempt to make the church an elitist place of morally strong people who deserve their salvation.

Augustine first quotes the same authority as the Donatists, namely Cyprian. In agreement with him he ascribes to the church mediation of Christian salvation.[102] Augustine also agrees that salvation includes sanctification, but then he distinguishes between the validity and the fruitfulness of the sacraments, stating that even the heretics must have the Spirit, because no baptism can be without the Spirit, but they may have it to their destruction rather than to their salvation.[103] However he disagrees with the Donatists and with Cyprian in their insistence that salvation can be communicated only by those who were sanctified.[104] Then Augustine turns Cyprian's radical statements against the Donatists themselves, quoting not passages concerning the *traditori*, the lapsed leaders, but the schismatics, whose crime is worse, according to Cyprian, because in their falling away from unity they drag many along.[105] Therefore, if the Donatists wanted to

99. See Leeming, *Principles of Sacramental Theology*, 144.

100. Ibid., 145.

101. Augustine considered the use of power as part of the ultimate pastoral solution of the church crisis (see Markus, *Saeculum*, 154–55). However, Peter Brown points to Augustine's long letter to Paulinus of Nola as showing Augustine's deep depression following the persecution of the Donatists. See Augustine, Ep.95.3 in Brown, *Augustine*, 243.

102. See Augustine, *DeBapt* I.iii.4.

103. Ibid., V.xxiv.34.

104. Ibid., V.xxvi.37.

105. See Cyprian, *On the Unity of the Catholic Church* XIV. He further claims that the

refer to Cyprian's authority, they must take into account that in his eyes a group that breaks from a big church cannot be a true church, and cannot be sanctified, and its merits from the time of persecution are not enough if they subsequently break unity.

AUGUSTINE'S THEOLOGY OF THE CHURCH

Despite its harsh nature, the Donatist controversy brought Augustine to a wider understanding of the true church and of orthodoxy than we find in Cyprian or in Augustine's own early Christian writings, when he was convinced that it was simply enough to belong to the right group.[106] Augustine came to realize the complexity of the question of what it meant to belong to the right church. When the church is divided, on both sides there are some people with material interests, and others with spiritual interests.[107] He does not deny that, in the case of controversy or schism, one side is more right than another. He does, however, recognize that the lapsed and schismatics partake in the life of the true church to the degree that they are in harmony with it: "whenever he [the one who severed himself from unity] desires to conduct himself as is customary in the state of unity, in which he himself learned and received the lessons which he seeks to follow, in these points he remains a member, and is united to the corporate whole."[108] And this participation is a source of their future conversion, which he sees not only in terms of acceptance of the fullness of such life, but also as a transition from belonging to the new covenant secretly to belonging to it publicly.[109]

Augustine is more and more aware that the true church is not identical with any of its institutional mediations. The human structures that carry it are imperfect, as are we, its human members, with our good and bad inclinations. Therefore in the church the wheat and the weed will continue to grow together till the end of the times: the gospel will be both preached and betrayed.[110] And yet, despite its vulnerability, and with the

---

crime of schism cannot be washed away even by martyrdom, because the one who does not belong to the church is not a martyr. See *ibid.*, XIX.

106. Compare Augustine, *DeVeraRelig* XI.

107. See Augustine, *DeBapt* I.xv:24. An idea that is later developed in *De civitate Dei* is outlined here.

108. Augustine, *DeBapt* I.i:2.

109. See Augustine, *DeBapt* I.xv:24.

110. See Markus, *Saeculum*, 157.

experience of its vulnerability, the church, whose "condition is such that every day the entire church says: 'Forgive us our debts,'"[111] continues existing in order to redeem a helpless humanity.

On the one hand, the question as to where the genuine church is and how it can be recognized takes on an eschatological character. It is here in its seminal form, not yet in fullness. On the other hand, it is directed to the concrete manifestations of church, to its orthodoxy and orthopraxis expressed or missing among concrete people and communities. Moreover, the theology of the church is supplemented by a theology of grace that not only completes the merits where they are missing, but shows again that the basis and life of the church does not consist of a perfect institution, but of a merciful and active God from which all else is derived.

CONFLICT OF AUTHORITIES

What makes an individual or community of people act in a certain way? This was my introductory question in this chapter. Is it church, tradition, or the Scripture? Is it faith in the works of the Holy Spirit, in the power of Jesus, or in the sovereignty of the heavenly Father? Various, often antagonistic, groups referred to these authorities in order to justify their convictions and practices. Yet whenever they moved too far towards embracing a coherence that can be orchestrated by people for their own interests, the need to break the neatness of their systems emerged, if what did not belong there and what was believed to come from God was to have any chance. In the following part I am going to examine, how, in times of crisis, different authorities came into conflict, how the conflicts were solved, and how in the process the transcendent divine authority became rehabilitated. I will start with Jan Hus and his rediscovery of the eschatological authority of Christ, before moving to John Henry Newman's emphasis on conscience as a guard of human integrity, and finally to George Tyrrell, in whose understanding of tradition the eschatological and the immanent are brought into a new relationship.

Hus's Appeal to the Eschatological Authority of Christ

Existential questions on the nature of the ultimate authority against which our beliefs and our actions will be judged and how this ultimate authority is accessible emerge in times of crisis. Our first example, Jan

111. Augustine, *Retractions*, 156.

Hus (c.1371–1415), undertook such questioning against the background of late medieval Christendom, which had lost its optimism concerning both the fundamental goodness of human nature and the possibility of educating people towards building a Christian society. Europe was a place of religious conflicts and wars, with the church involved on different sides, claiming to be the sole authority necessary for salvation. Efforts to resolve the crisis came from such different roots that, by the time of Jan Hus, they were in opposition. The Conciliarists sought new forms of administering the church from the top more efficiently. Others, like Hus, rediscovered a direct relationship with Christ as the starting point for each Christian and his or her contribution to just and peaceful relationships in the church and in the society. His involvement with the church from below was seen as a threat.[112] In this setting discernment was needed regarding not only who is the highest representative of Christ (whether one of the popes or a council), but also how we can recognize what is normative when different authorities stand against each other. The same was necessary to determine how the highest authority is related to mediated ones like the church and the Scriptures, and what role is played in the Christian life by one's own judgment and by inner peace.

Influenced by John Wyclif's "anti-nominalism,"[113] Hus was unwilling to accept the demands of obedience without exception, either to the Pope or to a Council. He claimed that none of the mediating authorities can stand in isolation from the others. The authority of the church is entwined with the authority of the Scriptures and tradition, and all stand or fall with the direct authority of Christ, whose presence can be recognized according to whether people are living in truth and in justice.[114]

112. In 1302 the Bull *Unam Sanctam* was issued by Pope Boniface VIII. It proclaimed that obedience to the pope was necessary for salvation; in 1378 two popes—Urban VI in Rome and Clement VII in Avignon—were elected. They anathematized each other and their followers and brought the church to war. In 1409 the Synod in Pisa suspended both Popes and elected a third, Alexander V. None of them was prepared to step aside. The papal schism lasted forty years, led Christians into wars and provoked strong criticism. Papalism, weakened by the schism, was complemented by the new movement of conciliarism. This came, however, from different roots than the reformers such as Hus, and therefore the two types of initiatives to help the church authority out of crisis ended up in opposition, as was the case at the Council of Constance (1414–1418).

113. John Wycliff (1329–1384) represented the second wave of anti-nominalist thought, reacting against Ockham and Scotus, and against their skepticism about the employment of the direct transcendent authority of God in Christian life.

114. For Hus general terms such as "truth" or "justice" represent real things, and not

Yet Hus's own understanding of this highest authority changed. First, he emphasized the law of Christ (*lex Christi*) as the basis of the true and just life of the church. This we find especially in his Latin writings from the time he was University rector and a welcome preacher at the church synods, protected by the king. Later he became a popular preacher in Prague's Bethlehem Chapel and concentrated on rebuilding the church from below. He began to speak about the authority of Christ's life (*vita Christi*), through which we can understand the law of Christ (*lex Christi*). In both cases, the mediation of Christ's authority by the church is not questioned, provided the church struggles like the apostles to follow the life of Christ and is not interested primarily in pomp and domination.[115]

A new dimension of the supreme authority emerged when Hus was drawn into direct conflict with the archbishop and lost the protection of the king. Placed under an interdict, he had to leave Prague. When in October 1412 Hus wrote his famous appeal to the highest authority of Christ, "the judge most righteous who most certainly knows, defends and judges, makes apparent and repays the just plea of any man,"[116] he had in mind the direct transcendent authority, unmediated by the church, or by anyone or anything else. The limit situation made Hus more radical. The direct judgment of Christ, standing above the church and no longer within the church, is seen as acutely needed, as the church embraced practices that were those of the anti-Christ.[117] Such judgment stands above every individual, giving each person a just and truthful ultimate hearing, even when the church refused to do so.

---

simple facts that we can agree to consider as real. These real things exist in God, not as passive ideas but as active matters of full power. They are not subjected to us and our opinion, but we are subjected to them, for they accompany God's acting. See Hus, "Výklad víry," 69.

115. See Topfer, "Lex Christi Dominum"; Molnár, *Na rozhraní věků*, 19.

116. *Husova výzbroj do Kostnice*, 30.32.

117. Though the limit situation radicalized Hus, in his Synodal sermon from 1407 we can already read: "However a false Christian . . . having received the name of Christ, clothed in the devil's arms and leading the struggle of the Antichrist, professing that he knows God, though denying him by his deeds, is a false Christ and true Antichrist." Hus, *Spisy latinské I*, 162. Similar statements can be found in the Czech writings where Hus shows that heresy applies not only to teaching, but also to Christian practice. See, e.g., Hus, "O šesti bludiech."

Nevertheless, the other mediating authorities are not ruled out as useless. The Scriptures and tradition[118] can help the church and each individual member of it to find a way back to following Christ, to standing under the personal authority of Christ in truthfulness and justice. As Hus prepared his defense for the Council of Constance, to which he was invited to prove that his teaching was not heretical, he further developed the inner personal authorities that complement the Scriptures, tradition, and the church, such as the "judgment of reason"[119] and inner peace.[120] Although he was never given a public hearing there and, despite the promises of safe return, was imprisoned on his arrival and burnt as a heretic, his search for an adequate relationship to the highest authority of Christ was even more influential after his death than during his life.

With the authority of a martyr, Hus's teaching and his life became themselves mediations of the highest authority of Christ, pleading for leaving the highest seat in our hierarchy of authorities vacant, so that we might give space to the living God. He pointed out that without justice and truthfulness (i.e. without orthopraxis) orthodoxy would never be achieved. We could say that Hus reformulated the topics present in the Scriptures and in the Greek and Latin traditions, and thus read these two main emphases as an "apophatic" challenge to the idolized certainties on which we base our actions[121] and that constitute "epistemological security" for us.[122] And yet even if Hus's theology stresses God's transcendence, and, underpinned by philosophical realism, prefers the perspective from above, his ecclesiology counters these emphases by developing a kind of "kataphatic" symbolism, oriented on social practices.

The question of the nature of the highest authority and of our access to it was not resolved after Hus. As we will see in the next section, it re-emerged with new vigor in modern times when Enlightenment phi-

---

118. Hus often refers to authority in the Scripture in his works, as well as to Latin and Greek Church fathers, saints (including holy Popes) and council statements. The Scripture and tradition represent a common authority for him.

119. See "Odpověď M. Jana Husi," §32.

120. Hus presents peace as one of important criteria for ascertaining whether someone is in the right relationship with God. He quotes Job (in the Vulgate): "Who has ever resisted him and lived on in peace?" (Job 9:4) See Hus, *Řeč o míru*, 31.

121. See Wittgenstein, *On Certainty*, § 11, 12, 189, 284, 550.

122. See Williams, *On Christian Theology*, 142.

losophy placed at the centre the knowing subject and his/her interests[123] and when theology began to search for a new relationship between God's transcendence and immanence.

Conscience as a Safeguard of Human Integrity in Newman

In nineteenth century Britain, the conflict of authorities involved different claims on the person who wanted to live a genuinely Christian life within a modern industrial society, yet within churches that still struggled with their medieval heritage. Both the churches and the society lacked a sense of stability at this time, even if for slightly different reasons. The societal instability was due to the memory of the French Revolution (1789), now revitalized by growing social tension and emerging communism (the Communist Manifesto was first published in 1848). The churches were much more afraid of intellectual challenges. In 1859 Darwin published *On the Origin of Species* and a violent debate started concerning whether, and if so how, human and other life is rooted in God. When Bishop Colenso of Natal (1814–1883) claimed to demonstrate that events concerning the beginnings of humankind, as described in the Book of Genesis, are historically unreliable, the conflict between religion and science grew in intensity.

John Henry Newman (1801–1890), originally an Anglican, later a Roman Catholic, strove to prevent the conflict by enabling a dialogue between the old and the new images of the world and of God, one building on free scientific research, the other on interpreting the sacred tradition. Newman's search for what is authoritative for a Christian in a time of crisis is based on a dialogue between the two ways of knowing, and on an attempt to place this dialogue within a person's spiritual life.[124] Newman sought an apostolic and at the same time intellectually credible Christianity, relevant in a society where the belief was growing that, in order to be good, one does not need to be a Christian.

---

123. See Descartes, *Discourse on the Method* IV.

124. Newman speaks of this dialogue in terms of the search for a *via media* (a middle way), which excludes extremes on both sides by means of mutual criticism and by the same means sharpens the good contribution of each side. The concept of *via media* appeared for the first time in Newman's Anglican period, when he (as a founding member of the Oxford Movement) sought a dialogue between Protestantism and Catholicism. In his Roman Catholic period he employed *via media* for a dialogue between religion, philosophy, and political power within Christianity. See Newman, *The Via Media.*

Together with a number of his secular contemporaries he accepted the value of human integrity and made no exceptions for Christians in this area. Likewise, he agreed that as we live in a changing world, we have to respond to the changes. For Christians, that meant responding to them in faith. This is not new or strange to Christian tradition, Newman claimed. Each new period of history had brought such a challenge to Christians, and they had not known before how they would think and act in new circumstances.[125] Similarly in his time, when Christians felt threatened by the new paradigm, their task was not to hide from the historical changes in some otherworldly shelter where they would remain immune to them, but to work with the otherworldliness of Christianity more creatively. They needed to ask what other visions of the world were excluded, to its own detriment, by this modern world of science, technology, and political liberalism. Conversely, they had to enquire in what sense these other visions of the world could enrich human life and contribute to human integrity. How can apostolic Christianity in this situation retain and rediscover its life-affirming strength?

In this context Newman examines what is truly authoritative for Christian life. As is typical for his dialogical approach, he does not single out one authority, but rather offers a map of relationships of different authorities, which together contribute to our intellectual, spiritual, or moral convictions. The external or objective authorities, such as the Scripture, tradition, and church, together with the internal or subjective authorities, such as reason and conscience, accumulate the wisdom of the insights on which a personal judgment is based.[126] Thus Newman speaks about a cumulative case.[127] Newman claims that in this manner a conflict between heteronomy and autonomy is overcome, without assuming a simple equality between the two. When Newman deals with the situation when different authorities are in conflict with each other, he returns to

125. In his work *An Essay on the Development of Christian Doctrine* Newman wrote: "In a higher world it is otherwise; but here below to live is to change, and to be perfect is to have changed often." (40).

126. See Newman, *Apologia*, 210 and 227. He does not ascribe this mutuality of external and internal principles only to Christianity, but claims that in the history of religion generally there are two major principles: authority, by which he means the objective external claims on a believer, and personal judgment (see 226).

127. Alternatively Newman speaks of an illative sense, emphasizing assent that turned the accumulated probabilities into a sufficient certainty to back up our attitudes and actions. See *Grammar of Assent*, 408.

the indispensable need for human integrity and argues for the supremacy of human conscience, i.e., an inner (subjective) authority, to act upon the insights from all other authorities and make the final judgment. As conscience is like all other authorities, fallible, it is possible that the judgment would be erroneous, but even with such an erroneous judgment one would not lose one's integrity, while in obeying a right thing for wrong reasons one would.[128]

Especially interesting is the section where Newman speaks of a possible conflict when someone is incapable in conscience of accepting a claim of the authority of the church represented by the pope. Even here, though, Newman claims supremacy for human conscience.[129] One is obliged, however, to take the arguments of the other side seriously. Only after a deep consideration, prayer, and various methods of assessment, when in all honesty a person can find no way of bringing themself to a genuine assent to the claims of the pope, is conscience allowed to prevail above the voice of the pope.[130] A similar engagement of the internal authorities is, however, required for an obedient assent. There is no genuine obedience without listening, without trying to understand, and without engagement of all human capacities, including conscience. Moreover, as Ian Ker points out, for Newman the loss of personal integrity is seen in terms of sin. Thus when someone is deeply convinced that the papal order (or some other external authority) is wrong, that person would sin in obeying it.[131]

Newman stresses again and again that, however confused and prone to error our conscience can be, we have nothing better to rely on. Conscience is not the voice of God, direct and non-problematic. It is a gift of God mediated through all our capacities and limits, but never fully reduced to them. Unlike in Hus, the supreme authority is internalized in Newman. It is not outside of us, like the eschatological judgment of Christ, but active within our life, making connections to other authorities participating in the cumulative case, and transcending them all, even its

128. See Newman, *Apologia*, 192.

129. The authority of conscience has priority even over the authority of Pope: "Certainly, if I am obliged to bring religion into an after-dinner toast (which indeed does not seem quite the thing), I shall drink—to the Pope, if you please—still, to Conscience first, and to the pope afterwards." Newman, *Sermons*, ii:261.

130. See Newman, *Certain Difficulties*, ii, 256–58.

131. Ker, *Newman*, 102–3.

own previous judgments, on the journey marked by what Newman calls "a divine method of Truth."[132]

There is a historical paradox that, while Hus was burnt as a heretic for similarly free claims to the divine truth, and shortly after Newman's death, theologians who elaborated his notions of development and of human interiority were persecuted by the Roman Catholic Church as modernist heretics,[133] Newman himself was made a cardinal in 1879 under Pope Leo XIII.[134] In the final part we will examine what happened when the ecclesial crisis over modernity deepened and the question of what is authoritative in Christian tradition arose with a new urgency.

The Meeting of Tradition and Modernity in Tyrrell

At the turn of the nineteenth and twentieth centuries the Roman Catholic Church took a defensive stance against what it perceived as secularism flowing into its body. The First Vatican Council (1869–1870) had already emphasized the need for certainty in a changing world and offered firm doctrine and institution as a wall against modern doubt.[135] A generation later those who were under suspicion of engaging with different views than those proclaimed by Vatican I started to be demonized and persecuted as enemies of the church. The elimination of these enemies had two stages. In the first, the demonic forces were attributed to the "Modernists,"[136]

132. Newman, *Apologia*, 192.

133. See the anti-modernist decree *Lamentabili Sane Exitu* (1907) and the encyclical *Pascendi Dominici Gregis* (1907), issued by Pope Pius X.

134. Even more paradoxically, this happened nine years after the First Vatican Council pronounced the dogma on Papal infallibility (1870).

135. The council opened with a dogmatic constitution *Dei filius* and concluded with the dogma on Papal infallibility.

136. On September 8, 1907 Pope Pius X issued the encyclical *Pascendi Dominici Gregis*, thus completing the decree *Lamentabili Sane Exitu* of July 4th 1907, which claimed to be a collection of Modernist heresies. The Encyclical talked about a clearly defined system, alleging that the "Modernists" wanted to destroy the very basis of the church structure. The two main heresies were "agnosticism," which rejected the validity of rational argument in the areas of religion as defined at Vatican I, and "immanentism," which derived religious truth from the inner needs of our life. The publication of these documents was accompanied by a process of excommunication of the followers of the so-called Modernist movement inside the Roman Catholic Church and culminated with the requirement of the anti-modernist oath from all priests, ordered by Pius X on September 1st 1909 (this was abolished by the Congregation for the Doctrine of Faith on May 31st 1967.) Nicholas Lash distinguishes between a "theoretical system," which

who were accused of undermining the church intellectually, and in the second phase to the "Communists,"[137] who were accused of undermining the church socially.

Here I look at the first phase, within which George Tyrrell (1861–1909), a Dubliner and, like Newman, a convert to Catholicism, formulated why and in what sense Christian tradition might be authoritative for modern people. The fundamental question that shaped his work is spelled out most clearly in his last book *Christianity at the Cross-roads*:

> How, then, must we, here and now, understand the apocalyptic and transcendental revelation of Jesus, so as to shape our spiritual life, feeling and action in harmony with His? How must we re-embody the same 'idea' if it is to live for us?[138]

Tyrrell criticizes attempts to reduce Christianity to rational knowledge or moral duty, whether coming from the side of Catholic dogmatism or liberal Protestantism. In both cases, he argues, transcendence is made inaccessible and thus practically eliminated or fully subjected to hierarchical ecclesial mediation. This life is thus identified with the next. As long as one is either obedient according to one system or moral according to the other, human life is eternal. Jesus' proclamation of the Kingdom, carried from generation to generation by the church, revealed the urgency of a different type of understanding of human life in relation to God. In it, God is stripped of moral and rational idols and, for redeemed humankind, worship in Spirit and truth is placed at the center of human life. Thus the spiritual side of life is freed and uniting all human potential in the service of God and of one's neighbor is made possible.

Behind Tyrrell's criticism as well as behind his rediscovery of the creative power of tradition there are two main inspirations, St Ignatius and Thomas Aquinas. Since 1880, when Tyrrell had joined the Society of Jesus, he had appropriated the depth of inner freedom present in the Ignatian

---

is presumed by the Encyclical *Pascendi*, and an actual stream of thought that the excommunicated theologians developed and shared. See Lash, "Modernism, *Aggiornamento* and the Night Battle," 53.

137. See the anticommunist policy of Pius XII in the 1950s, intuitive in its recognition of the forceful character of this regime and the impossibility of cooperating with it, out of proportion in regard to the weak criticism of Nazism, and providing insufficient base for any recognition that not every effort targeted at social justice, or society and church growing from below, must be "communist."

138. Tyrrell, *Christianity at the Cross-roads*, 114.

Exercises. Aquinas attracted him because of the honesty in his thinking. Tyrrell admired the fact that Aquinas was not afraid of conflicts with the fundamentalists of his time, and was thus an antidote to rigid late scholasticism.[139] Both St Ignatius and Aquinas helped Tyrrell to develop his theology from below, starting with a sense of God, which according to him was given to every human being. He understood that Christian tradition in its great representatives has worked with this starting point; it did not reduce or oppose it. With the inner sense of God and through the inner sense of God, it proclaimed Jesus' apocalyptic and transcendental revelation.[140]

The sense of God inherent in human interiority leads Tyrrell to two other themes; first, to pluralism concerning the ways God is perceived, second to discernment concerning which of the ways are authentic and which not. Both of the themes appear in his work *Lex Orandi* where he writes:

> Truth can and ought to be approached from many sides; it is not different because these aspects and approaches are different. The same city will offer as many distinct views to the sketcher as there are points in the surrounding horizon; but by no summing together of these sketches can we bring the whole within the compass of a single inward gaze. Religion too can be set before us under different presentations, all true in their way, but none, nor all together, exhaustive of reality. We can recognise under various descriptions a face that we have once seen; but if we have never seen it, no description can bring its full individuality home to us.[141]

Whether in the center of one's life there is a relationship to God, however distinctly lived, or something else, can be judged only from within the relationship, not "objectively" from outside. As in Newman, external authorities can help us to cultivate this relationship, but none of them is the final arbiter of whether a person lives it or not. From outside, however, the fruits of one's life can be observed.[142]

---

139. See Leonard, *George Tyrrell*, 8.

140. Tyrrell rehabilitates the "sense of God" in his works *Lex Orandi* and *Lex Credendi*. The anti-modernist decrees condemn it as a part of the heresy of "immanentism." See *Pascendi Dominici Gregis* §5.

141. Tyrrell, *Lex Orandi*, v.

142. In *Through Scylla and Charybdis* Tyrrell writes: "Life is the test and criterion for truth." (196).

Besides the notion of interiority Tyrrell also elaborates Newman's emphasis on development. Following the example of Aquinas, he takes seriously the arguments of his opponents and examines the development of Christian tradition from the standpoint of the Roman Catholic plea for stability. Thus he asks in what sense the revelation of Jesus remains incorrupt, and in attempting to answer this question he refers to the collective memory of the whole church:

> Avowedly the aim of the Church's dogmatic labour has been to preserve the original sense of revelation incorrupt. It is to the collective memory of the whole body that this guardianship has been committed. But memory needs criticism and correction, and this it receives from the understanding. In the measure that symbols were taken literally theology was at war with reason when reason, excluding the literal acceptance of apocalyptic imagery, seemed hostile to faith.[143]

What Tyrrell is saying here does not oppose, but radicalizes Newman. The original sense of Jesus' revelation is dynamic, not static. If the church wants to keep it incorrupt, it has to change. Tyrrell was convinced that if his church refused to change, it would die.[144]

Christian tradition is binding, according to him, not because it is a changeless truth but because it refers to its origins, in which there is life for each generation that appropriates them, including modern people with their worldviews shifting under their feet.[145] He was aware that in a time when his church was governed by fear and engaged in the anti-modernist controversy, holding such a position was dangerous, and that he was likely to be misunderstood, as Aquinas had been in his own time.[146]

143. Tyrrell, *Christianity at the Cross-roads*, 215.

144. See Tyrrell, *Medievalism*, where he explained the need to be faithful to what brings life to the church, despite the church's unwillingness and threats of excommunication.

145. As in Aquinas's times, so in modernity, "Religion cannot be the criterion of scientific truth, nor the science of religious truth. Each must be criticised by its own principles." Tyrrell, *Christianity at the Cross-roads*, xv.

146. Tyrrell first came into conflict with repressive church authority in 1899 after the publication of his article on "Hell" in the *Weekly Register*, in which he questioned theology based on fear. This conflict led at first to the withdrawal of the *imprimatur* for his writings. When the English hierarchy started to persecute the so-called Modernists, Tyrrell wrote: "The Modernist believes in modernity, but he also believes in tradition . . . Of the two, his belief in tradition has a certain priority." (*Lex orandi*, 4) He had to withdraw from the public eye and publish pseudonymously. Although the Society of Jesus tried to protect Tyrrell at first, in 1906 as the conflicts with the church hierarchy intensified, he was dismissed. Other

Despite having been gradually expelled from the church he loved and cared for, till the end of his life Tyrrell did not stop striving for its conversion, reminding the church that it was in fact killing what it wanted to defend, apostolic Christianity.[147] Modernism, according to him, offers a criticism of religion, of revelation, of institutionalism, of sacramentalism, of theology, of authority, but it does so in order to purify these categories and to contribute to the process of growth of the Christian tradition, in which the divine becomes something current and concrete.[148]

CONCLUSION: WHO AND WHAT MOVES OUR CONVICTIONS AND ACTIONS?

Returning to the initial question of this chapter, concerning what makes a person or a community of people think, believe, and act in a certain way, we can see a web of different authorities. We also see that, just as human convictions and actions are both good and bad, so are the authorities underpinning them. As Newman said, to the pure anything can become a divine method of gaining light,[149] but we can add that to manipulators anything can become a means for their scheming. History is full of examples of the parasitic use of divine authority, even of claims to human integrity and to conscience. But the situation is still more complex. It is not that good intentions always lead to good outcomes and bad intentions to bad outcomes. Already in the Bible, when we recall the story of the prophet Balaam bribed to curse Israel or of Saul going to Damascus to protect Judaism from what he considered its enemies, we can start to understand that even our motivations, however important, are not the deepest layer of the relationship with God and with the world in which we live. If we want to take seriously that divine revelation is relational, we have to count with all participants of the relationship. This relationality,

---

restrictions were imposed. He was forbidden to preach and celebrate sacraments publically. After the anti-modernist decrees, although, according to his bishop Amigo he was not excommunicated, his case was reserved to the Holy See. So he was forced to live outside the visible communion of his church. Tyrrell died aged 48. He received the sacrament of the sick conditionally, but was refused a Catholic burial. A friend of his, Abbé Bremond, who performed the burial despite the ban, was suspended.

147. Tyrrell accuses his church of using its apologetics as a "weapon . . . which simply murders the system it would defend." Tyrrell, *Christianity at the Cross-roads*, 20.

148. See Tyrrell, *Christianity at the Cross-roads*, xx, 115.

149. See Newman, *Apologia*, 192.

then, flows into a Christian understanding of what is authoritative and how and why.

In this concluding part I will first briefly summarize the main points discussed in this chapter and then return in somewhat more detail to the problem of the ideological use of authority in contemporary ecumenical theology.

Summary

When we speak of authority in Christian theology, it is important to bear in mind that we need to follow various examples of how believers in different times and cultures discerned what or who could make claims on their convictions and actions. The biblical traditions do not offer us one conceptual framework to deal with this plurality. When we try to grasp it and to speak about it, we generally use a concept derived from Latin law, *auctoritas*. With the help of this concept, we can discern in the Old and New Testament different strands of what is later called authority, and group them according to family resemblances. One way of doing so, which I referred to in this chapter, distinguishes between personal, traditional, and institutional authority. Another way, which became important especially as the church gradually entered modernity, concentrates on the difference between external (objective), internal (subjective), and transcendent (eschatological) authority.

The biblical examples analyzed above showed us that the main distinction in fact lay between the supreme authority of the Lord God and its different human mediations. They also indicated that we do not have an unmediated access to this divine authority without some symbolic mediation to either precede or accompany experiences of it. Concerning the symbolic mediating authorities, they often overlapped, although each one of them had a specific contribution to make, be it prophets, priests, and kings, Torah, or the church, Scriptures, and tradition. Likewise, each of them in human hands became corruptible, but that did not mean that its place could be left empty. The Scriptures were also aware of what were later called internal authorities, like inner peace or a good conscience (even if it did not use the precise terminology). Though these, too, were not seen as infallible, they were an irreplaceable test of being on the side of God.

The New Testament and the early church pointed out that what it means to be on God's side could be seen in Jesus, in his relationship with the Father, and his radical openness to the Spirit. Expressed in the later dogmatic formulation, Jesus Christ, both as fully divine and as fully human, proclaimed and embodied the eschatological authority-power (*exousia*) of the supreme God. The church, as the successor body of Christ's disciples, has struggled to understand how the Holy Spirit, which gave shape to Christ's earthly life, continued to work within as well as outside the church.

In the Patristic period we saw different attempts at clarifying criteria for continuity with the apostolic church and its teaching and way of life, usually in response to threats from outside or to controversies within the church. These caused inner divisions and threatened to replace the very core of divine generosity towards humankind with the smallness of human fear, shame, or pride. Although the authorities of the Scriptures, tradition, and the church received a more refined form, questions concerning their interpretation and the hierarchy of their claims passed on into medieval and modern Christian theology.

Finally, I examined the conflict of authorities that arose when the stability of the medieval societies had gone, and the process of individuation and secularization of modern men and women had begun. This conflict revealed the irreducible value of a transcendent eschatological authority, unpopulated by idols, a conditioning of the mediating authorities, both external (objective) and internal (subjective), and at the same time the need for human integrity, if a witness to the world in relationship to God was to be credible. The church stood right in the middle of the conflict, being the most easily corruptible authority and yet the most embodied one—as a womb where new life can be conceived and sustained.

The examples I have used to try to show how "authority" has been understood and what is "authoritative" in church history certainly do not exhaust the spectrum. There are many relevant topics I have not dealt with, such as different interpretations of the magisterium, conflicts between the universal and local church, between church and state, or what Christians, believers of other religions, agnostics, and atheists understand as authoritative. Here I can only refer to other books[150] and move to the last issue, the ideology critique of authority, which will take us up to the present.

---

150. See, e.g., O'Collins, *Fundamental Theology*, 186–91; Fries, *Fundamental Theology*, 602–33; Dupuis, "Interreligious Dialogue," 518–23.

The Ideological Use of Authority as an Ecumenical Problem

J. B. Thompson defines ideology as "the ways in which meaning (or signification) serves to sustain relations of domination."[151] Terry Eagleton highlights an important point regarding the use of the expression "ideology" in theology, namely that several negative and positive meanings are hidden behind it that might not necessarily be compatible.[152] Eagleton distinguishes sixteen areas in which ideology can appear. I will choose seven of them that are significant for an ideological understanding of authority. Ideology may concern the process of production and control of meanings, signs, and values in social life—or we can also say ecclesial life. It creates and sustains ideas that help to legitimate a dominant power, often at the expense of distorting communication. Ideology often operates with identity thinking and on the exclusion of those features of reality (and their bearers) that do not fit into the identity image. Ideology confuses linguistic and phenomenal reality. It claims that its enforced language expressions are based on experience or represent a natural—or in our case even revealed or eschatological—reality.[153]

I am aware that the institutional, traditional, and personal authorities in Christianity are never free of ideology. However, I want to focus here on the negative meaning of the ideologization of authority, and on problems caused by the ways in which meaning serves to maintain relations of power, and by what happens when the mediating authorities cease to refer to a higher transcendent and eschatological authority, and are instead ruled by their own interests. Ideologized authority may, then, adopt various forms and focus on any of the points just mentioned. Their common characteristic is that they either take control over the transcendent authority of God and thus deny its sovereignty, as we have already seen in Hus's struggle with the church hierarchy of his time, or they try to gain control over people's inner lives and explain away the inner authorities, such as conscience, in such a way that there is not sufficient place left for them. Then there are the unfortunate examples of justifying human interests by claiming as sacred or as directly meaningful something that

151. Thompson, *Study*, 4.

152. "The word 'ideology', one might say, is a *text*, woven of a whole tissue of different conceptual strands; it is traced through by divergent histories, and it is probably more important to assess what is valuable or can be discarded in each of these lineages than to merge them forcibly into some grand global theory." Eagleton, *Ideology*, 1.

153. See Eagleton, *Ideology*, 1–2.

is neither one nor the other. To give some examples, justifying social injustice by reference to the will of God, or claiming that violence and the deprivation of other people's freedom should be seen in terms of their sacrifice for God. In the eighteenth and nineteenth century "God's will" was used either as an argument on behalf of the desire to keep slavery going or against it. A century later the church is still divided, for example, in regard to issues of homosexuality, and the same arguments are used in a similar way. We can also notice references to "God's will" in other controversial or even taboo topics, as for example women's ordained ministry in the Roman Catholic or Orthodox church, the possibilities of sacramental life for divorced people living in new marriages, or the feasibility of intercommunion. Claims that reality is the way we see it (whether with an innocent naivety or with hidden agendas) often lie at the roots of exclusivist communal identities. To speak a different language than the majority means to criticize the system in which language conformity is required as a sign of faithfulness.

Some Protestant or Orthodox groups that insist, for example, on one single possible interpretation of the Scriptures and try to replace its aporetic plurality by a single harmonized image of how things are from "God's point of view," also work with ideologized authority. Instead of the source of faith, there is their own strong idea and the relations of power protected by it. We can find "leader" figures in charismatic, evangelical, and sometimes Catholic circles to whom are ascribed almost boundless knowledge and who enjoy almost boundless privileges (indeed these are claimed to be divinely guaranteed from above), including control over the forms of obedience of their subjects. In more experience-oriented churches and communities we can find implicit requirements of conformity to what is seen as a model of authentic spiritual experience and people can fabricate various accompanying phenomena that are supposed to belong to the power of such an experience. With different levels of consciousness, people who participate in such a process gradually substitute the reference to God for the reference to the idol of God. People can ideologize themselves, become their own inviolable judges and executors of their own images, forgetting that their conscience, their will, feelings, and judgment are fallible and corrupted.

None of the authorities of whom I have spoken in this chapter is free from the danger of ideological shortcuts, which necessitates a certain form of apophatic criticism. In my understanding the way Christian authority becomes an ideological authority is connected with the loss of individual or community freedom and the loss of their integrity. The realization of ways in which contemporary fixed meanings in different Christian denominations serve to maintain the relations of power can be of good service not only to the particular church but also to others, as it helps to rediscover authentic Christian authorities.

The apophatic way that I wrote of in the previous chapter can be helpful to us in this process, demanding as it does that the transcendent remain transcendent and the eschatological remain eschatological. On the level of mediating authorities, it is important to safeguard their dialogical nature, and struggle for a type of dialogue that is as far as possible not motivated by power interests. Newman's cumulative case can thus be complemented by Habermas's communicative action, which looks at the communal dimension of our assent.

Habermas's main interest is a healthy society, but his insights can also be employed when seeking healthy ways of being a church. Ideology critique, he proposes, should re-open the space where each of the actors exercises personal responsibility for their ideas and actions. It requires understanding of one's motivations as well as of those of others, and the recognition that in our social life autonomy and mutual dependence need to enter into a satisfactory relationship. For that we need to give up our identity ideologies and open ourselves to genuine plurality, where who we are and what we do is based on a consensus that emerges from dialogues uninfluenced by power. Right practice, then, depends on right communication, epistemologically grounded. This means that neither ideology of domination nor rhetorical skills are allowed to take over. Of course, he is aware that his project of communicative action is never finished and never completely free of the negative forces it fights. It requires an ongoing human conversion. [154]

---

154. See Habermas, *Knowledge and Human Interests*, 301–15.

4

History and Culture

When Jesus turned and saw them following, he said to them, 'What
are you looking for?' They said to him, 'Rabbi' (which translated means
Teacher), 'where are you staying?' He said to them, 'Come and see.' They
came and saw where he was staying, and they remained with him that
day. It was about four o'clock in the afternoon.

JOHN 1:38–39

Experience and judgment are always bound up with a horizon of
openness towards reality, in which a thing comes to view and can be
experienced and in which judgments become meaningful. A horizon of
this kind contains a certain anterior knowledge of that which we learn. It
is not a closed system, but includes also open questions and anticipations
and is therefore open towards the new and the unknown. Horizons of this
kind can come from our traditions, and they can also arise from the con-
text of our own experience and our familiarity with the world. They can
arise out of the incalculable significance attaching to specific experiences
we have undergone, and they can also have their source in ideas of our
own which we use for the purpose of attaining to knowledge of history.
Without a horizon of this kind, and in abstraction from it,
no event can be experienced or stated.

JÜRGEN MOLTMANN[1]

THIS CHAPTER SPEAKS ABOUT four contexts of theology: historical
and eschatological contexts (time-oriented contexts); and cultural and
utopic contexts (place-oriented contexts). The historical and the cultural

---

1. Moltmann, *Theology of Hope*, 190–91.

grounding of theology includes the actual, the particular, the given into which we step, in which we participate, and that we also shape and pass on to the next generations. The eschatological and utopic grounding of theology includes our hopes, based on our understanding of the nature of God's gifts and plans. It also includes our dreams and visions informed by the images of the unimaginable future of all things included in loving communion with God, images from which we draw our strength and that act as inspiration for the transformation of history and culture. All these four contexts contribute to what Moltmann calls a horizon of openness towards reality, within which theological reflection can become meaningful.

In the following pages we will first consider the biblical notions of time and space. Then we move to the modern debate, in which historical and cultural differences became a theological theme. We will track the way in which studying these differences helped Christian traditions to deal with the issues of faithfulness and innovation, with allowing plurality and striving for unity in a world that wanted to leave religion behind as something that did not belong to a modern progressive mind.

NOTIONS OF TIME AND SPACE IN THE SCRIPTURES

It would be beyond the scope of this book to examine how images of time and space developed in the Scriptures and how they influenced the writings and the organization of the canon. To examine the contextuality of theology, which is the main aim of this chapter, it is enough to work with the actual plurality synchronically. In doing so, we discover patterns of dealing with the tensions between the realized and non-realized images, values, and visions. We are challenged by the difference between particular understandings of hope (mediated by spatio-temporal symbols) and the idolatry that gives ultimate validity to what it has constructed on this side of history, from the material available to our minds and senses in the places where we live.

Symbolic and Chronological Time

When we read the biblical narratives, it is important to discern between two basic notions of time: symbolic and chronological. Here I will concentrate on how the two notions are connected.

Two Creation Myths

The two Old Testament creation narratives at the beginning of the Bible are not at the beginning of Israel's faith, but somewhere in the middle.[2] In the Scriptures, however, they form a prelude to all other stories about God's work amongst God's chosen nation and amongst all nations, with the church, with every human person, and all creatures.

Creation, according to the first chapter of the Book of Genesis, begins with light and darkness. These give rise to time: "Then God said, 'Let there be light'; and there was light. And God saw that the light was good; and God separated the light from the darkness. God called the light Day, and the darkness he called Night. And there was evening and there was morning, the first day." (Gen 1:3–5) After the creation of time there follows the creation of space[3] and the placing of creatures in time and space,[4] where time passes and is thus measurable. "And God said, 'Let there be lights in the dome of the sky to give light to separate the day from the night; and let them be for signs and for seasons and for days and years, and let them be lights in the dome of the sky to give light upon the earth.' And it was so." (Gen 1:14) A special, separate time, the time of rest, is also mentioned: "And on the seventh day God finished the work that he had done, and he rested on the seventh day from all the work that he had done. So God blessed the seventh day and hallowed it, because on it God rested from all the work that he had done in creation." (Gen 2:2–3) This cultic-etiological story works with symbolic time. We can talk about time in a symbolic way because we have an actual experience of time that establishes this symbolic speech.

An older story of creation from the second and third chapters of Genesis is more oriented towards space and its order.[5] Symbolic time is based on a memory that precedes the memory of humankind and the nation:

> These are the generations of the heavens and the earth when they were created. In the day that the Lord God made the earth and the heavens, when no plant of the field was yet in the earth and

---

2. Questions concerning the beginning and end of the world became a part of Israel's faith during the exile, amidst confrontations with the mythologies of the neighboring nations. They are connected with the need to relate the national God to other nations.

3. Gen 1:6–8

4. See Gen 1:9–13.20–31.

5. Gen 2:4—3:24.

no herb of the field had yet sprung up—for the Lord God had not caused it to rain upon the earth, and there was no one to till the ground; but a stream would rise from the earth, and water the whole face of the ground—then the Lord God formed man from the dust of the ground, and breathed into his nostrils the breath of life; and the man became a living being. And the Lord God planted a garden in Eden, in the east; and the tree of the knowledge of good and evil. (Gen 2:4–9)

The question of the beginning or the hierarchy of time is not dealt with here. People are situated differently, through the mythical memory of a place they inhabit. The longing for company as well as the desire to be equal to God, the pride and immaturity that destroy good relationships both vertically and horizontally, punishment and the promise of a new beginning, all are located in our first pre-historic home, the Garden of Eden. The topic of crime and punishment continues in the Flood narrative, and in the covenant God made with Noah. The theme of time emerges here, but time as differentiating between the past and the future: "the waters shall never again become a flood to destroy all flesh." (Gen 9: 15b) The non-repetitive character of the time of destruction that once came upon the earth is guaranteed by the covenant that will stay in God's memory: "When I bring clouds over the earth and the bow is seen in the clouds, I will see it and remember my covenant that is between me and you and every living creature of all flesh." (Gen 9:14–15a)

Time gives a dynamic to the biological order of growth, maturing, and ageing; likewise, it gives a dynamic to the cultic order given by the division of time into weekdays and holidays, and the celebratory repetition of those events that it is necessary to remember. Biological and cultic times, then, form the time of history. In the historical narratives, however, a different dimension of time is noted, namely that of God's intervention, an extra dimension marked by the experience of a power independent of the time of history.

THE TIME OF HISTORY

The symbolic time with which myths work unleashes human imagination and teaches us to understand that such imagination participates in what it tries to understand. The time of history used to be bound to the facticity of events as if "the past world" as such would be available to our analysis, description, and control. However, we do not have such a world at our disposal. The Old and the New Testament narratives can already teach us that the narrators always contributed to the image of the historical past, and their standpoints have been part of what they sought to testify.[6] The community of Israel forms and transforms its story of the covenant with the Lord and the words of the prophets add new dimensions and lead to a new self-understanding for Israel that forces a continuous critical revaluation of its relationship with the Lord, but at the same time sees it through difficult times. The church then, as well as Israel, depicts its history as the history of being called by the Lord, the history of God's faithfulness that time after time gives a chance to an unfaithful people.[7]

History, even in the biblical books, tries to give different events unifying themes, including those of promise, covenant, and salvation. The contemporary reader of what was in pre-modern times simply called the biblical history encounters a problem. What remains if we cannot count on a linear history demonstrable by material evidence, a history in which the events follow one after another in the right order? Attention has to be redirected to rediscover the value of these stories, to learn to work with texts in which it is impossible to draw a sharp dividing line between the mythical-etiological and historical features, because both of them form one unit. The texts also approach the events and their impact on the memory of God's people. The exodus of Israel from Egypt is a classic example of this. It also presents the founding moment of Israel that the next generations will remember, celebrate, and thus make present.[8]

> Remember this day on which you came out of Egypt, out of the house of slavery, because the Lord brought you out from there by strength of hand . . . You shall tell your child on that day 'It is because of what the Lord did for me when I came out of Egypt.' It shall serve for you as a sign on your hand and as a reminder on your forehead, so that the teaching of the Lord may be on your lips; for with a strong hand the Lord brought you out of Egypt. You shall keep this ordinance at its proper time from year to year. (Exod 13:3.8–10)

At the same time the text reveals its setting in a later state of affairs when it was necessary to explain why the Passover was celebrated. Here the Exodus served as a reference event: "And when your children ask you,

6. See Brueggemann, *Israel's Praise*, 12.

7. See Williams, *On Christian Theology*, 21–22.

8. See Ceresko, *Introduction to the Old Testament*, 72.

'What do you mean by this observance?' you shall say 'It is the Passover sacrifice to the Lord, for he passed over the houses of the Israelites in Egypt, when he struck down the Egyptians but spared our houses.'" (Exod 12:26–27) The cyclical time of festivals participated in forming the linear time of history in the memory of Israel to which it refers.

The Deuteronomist literature[9] tells the history of Israel at whose centre is the history of the glory and fall of the kingdom. I am not referring here to political and social history in today's sense, but rather a theological history that focuses on the explanation of the tragic fate of God's people, how it could be at all possible that God's people could end up in captivity. The story is narrated from the contemporary point of view of its authors, and its intention was to show that the situation of the lack of freedom on which the history was based was a consequence of Israel's long-term unfaithfulness. It relates therefore how the kings and people broke the covenant with the Lord and did what was bad in God's eyes. It is neither the whole history, nor the whole present. The texts that are available to us work with the time of history. This is a blessing when Israel is faithful to the Lord. Much more often, though, it is connected with the time of judgment, a tragic time, but also a time of catharsis that awakens new hope that the Lord will again intervene in the flow of things and redeem his people.

In these texts[10] we can distinguish the following moments: (i) Israel broke the covenant with the Lord, was unfaithful to the Lord, and thus sinned; (ii) therefore Israel was punished and suffered when the Lord let them fall into their enemies' hands; (iii) Israel cries to the Lord, begging for help; (iv) the Lord intervenes because God is always faithful.[11] These moments do not disappear even when we read about the time of blessing represented by the reigns of David and Solomon. We can, however, find a new eschatological dimension emerging in them that allows the preservation of the "validity" of the promises even when the authors of the Deuteronomist history experience their opposites. The promises, however, also have a non-realized element, one that has the potential to develop in the future.

---

9. Besides Deuteronomy, this includes Joshua, Judges, First and Second Samuel, and First and Second Kings.

10. See, e.g., Judg 2:7.10b–18.

11. See Ceresko, *Introduction to the Old Testament*, 120.

The description of the tragic history of Israel continues. As we noted in the treatment of the monarchy in the previous chapter, only three kings in the history of Israel and then of Judea are described positively: David, with some reservations,[12] Hezekiah, and Josiah.[13] Unfortunately, their efforts to purify the religion and keep justice were not enough to outweigh the long-term idolatry of Israel and the spilling of innocent blood in its midst.[14] The history of Israel is narrated as a recalling and radicalization of similar moments. The structure, found already in the beginnings of Israel's "history" in the Promised Land, is repeated when we read about the break-up of the Northern Kingdom (722 BC), as well as the fall of Jerusalem and the conquest of Judea (587 BC).[15]

Besides the emphasis on the tragic character of the time of history, we can hear in the Old Testament the emphasis on history as a time of the fulfillment of hope. Israel was strengthened by the period of exile and the people returned to rebuild the temple and, with it, their religious and social life.[16] They return with faith in the Lord as the creator of the world and the ultimate judge of all nations. Their God is at the same time God of all, and judge of all. The theological history of Israel is extended and becomes the theological history of the world.

The New Testament gives priority to an eschatological understanding of time over the historical, but even there traces of the time of history can be found. History is founded liturgically, as we have seen in the early Old Testament narratives. The liturgy is rather rooted in the eschatological memory—we do this in Jesus' remembrance until he comes in glory.[17] Time is counted from the other side—how much is left to the end of days. But there is also an emphasis on Jesus as a historical figure, continuing the history of Israel and the salvation history of the world, and the New Testament shows a new segment of this history, namely the history of the mission of Jesus' followers. The history of the church is at the same time a history of its common faith, witnessing to the works of the one God in the

12. See 1 Kgs 11.

13. 2 Kgs 18–20. 22–23.

14. The worst time was during the reign of Manasseh: see 2 Kgs 21; 23:26–27.

15. In contrast, a hopeful moment promising the beginning of the Lord's intervention is represented by the amnesty of Jehoiachin, king of Judah, in the Babylonian exile. See 2 Kgs 25:27–30.

16. See Neh 1–2; 4:1—7:4; 8–10; Hag 1–2; Zech 1–8.

17. See 1 Cor 11:26.

events of the earthly and resurrected Jesus, a history whose meaning and unity it is possible to understand only in the power of the Holy Spirit.[18] The unity of the church's history and the history of the world is given by the call to worldwide mission[19] and the knowledge that the new life given to Christians is to be good news for all.[20]

ESCHATOLOGICAL TIME

Many moments changed Israel's understanding of the nature of the redemption it could expect. There was the fall of Jerusalem, the destruction of the temple in the years 587–6 BC and the subsequent Babylonian exile, the delay of the expected golden era and the return to Zion of which Deutero-Isaiah talks, the persecution described in Daniel, the disappointment over the new introduction of the kingdom, the destruction of the Temple a second time in AD70. All these gave rise to a new form of expectation of redemption. In the Old Testament two basic types of eschatology can be found (i) prophetic and (ii) apocalyptic,[21] and, as we will see, each of them works with time differently. Prophetic eschatology is founded on the vision of the future for this life and this world as promised by the prophets: the end of violence and injustice among people, the end of poverty, and a new harmony not only in society, but also in nature, because Yahweh will transform this world into a better place to live in the future. A classic example is the text from Isaiah that speaks of a world in which the wolf shall live with the lamb without violence and babies could play above the viper's den without danger because the full knowledge of the Lord will heal all mechanisms of destruction.[22]

The prophet Ezekiel offers a broad vision of the future that stands on the border of prophetic and apocalyptic eschatology. In its accounts of particular events, times, and places it represents prophetic eschatology, but when Ezekiel's prophecy is broadened and includes other nations, we move on to apocalyptic eschatology.[23] The day of the Lord that is an-

18. See Rom 8; 2 Cor 3:6–8; Eph 1:23; 1 John 3:24; 5:6.

19. See Matt 28:19–20.

20. See Williams, *On Christian Theology*, 24.

21. Another distinction is between: (i) individual-universal eschatology; (ii) future-present eschatology. Individual eschatological statements concern the human being as an individual, whilst universal (or collective or general) ones refer to all people and the whole of creation.

22. See Isa 11:6–9.

23. In chapters 4–24 Ezekiel deals with the near future and what would befall Judah

nounced here, the day of judgment of all, although coming from the future, has an impact on each generation, including Ezekiel's contemporaries. Nobody knows when it will come.[24] The other eschatological theme is one of renewal. Ezekiel uses expressions such as "in years to come" or "in the latter days."[25] "The day" mentioned here is no longer the day of the Lord's judgment, but the following events. Israel's future is related to the covenant tradition, to Abraham, Moses, and David. Yahweh's promises are irrevocable, and so is his mercy.[26]

Apocalyptic eschatology constantly re-appears in late Judaism. It concentrates on the vision of the "other" world, as we read in Trito-Isaiah: "For I am about to create new heavens and a new earth." (65:17a) In terms of apocalyptic eschatology we still find an emphasis on the transformation of this world, as described in prophetic eschatology. Nevertheless, this transformation is put into the context of the coming of the God Yahweh, who will judge Israel and the whole world. Micah's vision of non-violence is preceded by a reference to judgment.[27] Elsewhere, there are references to the "Day of the Lord." Ezekiel says that it will be a "day of clouds, a time of doom for the nations" (30:3b), Joel says that "as destruction from the Almighty it comes" (1:15b), and Zephaniah offers a naturalistic description of this event as the destruction of the land when the judgment of the peoples will be carried out on the one hand, and salvation and renewal of the chosen people on the other.[28]

Apocalyptic "otherworldliness," however, appears as late as the second century BC. The book of Daniel, reflecting the Maccabean crisis,

---

for its trespasses. See, e.g., Ezek 7:1–27.

24. See Ezek 12:26–28. However, the end announced here is not the end of the universe or of history. It is the end of the holy city of Jerusalem.

25. Ezekiel develops them in chapters 34–48. See, e.g., 38:1—39:29.

26. The sequence of events described by Ezekiel resembles the moments that can be found in the description of the history of Israel in the Deuteronomist literature, and corresponds with the typical structure of the Ancient Near Middle Eastern tradition of judgment and restoration: (i) people sin; (ii) God is angry; (iii) God announces and sends a disaster; (iv) people call to God for help; (v) God remembers his mercy and makes a promise and starts the work of restoration. Ezekiel captures the following moments: (i) new disposition of God and God's people; (ii) new ruler of the people; (iii) rebuilding of the temple; (iv) return of God—restoration of the cult; (v) gathering of the scattered people.

27. See Mic 4:2b–4a.

28. See Zeph 1:14–18.

speaks of resurrection as a reward for the just, and thus a belief in life that continues after death was for the first time explicitly expressed in Judaism.[29] This new hope and faith, developed over the following centuries, also brought a new understanding of "time" beyond the limits of time, beyond the limits of death.

In the New Testament the fullness of time is the dominant theme. It is expressed by the references to "God's kingdom drawing near" or to the "last days."[30] Jesus opens his public ministry by announcing: "The time is fulfilled and the kingdom of God has come near; repent, and believe in the good news." (Mark 1:15)[31]

Beside the emphasis on the prophecy being fulfilled and the time of God's reign being already here, there are in Jesus' words statements balancing the "already" with the "not yet." When the disciples asked Jesus to teach them to pray, Jesus included in his prayer the phrase: "Your Kingdom come." (Matt 6:10) The Kingdom is mentioned in the future tense in the parables of the sower, of the weeds among the wheat, of the mustard seed, and of the yeast.[32] In these parables time for growing and maturing is still needed. The glorious future is here *in nuce*. This tension between the present and the future, between what is visible and what is invisible, between the prophetic and apocalyptic elements of God's reign goes through the whole of Jesus' life as far as the cross, where it culminates. The experience of resurrection does not disturb this tension, but interprets it apocalyptically as a breaking point in history:

> At that moment the curtain of the temple was torn in two, from top to bottom. The earth shook, and the rocks were split. The tombs also

---

29. See Dan 12:2–3.

30. In the gospels Jesus speaks of the kingdom as of something present: it "is among you." (Luke 17:21) The signs of God's kingdom are healing: "the blind receive their sight, the lame walk, the lepers are cleansed, the deaf hear, the dead are raised, and the poor have good news brought to them" (Matt 11:5) and exorcism broadly understood: "and the scroll of the prophet Isaiah was given to him. He unrolled the scroll and found the place where it was written: 'The Spirit of the Lord is upon me, because he has anointed me to bring good news to the poor. He has sent me to proclaim release of the captives and recovery of sight to the blind, to let the oppressed go free, to proclaim the year of the Lord's favor.' And he rolled up the scroll, gave it back to the attendant, and sat down. The eyes of all in the synagogue were fixed on him. Then he began to say to them, 'Today this scripture has been fulfilled in your hearing.'" (Luke 4:17–21)

31. See also Matt 4:17.

32. See Matt 13.

were opened, and many bodies of the saints who had fallen asleep were raised. After his resurrection they came out of the tombs and entered the holy city and appeared to many. (Matt 27:51–53)

The future then becomes the present in the Risen Lord, and in those who encounter him, and in him the defeat of death and the victory of life. Christians also understand the "last days" as their own present, sealed on the one hand by Pentecost: "This is what was spoken through the prophet Joel: In the last days it will be, God declares, that I will pour out my Spirit upon all flesh" (Acts 2:16–17a); and on the other hand by the "blindness" of their enemies and the appearance of the "Antichrist."[33] At the same time attention turns to the future, to the second coming of Christ,[34] to the approaching last day that will bring the final plagues as described in the book of Revelation,[35] the full and visible judgment of the world, as well as full and visible salvation.[36]

Topos and Utopia

As with historical and eschatological time, so with the spatial context of theology the symbolic and the factual are combined. We need to draw both on places as the actual environment we inhabit, places connected with the soil underfoot, particular people and their customs, as well as symbolic places, or, if you will, "non-places," where hopes and their shadows are placed.

THE LAND AND ITS WAYS OF LIFE

The emphasis on the particularity of places has already been noted in the chapter on revelation. There we saw how the tradition of Israel associated certain events of revelation in the lives of the ancestors with places that were important in its cultic life. Thus Shechem is the place where Yahweh appeared to Abram and promised to him the land of Canaan as well as numerous offspring.[37] The stories of Isaac and Jacob also contain similar references.[38] The particular wells and pillars are the special places

---

33. See 2 Tim 3:1–9; Jas 5:3; Jude 18; 1 John 2:18.
34. See, e.g., John 14:3; 1 John 2:28.
35. See Rev 15:1—16:21.
36. See John 6:39.44.54; 11:24; 12:48; 1 Cor 15:26.52–53; 1 Pet 1:5.
37. See Gen 12:7.
38. See Gen 12:2; 26:24.

where they encountered and worshipped the Lord.[39] Such places carry something that comes from the Lord's future, though at the same time they are here and not in the future. They serve to remind us of what is not yet here.

We can also note the connection between factual and symbolic places in respect of Egypt, Canaan, or Babylon. Each of these places represents a space inhabited by people with their culture, religion, values, customs, myths, and history. We are given information about Egypt. We learn where it is located, what the weather is like, how fertile it is,[40] about its origins, history, and rulers,[41] its industry, art, architecture,[42] and religion.[43] Compared with this admired and feared place Israel sees itself as unimportant, as a poor people, but a people who are saved from slavery by the power of the Lord, although they themselves would sometimes prefer the "fleshpots of Egypt."[44] Egypt is then a certain archetype of the "land of slavery," a symbolic place.[45]

Babylon plays a similar role.[46] It is a place of exile, but at the same time a place where the faith of Israel was changed and deepened. The symbolic story of the building of the Tower of Babel[47] also shows the need of independence from the attractive features of Babylon and the importance of reliance not on the finite Babylon, but on the infinite Lord.

Canaan is again an actual place.[48] It is at the same time a symbolic antithesis of Egypt and Babylon. It is a land that Israel defeated and this victory was attributed to the Lord who had promised it to Israel.[49] Here again we come to a very difficult blending of symbolic and factual meaning—and the question whether political consequences can be deduced from this symbolic meaning. Moreover, the tension between the

---

39. See Gen 26:24–25; 28:12–22.

40. See Gen 41:48; Deut 11:10–11; Zech 14:18.

41. See Gen 10:6; Ps 105:23.27; 1 Kgs 11:26.40; 12:20; 14:25; Jer 37:5–7; 44:30; 46:2.

42. See Exod 1:14; 14:7; Isa 19:9; Prov 7:16.

43. See Gen 41:45; 1 Kgs 12:28.

44. See Exod 16:3.

45. See, e.g., Pss 68:32; 80:9; 87:4; 89:11; 135:9; 136:10; Isa 11:16; Mic 6:4; Jer 2:2; Hos 2:15; Amos 2:10

46. On Babylon—or Chaldea, see, e.g., 2 Kgs 20:12–19; 25:27; 2 Chr 32:31; Isa 39.

47. See Gen 11:4–5.

48. See Gen 12:5; 16:3; 23:2.19; Josh 14:1; Judg 1:9.

49. See Ps 135:11.

territorial understanding and an understanding of Israel as a nomadic people wandering until the end of their days exists up to the present day. The Old and New Testament offer another example of factual-symbolic understandings of God's people, where the emphasis on territory is substituted by the emphasis on the community of people connected by language (whether it is a common language or common understanding of the meaning of things), common history, culture, and religion.

DESIRED PLACES OF HOPE

Places that do not exist yet but are desired or promised also feature in the Scriptures. They usually represent what is missing in the status quo. As not yet existing places they are symbolically mediated through what is known. We read, for example, of the agricultural vision of an ideal world where all "shall all sit under their own vines and under their own fig trees"[50] and will be brought to "a land flowing with milk and honey."[51] We are presented with a political vision of an ideal world in which a savior king will come as one who executes God's judgment, as a defender of the cause of the poor, as a deliverer of the needy, ruling to the ends of the earth.[52] There are even religious visions of ideal worlds, oriented partly to the "new temple" to which the Lord's glory will return, and partly to the covenant that will be put into all people's hearts.[53]

In the New Testament such visions become incarnated in the life of Jesus, and at least partly in the life of the church, when it functions as a society that has overcome social divisions and injustices, a place where people in the power of the Spirit decided they would have everything in common.

> Now the whole group of those who believed were of one heart and soul, and no one claimed private ownership of any possessions, but everything they owned was held in common . . . There was not a needy person among them, for as many as owned lands or houses sold them and brought the proceeds of what was sold. They laid it at the apostles' feet, and it was distributed to each as any had need. (Acts 4:32.34–35)

50. In 1 Kgs 5:5 this promise is projected into the past to the period of Solomon's rule; in Mic 4:4 and Zech 3:10 it has an eschatological perspective.

51. Exod 3:8.17; 13:5; 33:3.

52. See Ps 72:1–9.12–14.17; Ps 101:1–8; Isa 11:1–5.

53. See Ezek 40–48; Jer 31:33–34; Ezek 36:24–32; Isa 2:2–4.

Although it was a remarkable attempt to live the future now, we read later about the arguments concerning who is given priority when it comes to distributing portions from the common goods. So, the church had to accommodate itself to the fact that the ideal world is not present even in her midst,[54] or at least not yet.

Nevertheless, in creating a place in which something of the future hope is visible, God's promises and human desires coincide, although the realization of the ideals has to be subjected to the continuous need of purification. Like the church after Pentecost, and probably much more than that, we have to struggle with disordered human inclinations and desires to dominate, which can result in creating places where something else or someone else than God is at the center.

The places of the future come not only through our creativity and our visualization of the future, but also as places that await us. The New Testament uses a variety of images for this, including the heavenly wedding banquet, rooms in the Father's house, or the non-place where there will be fire or "weeping and gnashing of teeth."[55] The desired places of the future (and the feared non-places) show even more radically that the interweaving of the factual and symbolic understandings of space cannot be separated into two without destroying the meaning of both.

The two threads—the factual and symbolic—form a unity in the various concepts of time and place that the Scripture offers. However, at the same time it is important not to merge the two, as otherwise we would end up with the absurdity of political claims being made, based on what was promised in different religious-symbolic narratives. The factual informs and grounds the symbolic understanding, but we cannot move from the symbolic to the factual in quite the same way. There has to be a distance that prevents the symbols from becoming idols, mediating the eschatological as eschatological and the transcendent as transcendent, and allowing the plurality of different mediations.

54. See Acts 6:1–4.

55. See, e.g., the parable of the wedding banquet (Matt 22:11–14), the story of the last judgment, when the sheep will be separated from the goats (Matt 25:31–46), or the parable of the faithful and unfaithful slaves (Luke 13:22–30).

TIME IN THEOLOGICAL REFLECTION

Having sketched how the scriptural texts work with notions of time and place, let us move to the later theological debate underlying the modern controversies concerning the development and contextuality of theological truths. In this part I will concentrate first on theological reflection on time: time as coming from the past and recognized as a time of history; time as coming from the future and named as eschatological time. I will give some attention to modern understandings of history and progress, to the contribution of modern historical thinking to theology, and to criticisms of it. Here I will concentrate especially on the issue of finding past events "the way they were," on the need to revaluate this effort with the help of hermeneutics and ideology critique. Lastly I will deal with the understanding of history as living memory, for this concept rehabilitates areas that were pushed aside or not approached as themes in modernity. It is, though, precisely here that theology can rediscover itself as a historical and eschatological reflection on the human experience of God, to which both speaking from the past and listening to what comes from the future belong.

Historical and Eschatological Counting of Time

The symbolism of time as understood by contemporary Western theology is, to a great extent, influenced by Augustine. According to him, time has a beginning "at no time" and comes from "the Eternal Creator of all times."[56] We, as creatures made in time, measure time "in passage." Time is "extendedness" for us, stretching from the past towards the future. Augustine distinguishes three times, past, present, and future, as three modes of presence of things in the mind: "the present of things past is memory, the present of things present is sight, the present of things future is expectation . . . For the mind expects, attends and remembers: what it expects passes, by way of what it attends to, into what it remembers."[57]

Time moves from the past that is no more and is headed towards a future that is yet to happen. It brings and at the same time takes away the present.[58] We carry the past, according to Augustine; we carry the traces of things we discovered by our senses in our memory. The future, if it is to be real, must already include something present, predictable from

56. See Augustine, *Confessions*, XI.14.30.
57. Ibid., XI.20.28.
58. Ibid., XI.15.

present events.[59] Augustine's understanding of time moving from the past towards the future allows us to perceive as history the sequence of events printed into the memory of humankind, of the church, of the nation. It does not, however, provide any possibility of referring to past "reality" other than through what was preserved in the memory of a certain generation. Augustine's understanding of time does not reject eschatology, but subjects what can be to what already is.

The eschatological future, or in Augustine, rather the eschatological *telos*, as it is not a future time in terms of created time, a time that is consumed and passes, is expressed in terms of a Sabbath rest of creation, and as such is, for him, meta-temporal.[60] Eschatological hope is not, then, a hope in "a future," but a hope in God, who is the Lord of the past, present, and future, as well as a Lord above all time, to whose eternity all times are present, but who transcends all times.

A different eschatological perspective is offered by Jürgen Moltmann. According to him we can discover in time the lost dimension of growing towards fullness that comes from God's future.

> If we look back at these quantitatively different experiences and concepts of time, we can discover continuity in them, inasmuch as in each given case the experience of the coming time fulfils the earlier time and gathers it into itself. So, looking back, we can also say that what was earlier points to what comes afterwards. In the history of God, the different times and the different experiences of time are determined by what happens from God's side. Whatever happens from God's side has a certain direction, pointing from creation at the beginning to the eternal kingdom. For God did not create the world for transience and death. He created it for his glory, and therefore for its own eternal life. Augustine evidently did not take this dimension of time into account. [61]

Moltmann traces this dimension of time in the biblical traditions, where he reads that anything that happens is time-related, although there are different times to be distinguished:

(a) The time of the *right moment* is determined by the events. Every event has its time.

59. See Augustine, *Conf* XI.18.

60. "O Lord God, grant us peace, for Thou hast granted us all things, the peace of repose, the peace of Thy sabbath, the peace that has no evening." Augustine, *Conf* XIII.35.

61. Moltmann, *God in Creation*, 124.

(b) *Historical time* is defined by God's promises and events of God's faithfulness to them.

(c) *Messianic time* is defined by the coming of the Messiah and the beginning of the new creation in the midst of the time of this disappearing world.

(d) *Eschatological time* is defined by the prophetic line between the past and an announcement of a new, different future.

(e) *Eternal time* will finally be the time of new, eternal creation in the kingdom of God's glory.[62]

Thus Moltmann extends the notion of time, and unlike Augustine, allows different ways of measuring time, from the past to the present heading towards the future, and from the future descending towards the present. The different understandings of time here are complementary, rather than mutually exclusive, even if we need to treat each time in accordance with its own inner rules, and even if encounters between such times produce aporias and creative tensions. Yet precisely because of that, working with all these different times is beneficial for theological reflection, because in it our grasp of time-related contexts is prevented from being artificially harmonized.

Modern Concepts of History and Progress

The historical understanding of theology, as we know it today, is an offspring of the Enlightenment and modernity,[63] when people started to interpret time in terms of historical changes producing progress. During the Enlightenment the medieval model of the static world and its authority was broken. The church, tradition, and the Scriptures were desacralized and subjected to rational criticism. It was stressed that everything past, without exception, arose in time and was marked by the characteristics of

62. See Moltmann, *God in Creation*, 124.

63. Different landmarks in European history can be considered as the end of the Middle Ages and the beginning of modern times. They include: (i) the Renaissance period, concentrating on the human being, and the Reformation, with its different model of authority, influencing how the church and society operated; (ii) 1492—the "discovery" of America; (iii) the period when Copernicus (1473–1543) introduced his heliocentric model of the solar system; (iv) the time when Descartes (1596–1650) in his *Discourse on the Method* wrote: "*Cogito ergo sum*." (I think, therefore I am); (v) 1648—the end of the Thirty Years' War, when the newly-established peace changed the political situation of Europe and gave rise to absolute states.

its day. In the name of progress it was claimed that the past took place on a lower evolutionary level than the present, and people were expected to rid themselves of the layers of myths and legends, as in the modern "now" they were in an age that operated with verifiable facts.

Modern Europe, tired from the Thirty Years' War, achieved religious toleration with this new hermeneutic principle for the interpretation of history. The same principle brought the relativization of Christianity, as it (or any single expression of it) was no longer seen as a static eternal religion, but a historical contextual one.[64] The modern concept of history, supported, for example, by von Ranke,[65] begins with a distrust of tradition. Its ambition is to subject tradition to history as a faithful, evidence-based account of events "as they really happened."[66] Tradition was accused of preventing people from developing freely, of binding them with dogmas, forming their prejudices, and controlling them through fear. It was seen as dogmatically distorting the past.[67]

Historical criticism within Christianity concentrated on the Bible, especially on the first chapters of Genesis dealing with creation of the world, with the flood, then with the miraculous stories from the lives of the ancestors, the calling of Moses at the burning bush, and the exodus of Israel from Egypt. In the New Testament, it focused on Jesus' conception, miracles such as the walking on water or healing, Jesus' resurrection and ascension, as well as on whether Jesus really established the church as we know it, whether he instituted the seven sacraments, and whether the authors of the New Testament really were the apostles.[68] The efforts to find pure, empirically verifiable facts, evidenced by written documents or excavations, without previously accepted dogmatic schemes of interpretation, represented the base for the search for the historical Jesus, contrasted with the Christ preached by the apostles and represented by the dogmatic teaching of the church.[69] Themes that exceed the limits of nat-

64. See, e.g., Leibniz, *Neue Abhandlungen*; Lessing, *Schriften 2*.

65. See, Ranke, *Geschichten*, especially the appendix „Kritik neuerer Geschichtsschreiber."

66. Compare Moltmann, *God in Creation*, 108–10.

67. See Moltmann, *God in Creation*, 108; he refers here to Strauss, *Die christliche Glaubenslehre*, 71; Scheller, *Die Stellung*, 31.

68. The historical-critical approach was taken to its extremes by theologians representing Protestant Liberalism, such as D.F. Strauss, F.Ch. Baur or A. Von Harnack.

69. See Strauss, *The Life of Jesus* (1835); Baur, *Paul, the Apostle of Jesus Christ* (1845);

ural-scientific reason were interpreted with extra care, for they were seen as the best examples of the dogmatic, non-historical layers that had kept believers in the darkness of ignorance. Scripture texts were researched as any other literature with consideration given to the context in which they originated, to issues concerning authorship, and the chronology of the texts, along with the use of other sources to deal with the subject.

Nevertheless, critical research, which is now considered a necessary part of biblical studies and the history and teaching of the church, would not be here without struggles over the legitimacy of the historical-critical method. At the same time it is necessary to revaluate the modern understanding of the facts and of progress, as well as its absolutization of one scientific point of view, namely that of the natural sciences.

Postmodern Criticism and New Possibilities

The move from modernity to postmodernity[70] is marked by mistrust in history, progress, and scientific objectivity. This mistrust is motivated at least partly by the fact that the modern ideas of the "adult" world were as vulnerable to abuse as all previous concepts. Their proponents also used them as an alibi for the defiance of freedom and human rights. What was claimed to serve human emancipation also led to new forms of exploitation and violence. In this part I am going to explore two critical voices: Jean-François Lyotard and his analysis of developed European societies and their ideologies, and Johann Baptist Metz, who directs our attention to history as a "memory" that confronts us with where we came from and puts before us the possibilities of realizing that which we will become.

---

von Harnack, *What is Christianity?* (1901). Such views were opposed by more moderate users of the historical critical method among the Catholic Modernists. See, e.g., Loisy, *The Gospel and the Church* (1901); Tyrrell, *Christology at the Cross-Roads* (1909).

70. The expression "postmodern" was first used in architecture and described a movement in the 1950s and 1960s critical of the international style of buildings reminiscent of gigantic machines. From here the expression "postmodern" spread to other arts, as a protest against the so-called "modern." In the seventies post-modern philosophy appeared and this expression is often taken as a synonym for deconstruction, represented especially by the French literary critic and philosopher Jacques Derrida, as well as for post-structuralism. Issues that so-called postmodern thinking deals with were already hinted at in Marx (1818–1883) and his social theory, in Nietzsche's (1844–1900) philosophy of the announcement of the death of the old god and the freedom of man, in Freud's (1856–1937) depth psychology, in Durkheim (1858–1917) and his sociological analysis, in Wittgenstein's (1889–1951) analysis of language and revaluation of certainty, and in Heidegger's (1887–1976) hermeneutics.

Lyotard's Deconstruction of the Metanarrative of Progress

In *The Postmodern Condition: A Report on Knowledge*,[71] Lyotard identifies "metanarratives" as ultimate explanations offered to a society that are assumed to be superior to other explanations, because they are supposed to disclose timeless truth.[72] In fact, however, they are tools used to fix the given conditions of a society—the ways in which access to power and wealth is distributed, for example—and to provide those who control these mechanisms with means to justify their positions. Thus metanarratives are not innocent.[73] Lyotard's two favorite examples of metanarratives from the past are to do with knowledge, either as produced for its own sake or as produced for general human emancipation. Both contributed to the modern idea of progress. These two metanarratives, Lyotard argues, lost their credibility after the Second World War. Yet the desire to construct new metanarratives remained. With the spread of globalization, this desire became even more dangerous, as people in power now have the possibility to construct an even more perfect universal dictatorship.

In Lyotard's critique the metanarratives concern society as a whole. He pays attention to the negative aspects of the power relationships that stood behind knowledge and emancipation, which defined the modern concept of "progress," and made it possible to understand the present as something absolute, superior to the past, and determining the future. Metanarratives can be found at the base of all totalitarian systems and, because they essentially tend towards totality, it is necessary to strip them of their power.[74] In order to gain freedom over them we have, according to Lyotard, to deconstruct their basic principles—and at the same time avoid the tendency to replace them with other absolute principles.[75]

71. Lyotard wrote this book in 1979 as a report for the Quebec government on the state of knowledge, science, and technology in advanced Western European societies.

72. Lyotard's analysis draws on the sociological model of Durkheim, treating society as an organic unity, the functional system of Parsons and the class system of Marx, arguing that each of them attempted to explain society by means of a single theory. See Lechte, *Fifty Key Contemporary Thinkers*, 246.

73. "Its [referring to the performance of grand narratives] only validity is as an instrument to be used toward achieving the real goal, which is what legitimates the system—ppower." Lyotard, *The Postmodern Condition*, 61.

74. Ibid., 61.

75. Lyotard blames Kant for the widespread conviction that there is "one right way" for everybody to behave in a particular situation. Lyotard argues that such a conviction

Metanarratives of progress legitimate the privileged position of powerful people in Western societies. Such people have money and thus access to technologies. They can finance research and decide the direction "progress" will take, and who will and who will not participate in it. They will work with the category of "objectivity" that they themselves have determined, just as they decide whom they want to silence or exclude from their game. This type of behavior, although it is justified by the effort towards progress, is, according to Lyotard, equivalent to an act of terrorism and might have disastrous consequences.[76]

Lyotard deals with the issue of how to determine a person's moral duty after the deconstruction of metanarratives of progress. He wants to ask what would prevent the abuse of power whilst avoiding slipping back into a world of dead, objective norms. Thus he sees the need for continuous change. Here the emphasis on everyone having to find a concrete form of moral duty in his/her individual situation is not enough for Lyotard. He is aware that our contemporary era deals too much with the question of "my" rights and too little with the question of the rights of the "other." A person in his/her judgment must take into account a "different" person with his/her rights, needs, freedom, someone who is not reducible to a principle. Lyotard's original emphasis on the relativity of the criteria here changes into an emphasis on relationality to the other.[77]

The issue of the necessity of some conception of "progress" returns with the knowledge that it is necessary to revaluate our understanding of time and the future. We need to recognize that we no longer shape time, but time also shapes us, the time in which we live, think, remember past things, and dream of the future. Here new possibilities emerge for the inclusion of memory and hope in redeeming events into the empty space left behind after the deconstruction of "progress."

---

ignores the arbitrariness of our choices, and simply gives to one arbitrary choice authority over others. This is something that we have to act against, if we do not want to support the exclusions and injustices that metanarratives impose. Against Kant he claims: "'Always act in such a way that the maxim of your will may'—I won't say 'not be erected,' but it is almost that—'into a principle of universal legislation.'" Lyotard, *Just Gaming*, 94; compare to Kant, *Critique of Practical Reason*, 119.

76. See Lechte, *Fifty Contemporary Thinkers*, 247.

77. Lyotard dealt with these issues in his later work, *The Differend*.

The Rehabilitation of Memory in Metz

We find just such an attempt in the German theologian Johann Baptist Metz. Metz rejects any notion of history as a set of objectively provable events, progressing towards aims decided by those in positions of power. Instead, he claims, history is rooted in a living memory, *anamnesis,* which is ultimately rooted in the memory of God. From there both our historical memory (*Eingedenken*) and meditative reflection (*Angedenken*) arise.[78]

Metz points out that Christianity works with the memory of previous events and people in the light of eschatology. First, the memories are brought back and become alive through the power of the Spirit, the power that comes from the future. Second, Christian understanding of *anamnesis* includes the tension between the "already" and the "not yet." In the commemorated events of salvation in human history God's kingdom has already come near, the last days have already touched us, but the Lord has not yet come in glory. The presence of the active Spirit and the eschatological tension both contribute to the dangerous quality of the memory. In other words, when we give up control over what is allowed to be said about what happened, other unpredictable aspects of the past coming from the memory of God may come to challenge us.[79]

It is, however, the dangerous quality of memory—memory vivified by the Spirit—in which we can find how Christ's liberating power descends to all the hells of this world, how Christ frees the captives and restores life.[80] It is a shocking power, and has little to do with religious dogmatism, which tried to tame what had really happened by creating a Christian (or other) identity, tradition, or collective memory, in which

78. According to Metz, Christianity took both of these emphases from Judaism and used them to enrich the Platonic understanding of anamnesis, focused on the recollection of ideas. See Metz, "Anamnestic Reason," 190.

79. These dangerous memories, like the dangerous memory of the Crucified, hide not only the potential for destruction, but also a potential for redemption, for a genuinely new life. As such, they belong to the in-depth structures of the truths of Christian faith. See Metz, "Anamnestic Reason," 189–94.

80. See Metz, "Anamnestic Reason," 189–94. The potential for redemption cannot be found anywhere else than in what has happened. We find it to the extent that we accept responsibility for what has happened and for who we have been and what we have done in that context. In this process we can, however, find hope, as we realize that we have not been only the movers, but also moved by the Spirit of life, who remembers the memory of God within us, who "helps us in our weakness," and "intercedes with sighs too deep for words," as Paul says in Rom 8:26.

salvation became an empty concept, deprived of the dangerous quality of the Spirited memory. The religious substitution of the dangerous memory is then concerned solely with maintaining a religion that is no more than a reproduction of an authoritarian institution, and where public responsibility for sharing the memory that we cannot control has disappeared.[81]

At the same time Metz is skeptical about non-institutional religiosity. He points out that the dangerous memory needs a tradition in which it is carried on as something that is never fully owned by the tradition. Such a tradition needs an institutional home where self-preservation would not dominate. Without such roots it might be possible that a particular person would be able to feed from the sources of a Christian faith, but it would hardly be possible to pass these possibilities on to the next generation. They would, according to Metz, face the loss of symbolic memory, and with it the loss of history.[82]

Keeping memory alive and redolent of its dangerous quality does not only make it possible for us to confront our guilt as we are made to see the non-realized possibilities in history. It also opens up a journey of conversion. As such it has a constitutive meaning for theology, which in the last analysis is not an independent science, but a discourse dependent on the memory of God, and on the revelation of such memory.

PLACES OF THEOLOGICAL REFLECTION

Now let us move on to the spatially-oriented contexts of theology, culture, and utopia. I will start with the historical and terminological grounding of the subject, continue in examining three modern conceptions of culture, inquiring into the relationship between Christianity, church, and culture, and finally subject them to a postmodern critique, and point out some alternatives this critique suggests. In the end I will consider the relationship between memory and cultural and utopian heritage.[83]

81. See Metz, *Faith in History and Society*, 202.

82. Ibid., 201–2.

83. I deal with the subject in much more detail in my forthcoming book: Noble, *Theological Interpretation of Culture*.

Culture: Defining the Subject

Culture as a topic of study is relatively new. It first appeared in the second half of the nineteenth century.[84] In the second half of the twentieth century it developed into a subject called cultural studies in European and American universities. This subject complements anthropology and helps it avoid becoming mere folklore studies. Cultural studies first concentrated either on "moral activities," where culture played the role of a hidden censor of what was acceptable in society, or it focused on culture as creating meaning in a society.[85] Cultural studies also helped in distinguishing not only time periods, but also local situations, values, customs, and so on. The field of cultural studies has undergone a similar process of transformation to historical studies, as the idea of one coherent culture began to fall apart, and was replaced by an awareness of the fragmentation and plurality of cultures that share the same space in the same time.[86]

According to Edward Tylor's classic definition, culture includes: "knowledge, belief, art, morals, law, custom and any other capabilities and habits acquired by a man as a member of society."[87] Culture is not the antithesis of nature, but more like its evolution, the cultivation of human abilities and possibilities in a definite context. Culture develops and is handed down in symbolic words by which the developing and traditional meanings and values are captured.[88]

Three Modern Approaches

The relationship between theology and culture as a theme of study emerged in the 1950s. Richard Niebuhr with his pioneering work *Christ and Culture* initiated the discussion in Protestant theology. Paul Tillich, on whom I will focus in more detail shortly, continued the discussion. Catholic theology started to pay attention to culture as a space of theological reflection around the time of the Second Vatican Council, when the church became willing

---

84. See Arnold, *Culture and Anarchy* (1869); Tylor, *Primitive Culture* (1871). For comments see Gallagher, *Clashing Symbols*, 11–13.

85. See Gallagher, *Clashing Symbols*, 4; Gallagher also refers to Carter, *The Culture of Disbelief*.

86. See Cady, "Loosening the Category That Binds," 18–22; Libanio, "Hope, Utopia, Resurrection."

87. Tylor, *Primitive Culture*, 1.

88. See Geertz, *The Interpretation of Cultures*, 89.

to acknowledge not only that its teaching develops in history, but also that it develops in relationship with the cultures it passes through, and that they influence one another. Hans Küng was one of the post-conciliar theologians who dealt with this topic. He introduced into theology the concept of paradigm, which enabled him to integrate both the historical and cultural plurality of theology. In Orthodox theology the need to study culture arose along with the rediscovery of the Patristic heritage, and as we will see in the work of Paul Evdokimov, in this light it reflected upon present cultures, and their call to cultivate the world in which we live.

CHRISTIANITY AND SECULAR CULTURE IN TILLICH

Paul Tillich tried to define the ways in which Christianity relates to secular culture and at the same time to show the religious dimension of human culture as such. He began by challenging what he often came across as a false opposition between the sacred and the profane. According to such views, the secular world and its cultures have nothing to do with God. Religion alone is the holy, separated realm, where the Holy Spirit speaks. Against such positions he formulated his method of correlation. This method presupposes that religious symbolism gives foundations to culture, and culture in return offers to religion new forms of expression in each new situation.[89] Thus they are co-related. This is valid even in those situations where culture becomes more a protest against religion than its expression. As long as it mirrors the situation of people of its time and asks existential questions, it remains related to the same sources of being as religious symbols, in which essential answers are revealed.[90] Tillich insists that both theology and culture are in their "ultimate concern" related to the "Ultimate Reality."[91]

In considering the culture of his day, he agreed that it saw itself as emancipating itself from religion and from God. But he also regarded it as necessary to add that this was a protest against a narrow definition of religion, in terms of its myths, teachings, rituals, and laws. The atheist-

89. Although I agree with Tillich's basic insight, I find his Aristotelian language of substance and form problematic. He says that "religion is the substance of culture, culture is a form of religion." Tillich, *Theology and Culture*, 42.

90. See Tillich, "Philosophy and Theology," "The Two Types of Philosophy of Religion," "The Problem of Theological Method" and "Biblical Religion and the Search for Ultimate Reality."

91. See Tillich, *Theology and Culture*, 42; "Biblical Religion and the Search for Ultimate Reality," 357.

existentialist culture tried to analyze the situation of humankind and capture artistically the technically transformed world in which human beings had lost the depth of encounter with reality. Reality was stripped of its transcendence and eternity was eliminated. The world explained itself on the basis of a system of temporal relations.

So even atheist Existentialism is a protest against this type of industrial society and shows that people are left with nothingness, having lost their meaning and their humanity and thus alienated themselves. Art, music, or poetry have not returned to the forgotten God on a large scale, but they depicted what meeting non-being feels like. Their statements, although they do not speak of God and God's order of things, are theologically significant. They ask questions to which theology must find answers. The answers cannot be offered in the form of a repetition of the catechism. Tillich urges a deeper immersion into the abundance of Christian symbolism and the rediscovery of a wider and deeper Christianity for the church and culture of his time, which no longer want to be connected. Existentialism alone, he claims, cannot give the answer, but it might determine a form of the answer that is acceptable for an artist or philosopher, an answer that can become a source of revelation for him/her.

Tillich's method of correlation and his very positive reading of contemporary culture had a great impact on later theology, even if we might question Tillich's distinction between the questioners and those who have the answers, and hold that both religion and culture formulate existentialist questions and give symbolic answers; in other words, the correlation goes both ways. The next important task was to move beyond the dry Christianity of rational doctrine and moral prescriptions, to the largely forgotten symbolic wealth. As he sought to do this, Tillich was confronted with the theological problem of how to relate what is absolute to our human relativity.[92]

According to Tillich, our life is multidimensional. We can find the divine and demonic in it, the spiritual and material, the heavenly and

---

92. The Ultimate, according to Tillich, is Godself, which is the foundation and depth of our existence. It has no multiple meanings. It is eternal, beyond the division of subject and object. In comparison our human world is relative. We can recognize the separation from God in it (separation of our essence from our existence). It is the world where we experience finitude, solitude, guilt and suffering, doubt, absurdity, and death. The source of our existence is in the absolute, in God from whose being we take our power of being, from whom we are separated by sin, with whom we are reconciled in Christ and called back in the power of the Spirit. See Tillich, *Dynamics of Faith*, 41–54.

earthly, being and non-being. Its basic dimension, however, is that of the Spirit, relating our existence to our essence. The human ontological question about God's beginning and God's answer provided by revelation are tied together. Correlation is mediated through symbol and myth in which the human situation and God's revelation meet.[93] Symbol and myth represent the only adequate religious language. They are the forms of language that participate in what they refer to. They participate in the meaning of God's unconditional character, of God's transcendence. That is the reason they cannot be replaced by other forms of language that are not referential and participatory in the same way.[94] Christian myths and symbols, according to Tillich, were pushed aside by the descriptive understanding of God and God's work, but they are not dead. Secularization might paradoxically help by removing description and creating space for symbol and myth to return.[95]

PARADIGM CHANGES IN KÜNG

The Second Vatican Council rehabilitated the positive role of human culture, and began to integrate the notion of cultural plurality into its decrees.[96] For Roman Catholic theologians after the Council it was there-

93. Tillich formulated his concept of symbolic mediation against the background of secularization, especially in the time of his American exile. But he writes also about the beginnings of secularization in Germany in the 1820s. According to him, secularization was caused partly by social changes, partly by the inability of theologians who interpreted the teaching of faith too "supernaturally," and allowed theological reflection to become isolated from the problems of contemporary society. Clayton, "Introducing Paul Tillich's Writings," 18–19. See also Tillich, "Rechtfertigung und Zweifel."

94. Tillich stresses that symbols and myths are of a different dimension to statements that demand or at least enable rational verification. Their authority is in their immediacy, which puts them at the centre of religious traditions and as Clayton summarizes "these traditions live only until their constituting symbols lose their power!" (Clayton, "Introducing Paul Tillich's Writings," 18).

95. Three of Tillich's shorter texts concentrate on the power of symbols and myths in more detail: 'The Religious Symbol/ Symbol and Knowledge' (1940–41); 'Religious Symbols and Our Knowledge of God' (1955), published also as a part of his essay *Dynamics of Faith* (1957) and in *Theology of Culture* (1958), and 'The Meaning and Justification of Religious Symbols' (1961).

96. "The human being comes to a true and full humanity only through culture, that is, through the cultivation of the goods and values of nature. Wherever human life is involved, therefore, nature and culture are quite intimately connected one with the other. The word "culture" in its general sense indicates everything whereby humans develop and perfect their many bodily and spiritual qualities; they strive by their knowledge and labor to bring the world itself under their control. They render social life more human

fore necessary to develop new theological methods that would make it possible to work with such a plurality and move beyond the idea of a single ideal cultural expression of Christianity. Hans Küng's work with paradigm changes in Christianity is one of the contributions to this new area. I have included his concept among the modern ones because of his attempt to grasp all the historical and cultural variety within one interpretative scheme. It may otherwise be rightly argued that in other aspects of his treatment he would fit in postmodernity.

Küng traces the dynamics of the development of Christianity and its dramatic transformation, first from a narrow circle of Jewish disciples to the encounter with Hellenistic culture. He then notes the ecclesio-legal culture of the European Middle Ages and the Protestant religion of morality and inwardness. Fifthly, he points to the struggles with the modern world of a religion hanging on to a fast disappearing social, intellectual, and cultural supremacy. Finally he refers to postmodern cultural and religious plurality and the challenge to find common values that have survived the time of critical reason. He places the changes of the form of Christianity to the context of the changes of epochs that every society goes through. To do this, he introduces the term "paradigm," taken from the sciences and sociology.

Küng's theory of paradigmatic changes comes from T. S. Kuhn who defines paradigm in his *The Structure of Scientific Revolution* as the whole order of beliefs, values, techniques, and other things that are shared by the members of a particular community.[97] Küng perceives Kuhn's definition of paradigm as a way of grasping variety, without having reality divided into disconnected elements. The transformation of paradigms does not

---

both in the family and the civic community, through improvement of customs and institutions. Throughout the course of time they express, communicate and conserve in their works great spiritual experiences and desires, that they might be of advantage to the progress of many, even of the whole human family. Thence it follows that human culture has necessarily a historical and social aspect and the word "culture" also often assumes a sociological and ethnological sense. According to this sense we speak of a plurality of cultures. Different styles of life and multiple scales of values arise from the diverse manner of using things, of laboring, of expressing oneself, of practicing religion, of forming customs, of establishing laws and juridical institutions, of cultivating the sciences, the arts and beauty. Thus the customs handed down to it form the patrimony proper to each human community. It is also in this way that there is formed the definite, historical milieu which enfolds the person of every nation and age and from which he or she draws the values which permit them to promote civilization." GS 53

97. See Kuhn, *The Structure of Scientific Revolutions*, 175. Cited in Küng, *Christianity*, 60.

mean the loss of Christian identity. On the contrary, it is, according to Küng, a part of this identity. We could say it belongs to the essence of Christianity that it is always new and always old. The change of paradigm does not influence only its outer form and so he rejects the separation of form from content. The change of paradigm changes the whole of Christianity, because the whole of Christianity is shaped by the historical and socio-cultural context. At the same time the whole of Christianity is called to faithfulness, to stability, to not abandoning its mission, which is given by hoping in God, a radically Christ-like orientation, and a life of practice growing from the power of the Spirit. Here we will not find too much space for dogmatism, traditionalism, or fundamentalism.

Küng distinguishes between the early Christian apocalyptic paradigm, the early Church-Hellenistic paradigm, the medieval Roman Catholic paradigm, the Reformation Protestant paradigm, the Enlightenment modern paradigm and the contemporary ecumenical (postmodern) paradigm. He deals with the dominant traits of each paradigm, but also with particular forces that initiated the course of change from one paradigm to the next, such as, for example, the legalization of the church by Constantine, the experience that the church is capable of Crusades and the Inquisition, the scientific, technical, and cultural revolutions, and so on. According to him, individual paradigms do not refer only to the past, but also represent present religious-cultural minorities that go to forming the plurality of our contemporary scene. Here Orthodox traditionalism, Roman Catholic authoritarianism, Protestant fundamentalism, and liberal modernism all belong.[98] Küng uses this roughly-sketched picture of paradigmatic changes for a more general question concerning the criteria of possibility for paradigm change. Küng names three: (i) when a new movement announces its arrival in not only the personal but also the public sphere; (ii) when what it understood as opposition becomes representative in terms of the whole; (iii) when the thoughts and examples of newly formed norms break through the boundaries of experiment. Then a change of times, formation of epochs, and macro-change of paradigm happens.[99]

Within his one very general and largely simplified scheme Küng tries to understand contemporary Christianity, taking into account its aporias and postmodern fragmentation. Besides Kuhn, we can trace here

98. See "Table 1" and "Table 2" in the flyleaf of Küng's book *Christianity*. The chapters of his book are organized according to this schema.

99. Küng, *Christianity*, 651.

other influences, namely that of Hegel's universalist dialectics,[100] and of Harnack's tendency to search out the "essence" of Christianity.[101] These two influences make him stay within the modern frame of mind. Despite his (and Hegel's and Harnack's) recognition that religion does not stand outside history and culture, Küng seeks for the continuity of the "essence" of Christianity, and even sees it as a condition for continuing to carry Christ's message of reconciliation and the redemption of humanity.[102] In this search cultures have a factual, rather than positive, place. Küng does not develop a positive theology of culture in a similar way to Tillich. Instead he insists that the facticity of culture has to be taken into account. Moreover, in his examples the facticity comes more often through negative than positive examples, as he keeps asking how Christianity, after having survived the antagonistic cultures of Nazism and Communism, can live up to Christ's call in the culture of consumerism and secularization.

CHURCH AND CULTURE IN EVDOKIMOV

In Paul Evdokimov, the Russian-French Orthodox theologian,[103] we find both a positive theology of culture and a deep awareness of how culture can miss its call to cultivate this world. His theology of culture starts with an assumption that is, for those of us with a western theological formation, highly unusual. According to him, each culture has its beginning and source of power in the church, and the church has its origin in paradise. Thus the church is seen as universal in the sense that it concerns all people, and it is home for any desire of a lost paradise. Culture grows from this home, and develops throughout human history as an expression of human endeavor to cultivate the Garden of Eden.[104] It is rooted in the commandment to "cultivate," to partake in God's creative power. Thus

---

100. Compare with Hegel's philosophy of history and spirit, *Fenomenologie ducha* and *Philosophy of History*.

101. Compare von Harnack, *What is Christianity?* and Küng, *Christianity*, 1–12.

102. See also Küng, *Theology for the Third Millennium*, parts BII–IV, CI; *Global Responsibility*, part c.

103. Paul Evdokimov, although born in St. Petersburg, spent most his life in France, where he studied at the Sorbonne and then taught in the Institute of Saint Serge. He was one of the most energetic Orthodox representatives in the ecumenical movement and took part in the work of the World Council of Churches, as well as being an official Orthodox observer at Vatican II.

104. See Evdokimov, "La culture et l'eschatologie," 15–24; *L'art de l'icone*, 54.

culture has a mediating position, a priestly function in uncovering God's mystery, holiness, and glory.[105]

Culture participates in the cosmic liturgy. It has an eschatological perspective. It goes from symbols to the matter that is symbolized, to the transformation of the world and church into a new earth, into God's kingdom. Earthly culture is seen as an icon of the heavenly kingdom, pointing to the kingdom by the power of the Holy Spirit.[106] But culture is also corruptible. It can become an empty symbol when it collects and petrifies human art and puts it into a museum, when it creates lifeless values or when it puts the pre-ultimate to the place of the ultimate. Then it is also possible to say that the great success of creatures becomes a failure of creation because the creators of these products do not transform the world.[107]

In Evdokimov's theology there is no opposition between the profane and the sacred, simply because all that is is sacred, as it has the potential to point to God.[108] Thus neither culture and nature, nor culture and church, are in enmity, but are all called to cooperate in the process of hierophany.[109] The opposition lies between this call and its betrayal. Instead of ontological dualism, Evdokimov speaks of moral dualism, where the "new person" and the "old person" stand against each other, where the sacred and the demonic (the caricature of the sacred) stand in opposition.[110] It is important to note that Evdokimov's notion of sacredness is based in a Trinitarian theology. All that is is sacred because God has created it, because it was redeemed in Christ, and because God intends it to achieve deification.

Evdokimov asks how to approach culture as a human activity that simultaneously takes place in history and shares in eschatological fullness. He finds unacceptable those extreme solutions that give up historical conditionality in the name of "hypereschatologism" (glorifying a timeless spirit without flesh); or on the contrary those that reject the eschatological in the name of total historicity (making efforts towards perfection within the world, locked in its finitude). Evdokimov shows that the first extreme puts culture in the position of rebellion, where culture refuses to be used

105. See Phan, *Culture and Eschatology*, 59.

106. See Evdokimov, *L'art de l'icone*, 65.

107. See the summary of Evdokimov's position in Phan, *Culture and Eschatology*, 60.

108. See Evdokimov, *L'art de l'icone*, 107.

109. Ibid., 108.

110. See Phan, *Culture and Eschatology*, 68.

as a tool by the church. Thus, in rebellion (however understandable) it separates itself from its religious sources. In extreme cases it sets itself in the position of the ultimate home, a place that belongs to the church, and thus turns itself into an idol, into an anti-church.[111]

In the second case humanity is stripped of its humanness because it stands and falls with its religious setting. Marxist or existential experiments to limit the world to its materiality lead to agnosticism, skepticism, and in the end to hopelessness. In our technical civilization, in which we have learnt to look at things from a utilitarian point of view, culture, too, faces the temptation of accepting this restricted view. Evdokimov complains that a prophet, philosopher, or poet has become "a useless thing."[112]

Yet, according to Evdokimov, we have access to God's kingdom only through the chaos of the world.[113] Culture, despite its ambiguity due to the fact that it is both created and fallen, has not lost the power to point towards what is coming from God's future.[114] Culture, in the same way as people and nature, is not destroyed by the Fall, but it is "reduced to ontological silence."[115] Thus culture must wander through the desert, on the journey from death to life, ascend from hell to God's kingdom, to be cleansed. Culture is not self-sufficient, but needs the Holy Spirit to work in and through it. The Spirit helps culture to transcend its limited capacity. The Spirit takes and transforms it to rediscover its primary *telos*, heading towards its fulfillment.[116] Culture needs the church and the church needs culture. Culture is a mediator between the world and the church. In culture faith and reason can become reconciled, the world and the church integrated, history and eschatology brought into a mutually enriching relationship.[117]

Evdokimov's very positive theology of culture can be inspirational, despite a difficulty we may have with his understanding of the church, and the need to elaborate how such a broadly understood home is related to the actual churches here and now, and to believers of other religions

111. See Evdokimov, "La culture et l'eschatologie," 15–24; compare Phan, *Culture and Eschatology*, 58–59.

112. See Evdokimov, *L'art de l'icone*, 58.

113. Ibid., 314.

114. Ibid., 315.

115. See Phan, *Culture and Eschatology*, 76.

116. See Evdokimov, *L'art de l'icone*, 122.

117. See Phan, *Culture and Eschatology*, 56.

and their institutional life. His shift from ontological to moral dualism asks to be complemented by Tillich, which would lead us to saying that a culture can remain faithful to its *telos*, imperfect as it is, like most of our life here and now marked by ambiguity, without a conscious relationship to its religious roots. Evdokimov makes this step possible, even if he does not take it himself.

Postmodern Criticisms

Where Tillich's, Küng's and Evdokimov's concepts of the relationship between theology and culture present one universal explanatory theory, they are vulnerable to Lyotard's critique of metanarrativity. In Evdokimov's case the critical point comes when he places all human culture into a relationship of dependency, not only on the Spirit, but also on the church.[118] Even if he offers a very broad understanding of the church, the priority of one religious institution over others, as if from the point of view of God's mind,[119] presents a problem. Here Evdokimov seems to endanger the iconicity of culture precisely by the means he employs for its defense. In Tillich the vulnerability comes through the one-sidedness of the correlation method. Culture asks only existential questions, religion gives only symbolic answers. Besides the emphasis that the Kingdom of God includes both and transcends both, it is necessary to reconsider their interchangeability.[120] While Evdokimov and Tillich's concepts tend to give religion or, more explicitly, the church a slightly better position, despite their criticisms of deviations found in the actual religious state of affairs, Küng's concept of paradigm changes, which is located within the developing postmodernity, bears most of the features of metanarrativity. It tries to capture the pluralist development of Christianity, as it were objectively, within one scheme. Its ambition is to track down the "identity of Christianity" by singling out the "substantial" from the "insubstantial," the "kernel" from the "outer layer."[121]

118. See Evdokimov, *L'art de l'icone*, 99.

119. Evdokimov claims that the church was here before creation, in God's mind; therefore it has priority over the world and institutions that have their beginning in the world. See Evdokimov, "La culture et l'eschatologie," 15–24; *L'art de l'icone*, 54.

120. Tillich, *Theology and Culture*, 51.

121. See Küng, *Theology for the Third Millennium*, parts BII–IV, CI; *Global Responsibility. In Search of a New World Ethic*, part c.

In the following part I will consider two critical positions related to the modern concepts of the relationship between theology and culture. The first comes from Theodor Adorno, who did not locate himself within postmodernity. His analysis of what he called identity-thinking would be a helpful complement to Lyotard's criticism of metanarratives. The second point of criticism, from Lamin Sanneh, is directed to the problem of cultural relativism, which, according to Sanneh, is not a postmodern invention.

ADORNO'S NON-IDENTITY THINKING

The German philosopher Theodor Adorno (1905–1969) encountered the problem of totality and the deep roots of totalitarian thinking both in pre-war and post-war Germany,[122] and during his emigration in the United States. Coming from a cosmopolitan Jewish family background, he was brought up to appreciate German romanticism and modern art, as well as materialism and critical Marxism. These contradictory influences then flowed into his critique of any form of totalitarian system, be it fascist, communist, or an oligarchy of experts and elites. Adorno showed that political or economic totalitarian systems did not rest on their own ideological foundation, but grew out of deeply-rooted convictions that allowed them to administer the world and dominate it by their power. He did not blame the world of the Enlightenment for the invention of totalitarian thinking, although he criticized it for the fetishism of technology, class domination, and the repressive exclusion of those who did not fit. Instead he showed that totalitarian thinking was a much older problem, and that in fact the Enlightenment remains an unfinished project.

Adorno's critique of totalitarian thinking rests on two pillars, his negative dialectics and his aesthetical theory. Both represent a criticism of metaphysics and offer ways of overcoming "the identity thinking" we have inherited from metaphysical traditions.

Negative dialectics relies on Adorno's conception of the non-identical, which stands in opposition to identity thinking in three areas:

---

122. Brunkhorst vividly shows Adorno's personal situation in the wider context of post-war German academia, where former Nazi professors became overnight mere scientists, who had never been interested in politics, and proclaimed they had been in silent opposition. Yet, as he demonstrates, from these mere scientists Adorno experienced an ongoing anti-Semitism, and after his return to Frankfurt University it took him 12 years to become a professor, and only posthumously, through the work of Habermas, was his critical theory to gain academic respectability. See Brunkhorst, *Adorno and Critical Theory*, 54.

(i) "labeling"—using general terms to mark concrete events and objects so that they are forced to have a false identity because general terms always include only some aspects of an event or a thing and exclude others;

(ii) idealistic metaphysics, which mistakenly separates the "essence" of things from their "surface," which includes events and forms of life, everything to do with our bodies, feelings and desires, and is seen as largely irrelevant for the knowledge of the world, complete and final;

(iii) instrumental reason, aware of the fallibility and changeability of our opinions, but at the same time acts in a way that its technical interest dominates the object and world and excludes the perspective of "the other."

While the first steps towards identity thinking cannot be avoided to some extent, otherwise we would lose the ability to communicate that includes the naming of the event and thing in partially truthful words, the other areas should be avoided.

All three areas are subjected by Adorno to a radical criticism that forms his negative dialectics. The aim of this criticism is to rediscover the inconsistency between our image of the world and the world itself. This helps to get rid of our self-centered narrow view of the world and our special place in it. In Adorno any claim to truth that we make is necessarily limited and conditioned by our perspective, and if we deny that, we construct some form of egocentrism. In history an extreme form of egocentrism is seen, for example, in anti-Semitism, which grows from a morbid expression of repressed mimesis. Mimesis imitates the environment, but false projection makes the environment like itself.[123] We can say that in such cases egoism grows like a cancer through political culture. Paranoiacs who create a world in their own image at the same time deny or repress all contradictions between their image and the world. They idolize the image.[124]

Here Adorno's negative dialectics meets aesthetic theory. Adorno starts from the Jewish prohibition of making images,[125] which according to him prevents us from creating a copy of the world. The Bible as well as modern art demand authenticity, a non-reduced experience, a con-

123. See Adorno, *The Dialectic of Enlightenment*, 187.
124. See Brunkhorst, *Adorno and Critical Theory*, 27.
125. Compare to Exod 20:4–6.

stitution of an original of a kind, not a copy. According to Adorno, the same requirement should be used for any explanatory theory. It has to be an original, consciously working with its own situatedness, and not a copy. It cannot claim objectivity. Such claims are a disguise for desiring domination.[126]

Adorno requires an original, in other words, a development of a certain type of reflection, which is not a return to the world before aporias and conflicts, but a critical immediacy that reaches new solutions of problems by means of a free, responsible, and creative relationship to the world. Like a Cubist picture or dissonant music, which offer several perspectives at once and give space to the non-identical, such reflection should enable communication instead of pretending that it is a conclusion to it. The condition of communication is that each of the perspectives offered freely relates to truth in some way (necessarily partial and fallible). Freedom is according to Adorno "experimental freedom," a conscious self-exposure to the aporetic situations that cannot be dominated or controlled. The original and free approach to reality, then, is not reserved to the elite only, those who would be equipped to take the consequences upon themselves. Both our fragmented existence and experimental freedom concern all those who take part in it.[127]

SANNEH'S CRITICISMS OF CULTURAL RELATIVISM

In his book *Religion and the Variety of Cultures: A Study in Origin and Practice*, Lamin Sanneh, a professor of history at Yale Divinity School, deals with the relationship between Christian mission and modern culture. Coming from the African and British colonial background, he embodies life in a plurality of cultures, which makes him sensitive in dealing with its problematic areas, which, besides the tendency to totalitarian thinking as addressed by Adorno, also include cultural relativism. Thus Sanneh unmasks what can be seen as a negative mirror image of an egocentrically oriented world, this time supported by an ideology claiming that nothing really matters (apart from its own agenda, of course). Such relativism, Sanneh claims, comes as a fruit of secularization, introducing a sharp dichotomy between culture and religion, and preventing a creative dialogue between the two.[128] Sanneh concentrates on the problem that arises when

---

126. Brunkhorst, *Adorno and Critical Theory*, 103.

127. See Adorno, *Aesthetic Theory*, 321.

128. See Sanneh, *Religion and the Variety of Cultures*, 1–3.

a culture sees itself as ultimate and fit to replace not only those religious mediations it sees as inopportune, but also faith in God as such.

If human culture is anthropologically based and anthropology is deprived of any genuine transcendence capable of making claims on human life, culture tends to see itself even as a final arbiter and interpreter of God's images. There is nothing left outside, which could relativize the convictions and values within the given culture. Culture thus succeeds in depriving religion of its critical voice, and rejects, or at times even suppresses, the representation of values that would transcend the given cultural background, including the value of human life. This is what Sanneh calls cultural relativism.[129]

Sanneh gives the following example. During World War II the American War Council organized a special meeting of cultural anthropologists. It asked them for help in a psychological campaign against German National Socialism. One of the anthropologists protested against the goal of this meeting, saying that scientific anthropology was an objective discipline with no ethical agenda and so they could not judge the values of others. He continued that if Germans preferred Nazism, they had the right to do that just as democratic Americans had a right of choice, because preference is simply an expression of the cultural climate in which people find themselves.[130]

Sanneh's critique of cultural relativism shows the impotence of absolutizing culture and cultural plurality, and the dangers of buying into such an apparently tolerant ideology. It represents the opposite problem to that of subjecting culture to religion, but eliminates transcendence and human solidarity even more effectively. Because, while all world religions have both of these safeguards in their holy texts, and in their ritual and ethical practices, culture, which claims a complete sovereignty, can do away with both transcendence and solidarity simply as its preferred option. When religions become totalitarian, they have to have done some violence to their own traditions, but when a culture becomes totalitarian, using relativist ideology, it can praise itself for its consistency in making free choices, completely incapable of outside criticism.

---

129. Ibid., 43; see Bindney, "The Concept of Value," 684.

130. Ibid., 45–46; parts of the quotation are taken from the report of Adams, "Introduction," 7.

Relations between Culture and Memory

In this last section I want to bring into relationship the understanding of history as living, dangerous memory, as spelled out by Metz, and new possibilities of grasping culture non-ideologically. I will focus on Bloch's understanding of "cultural heritage" and its application to theology, and then on the rehabilitation of "utopia" and "utopian heritage," introduced by Libanio.

CULTURAL HERITAGE ACCORDING TO BLOCH

Another German philosopher of Jewish background and a friend of Adorno, Ernst Bloch, focused on the non-ideological elements present in the cultural heritage of each society.[131] Bloch understands cultural heritage as a critical non-present that contains explosive power to change. Myths, images of the past, social groups and structures of the past are not dead matters, but constitute a potential for further development. Bloch, like Adorno, took as a starting point twentieth century European experiences of the reduction of memory and totalitarization of culture. He started with the negative example of Nazism.

With reference to the cultural heritage Bloch explains why Marxist theory[132] was not sufficient for the critique of Fascism. For Marxism, history and society are dominated by economic interests, as we can see in the class war theory. Fascism could not be explained only by reference to decadent capitalism. Fascism, on the contrary, established its success by reviving nationalist myths and images of the past that appealed to all social groups. Fascism prided itself on bringing employment and social security to the working class. In this sense it was a protest against the impoverishment of its day. It brought new meaning and new identity to the middle class, and succeeded in including farmers, praising their relationship to the land in a way socialism never managed.[133]

Cultural heritage stands as an antithesis to an understanding of the history of culture that limits the voice of the past to the past only and sees

---

131. I have taken the concept of "cultural heritage" in reference to Bloch from Fiorenza, "Religion and Society," 29.

132. Bloch valued Marx for his social critique, and was even considered a Marxist-oriented philosopher. This, however, did not prevent him from criticizing the ideological strands in Marxism itself and the totalitarian systems it led to. See Bloch, *The Principle of Hope*, III: 1370.

133. See Fiorenza, "Religion and Society," 29.

it as overcome in the next stage of development. For Bloch, history is a space where the past talks to the present and offers a critique of which the present itself is not capable. The foundational images, values, and visions that cannot be reduced only to the present are found in the cultural heritage of the past. They represent a contrast to what has not been realized in the present. Besides the negative examples of Nazism or Communism, where the new ideology exploited people through what was missing in their situation, Bloch deals more positively with hope embodied in images of a better world, in other words, utopian hope.[134] Bloch talks about the particular utopian horizons of human culture,[135] which include the "contents" of hope as we encounter them in various periods of history, first in the form of ideas, then as encyclopedically processed "real" evaluations of the human situation.[136]

Bloch's concept of cultural heritage, though set in modernity, does not rely on modern thoughts of progress. "Progress," according to Bloch, does not emerge as heading towards a clearly defined target.[137] Instead he speaks of a dialectic relationship between the present and the past. The past raises its criticism in regard to the present. But this cultural heritage of the past cannot be repeated. It is necessary for it to continue in a creative way in the present and be open to new development and changes.[138] Here there is an overlap with a future that does not come from some unknown realm, but from the present. Bloch says that tomorrow lives in today. People seek it, ask for it. Of course, faces turned in the direction of utopia have different expressions at different times, just as everything they believe they have seen differs in every single case.[139] What does not change is the materiality of their vision of happiness, freedom, a land overflowing with milk and honey. If hope were stripped of its materiality, it would easily lose its direction. Images, values, and visions belonging to

134. In the second part of his *Principle of Hope* Bloch elaborates in detail various forms of utopias. He distinguishes five basic types: (i) medical utopias oriented to the struggle for health; (ii) social utopias oriented to freedom and just order; (iii) technological utopias oriented to the victory of humankind over nature; (iv) architectural utopias oriented to buildings that would depict a better world; (v) and lastly geographical utopias oriented to the rediscovery of the lost paradise. See Bloch, *The Principle of Hope*, II: 454–794.

135. Bloch, *The Principle of Hope*, I: 146.

136. Ibid., I: 146.

137. Ibid., III: 1374.

138. Ibid., III: 1375–76.

139. See Bloch, *The Principle of Hope*, III: 1374–75.

our cultural heritage contain the "realized" and the "non-realized." Both of them, according to Bloch, are rooted in the material world.

UTOPIAN HERITAGE ACCORDING TO LIBANIO

The theme of utopian[140] heritage is widely developed in various forms of liberation theology. As in Bloch's cultural heritage, here also utopia represents the "world" that has not been adequately included into the contemporary model of socio-cultural relationships, the world that lives in promises, longings, images, or dreams of better tomorrows. The "utopian world," as Bloch pointed out, has its roots in the past as much as the "realized world." They are both included in the cultural heritage, they both inform (or deform) people's faith, hope, and actions. Here I will concentrate on the understanding of utopia and its role developed by the Brazilian theologian João Batista Libanio.[141]

In Bloch's categories, we can say that Libanio concentrates on the social utopia originating from the situation of the great poverty of the third world.[142] Libanio shows the twofold etymology of the word "utopia": *ouk topos* (no place) and *eu-topos* (good place). Using this twofold etymology, he explains the tension between reality and unreality that contains human longing for happiness, joy, peace, and fulfillment of life, and that underlies our utopian heritage. According to Libanio, utopia expresses human longings for a truly just order, a truly humane social world that corresponds with the dreams, needs, and ultimate goals of human life. Utopia is an image of a perfect society that creates a horizon for real projects in history and the desire for alternative projects in regard to the current situation and enables them to move towards their goal.[143]

Utopia also has another function: it accuses the contemporary world of not providing space for the positive alternatives represented by the images of the possible good places. Thus the utopian "world," though resented by the dominant world, subverts with its very non-existence what actually exists.[144] Utopia is born in a time of crisis and change, and such

140. The expression "utopia" is attributed to Thomas More who gave his political satire (1516) that title.

141. See Libanio, "Hope, Utopia, Resurrection," 279–90.

142. See also Libanio, "The Current State of Theology in Latin America."

143. Libanio, "Hope, Utopia, Resurrection," 281.

144. See Libanio, "Hope, Utopia, Resurrection," 282. Libanio shows that a similar theme is already present in the Bible, although not the expression itself, which, as noted,

time marks both of its functions, that of providing a positive figurative goal, and that of subverting what does not allow the positive transformation. Thus, Libanio says, the passage from feudalism to early capitalism brings Renaissance utopias (More, Campanella, Bacon); the struggle between the bourgeoisie with its growing power and feudal rulers gives rise to liberal utopias (Harrington, Rousseau, Locke). The protest against the oppression of the working classes gives rise to social utopias (Saint-Simon, Fourier, Owen, Blanc). The dehumanizing influence of technology, progress, and functionalist approaches to human relationships gives rise to communal types of utopia (Hippies), etc. The utopian visions of better worlds and of the subversion of the momentary unbearable state of affairs are always historically and culturally conditioned. None of them represents an absolutely good future, the completion of all eschatological promises. [145]

The utopian imagination is not, according to Libanio, the same as hope. Sometimes the reality is so brutal that there is no strength to even dream of a utopian world, but hope that God stands up for God's people still remains. This hope is no longer connected with human abilities, with their power, their ideas, but it comes from hope in God's promises and in God's power. Abraham is a representative of such hope, one who hopes against hope.[146] Utopias, concrete alternatives to an unbearable state of affairs, might indeed nourish this theological hope, give it strength, show that we experience God in our human courage and that we meet God in our human dreaming of a better, fairer world. Libanio is aware that what we want and what God wants meet at the deepest level. So, our concrete, historically conditioned ideas about the hoped-for world must leave room for eschatological hope, and for knowing that the world without blemish and stain will only be in heaven.[147]

A postmodern critique might add that none of our dreams of how to create a better world in history is free of the desire to dominate or to order things so that they are advantageous for me at the expense of someone else, whether this shadow is manifested at the beginning, during, or at the end

---

appeared only in the 16th century. Israel knows agricultural, political, and religious utopias. In the New Testament we can find a social utopia that served as a model for the communist utopias, utopias about sharing spiritual goods, and apocalyptic utopias. For more detail, see Pixley, J. "Las utopias principales de la Biblia."

145. See Libanio, "Hope, Utopia, Resurrection," 282.

146. Ibid., 282–83; compare Rom 4:18–22.

147. See Pixley and Boff, *The Bible, the Church, and the Poor*, 213.

of the realization of my dream. Utopia can become an apology for what already exists. Thus the utopia dies and its remains assault living utopias. Here Libanio criticizes Marxism. Marxist socialism became an attack on political utopia, on an alternative vision of the world. It marked utopia as alienation. It was accused of idealism, of building castles in the air, depriving people of responsibility for political struggle for a new society and stealing the power to act, so that its lack of realism would lead to frustration. Marxism, according to Libanio, raised itself to be a scientific view, a scientific reading of reality incompatible with the utopian reading, with its vague character and lack of scientific seriousness. Marxism introduced in practice its understanding of equality and social policy, but it took away people's freedom. The second extreme can be seen today in European consumer society. It profits from the ruins of the utopia of the boundless spontaneous freedom of humankind and, in the name of a utopia already deprived of its positive power, it creates new situations of conflict and injustice.[148]

Utopia stresses the horizontal dimension of hope, a hope that has its place in this world, its history, peoples, societies, cultures; eschatology opens the vertical dimension of hope, pointing towards the "ultimate" future in God, towards the future that is for us a mystery of resting in God, something we have not reached yet, that we do not yet know. This future is the basis of all our hopeful futures in history, but at the same time it relativizes each one of them, for this future comes from the other side, from where the Father resurrected his Son.[149] Eschatological hope continues to be a possibility even as society deems it unnecessary, but it is and remains God's gift and, according to Libanio, also a certainty. The one who resurrected Jesus will also resurrect others, and will change the state of things in the direction the Beatitudes indicate.[150] And because God is the God of life, he will not cease to inspire efforts to protect life and make it more plentiful, efforts that we will not stop including in our utopian heritage. In the end we can say that although hope represents a more permanent value in Libanio, it is not quite separable from utopia. Both present a positive alternative and critique of what is; eschatological hope from the point of view of eternity, and utopia from the point of view of a possible historical world. Both blame the contemporary world when

148. See Libanio, "Hope, Utopia, Resurrection," 279, 284. Libanio refers to Marcuse, *El final de la utopia*, 10.

149. See Libanio, "Hope, Utopia, Resurrection," 280–82.

150. Compare Matt 5:1–12; Libanio, "Hope, Utopia, Resurrection," 289.

it does not provide space for them, and with their very "non-existence" they subvert what exists.[151]

CONCLUSION: CONTEXTUALITY AS A REQUIREMENT OF ONGOING TRANSFORMATION

The four contexts examined in this chapter in relation to the biblical and traditional understanding of time and space helped us to see how theological discourse is conditioned by the historical and cultural situations in which it arises, as well as by the eschatological hope and the utopic imagery that partake in the actual settings and subvert its finality. We have also seen how theologians, on the borders between pre-modernity, modernity, and postmodernity, struggled with such conditionality. Keeping the ultimately important difference between what is true and what is false, what is just and what is unjust, and so on, while admitting that particular representations of these would always be subjected to further transformation represents an ongoing challenge. In the conclusion to the chapter I first offer a brief summary of the main ingredients of this challenge, and then look at the problems arising from the attempts to avoid it.

Summary

In this chapter I focused on the issue of time and space, of how various times and cultures transform the context that gives rise to theology—and thus theology itself. The inquiry into the symbolism of time in the Scriptures led me to the relationship between the time of history and time of eschatology and provided wide possibilities of "commemorating" past events and promised futures. The symbolic grasp of space then captured both the concrete places we inhabit and their culture, and the utopias we dream about, and from where we draw our strength and inspiration to transform culture. These biblical foundations were important as we moved to the controversies that the pioneers of modern theology had to face, as they challenged both the narrow Enlightenment understanding of scientific facts, and the ecclesial desire to control what people are to remember and what they are to hope for.

Theologians of the end of modernity, Evdokimov, Tillich, and Küng, stressed the multilayered character of history and culture. They overcame a single understanding of progress based on one interpretation of the

---

151. See Libanio, "Hope, Utopia, Resurrection," 282.

world, where it is "clear" what the lower and higher evolutionary stages are. Yet their desire to grasp the plurality with the help of one interpretive scheme needed further revision. Here the postmodern critique was helpful as it uncovered the ideological tendencies present not only in any universal concept of the world but also in any universal explanatory theory. At the same time, it radicalized the need to consider whether Christianity can really do without any understanding of progress and without any desire to find a unifying meaning in our heterogeneous world.

Adorno and Metz, as well as Bloch and Libanio, offered alternative perspectives, which integrated ideology critique into the challenge to keep the difference between the ethical and the aesthetical opposites. Each of them worked with some form of real "subversive power." They understood memory as more abundant, more complex, and more inconsistent than any of its social or individual representations. In the end they saw the need for a living hope that subverts even what seems to be the ultimate fragmentation of meaning and the loss of the ability to distinguish between good and evil, justice and injustice, progress and regression.

Attempts to Restore Past Times

Hans Küng, in his paradigmatic scheme of the development of Christianity, showed that individual paradigms did not disappear, but even today they form religious-cultural minorities contributing to the plurality of the current religious scene. Thus we find groups that adhere to Orthodox traditionalism, Roman Catholic authoritarianism, Protestant fundamentalism, and liberal modernism. To an outsider these groups seem to behave as if they lived the past in the present.

Ernst Bloch, on the other hand, claims that it is not possible to live in the past. If somebody wants to live in the past, they live in an illusion of the past because the past has gone, and it is impossible to return to it. It is only possible to continue creatively. Is then Orthodox traditionalism a creative continuation of the Hellenistic paradigm of Christianity, Roman Catholic authoritarianism a creative continuation of the medieval paradigm, Protestant fundamentalism of the reformation paradigm, and liberal modernism of the Enlightenment paradigm? Do they not also try to revive forgotten memory and return the forgotten values to circulation? What role do the repressive mechanisms we talked about in connection with the critique of ideology play in these minority countercultures?

What role does the freedom of humanity and an "epistemology of se-curity" play? Do these "countercultures" leave space for openness and solidarity with others? Is their hope for all or for them only?

These and similar questions keep coming to mind as I read books by authors such as John Milbank and Catherine Pickstock. They represent the more radical wing of a group of thinkers associated with "Radical Orthodoxy," a movement that aims to combine a deep understanding of contemporary thinking with a theological perspective that looks back to the beginnings of the church. In *Theology and Social Theory* Milbank demonstrates an excellent knowledge of the postmodern terrain, but this knowledge serves him in order to remove the modern theological efforts from the scene and plead for a return to a Christian empire and its power relations whose idyllic picture is built upon a selective reading of St Augustine.[152] Milbank rehabilitates the sacrifice of human free will to God's service,[153] and to the teaching on satisfaction.[154] He places the uniqueness of Christ's journey on the same level as the journey of the church,[155] and chooses to stress the universality of Christian faith that has a timeless character and is given ontologically, so that all people at all times bear the traces of the Trinity.[156] Catherine Pickstock shares a similar vision. The time of a Christian fullness is in the past, and thus we need to adapt to that time, if we want to have a share in the best of Christianity.[157] Pickstock sees the Latin mass of the Late Middle Ages as an ideal, with its unfamiliar language, the passive attendance of lay people with the at-titude of veneration of the gift of Christ's body.[158] She returns to sacrificial thinking and to the defense of transubstantiation, something that is, ac-cording to her, a condition for the possibility of all meaning. She pulls out the Consecration formula from the whole of the liturgy and claims that

---

152. See Milbank, *Theology and Social Theory*; "Postmodern Critical Augustinian-ism." Richard Roberts named Milbank's project as "postmodern critical Augustinian-ism" and Milbank identified with the description. See Milbank, "Postmodern Critical Augustinianism," 278.

153. See Milbank, "Postmodern Critical Augustinianism," 271, point 20.

154. Ibid., 274, point 32.

155. Ibid., 277, point 40.

156. Ibid., 277, point 41.

157. See Pickstock, *After Writing*, xv.

158. Pickstock, *After Writing*, 176.

these are the only words with a meaning that is certain, and thus they give meaning to all other words.[159]

Although such attempts to restore Christianity to the time of its power and glory need to be subjected to the hermeneutics of suspicion in order to find out what power and interest stand in their background,[160] the effort to revive temporarily unrealized values that our Christian memory contains is not exhausted by them. Even the previous analysis of the yearning for "epistemological security" does not exhaust the question as to why fundamentalism presents an attractive "postmodern" possibility. As J.M. Domenach puts it, the journey that takes a person to the limits of "scientific possibilities," where they touch the abyss of nihilism, might convert them and bring them to those very things that they thought they had left behind.[161]

---

159. Ibid., 261.263.

160. Compare to Habermas, *Knowledge and Human Interests*, 311.

161. See Domenach, "Voyage to the End of the Sciences of Man," 159.

5

Religious Experience

Six days later, Jesus took with him Peter and James and John, and led them up a high mountain apart, by themselves. And he was transfigured before them, and his clothes became dazzling white, such as no one on earth could bleach them. And there appeared to them Elijah with Moses, who were talking with Jesus. Then Peter said to Jesus, 'Rabbi, it is good for us to be here; let us make three dwellings, one for you, one for Moses, and one for Elijah.' He did not know what to say, for they were terrified. Then a cloud overshadowed them, and from the cloud there came a voice, 'This is my Son, the Beloved; listen to him!' Suddenly when they looked around, they saw no one with them any more, but only Jesus. As they were coming down the mountain, he ordered to tell no one about what they had seen, until after the Son of Man had risen from the dead. So they kept the matter to themselves; questioning what this rising from the dead could mean.

MARK 9:2–10

*For what fills and satisfies the soul consists, not in knowing much,
but in our understanding the realities profoundly
and in savoring them interiorly.*

IGNATIUS OF LOYOLA[1]

MARK'S GOSPEL SHOWS THE contrast between different layers of our experience. Jesus was different on the mountain of the transfiguration than the disciples had been used to from their everyday life with him, and yet, retrospectively, one type of experience shed light on the other,

---

1. Ignatius of Loyola, *Spiritual Exercises*, 121: "The second note to the spiritual exercises."

and together they started to form a fuller understanding of who Jesus was. It is important to concentrate on the experiential base, even if this can never be isolated from the symbolic categories in which it is expressed, and that belong to the religious and cultural context of each generation. St. Ignatius demonstrates in the introductory notes to his Exercises another important aspect of dealing with experience, namely that knowledge itself does not nurture the human soul. This happens, rather, when one catches a glimpse of one's own life, of other people, of the Lord God, as they are. Only then does the inner perception and feeling of things become clearer. We are led from the realm of rational speculation to the realm of experience, where humanity meets God. To understand things in their depth, to experience and feel them inwardly, presupposes a transformation of the way in which we had previously thought of ourselves, the world, and God.

In this final chapter I will concentrate on religious experience as a source of theology and on the way the emphasis on direct and handed-down experience appears in the Scriptures and how it was re-introduced into modern and postmodern theology through the rehabilitation of, especially, the non-dogmatic aspects of Christian traditions.

Alongside the Scriptures, tradition, and the church, we will take religious experience as a source of theology. While emphasizing the importance of acknowledging and working with our own experience, I will mostly focus on experience testified by the tradition and mediated and corrected by the church. In this, however, the possibility of speaking from mediated experience to direct experience will be safeguarded.

This approach must be aware of two factors. One of them is expressed by Zdeněk Trtík when he writes: "Theology that does not originate in immediate religious experience . . . does not contain any religious knowledge at all."[2] Immediate religious experience is not to be underestimated. It plays a key role in theology. It cannot be replaced either by tradition or the Scripture. Only in it does faith become a personal faith, only in it can I talk about God as my God and come to my own theological statements. The other factor is implied by Küng when he says: "Any faith based on illusion is not really faith but superstition."[3] Küng refers us to the issue of discerning between religious experience and illusion, between the person

2. Trtik, *Vztah já–Ty*, 71.

3. Küng, *On Being a Christian*, 418.

of faith and someone living in an unreal world. This area is very compli-cated and we will see how difficult it is to give unambiguous criteria to show this difference. Nevertheless, in dealing with religious experience, it is not possible to avoid this issue completely.

Bearing in mind these two factors, we will try to elaborate what religious experience is. We will briefly summarize mediated religious experience as testified by the Scriptures and tradition, and we will look at the extent to which the immediate religious experience of modern and postmodern people contributes to a theological understanding of life as a whole. How can a reflection on religious experience help in distinguishing whether a particular experience is about feeling and experiencing things inwardly, about meeting God and God's world, or about illusion?

In the first part of the chapter I will examine different ways of "expe-riencing" the Lord, the Lord's presence, and the Lord's actions, represent-ing a counterpart to the Lord's word in the Scriptures. Then I will explore two different approaches to prayer and religious experience, as presented by classic Eastern and Western theology. First, I will concentrate on Symeon the New Theologian and his Three Types of Prayer, and secondly on Ignatius of Loyola and his understanding of the dynamics involved in experiencing God. The third part of the chapter will describe the pro-cess of the rehabilitation of religious experience in modern times. I will clarify its purpose and introduce authors who significantly contributed to this process: Schleiermacher, Brentano, Otto, and James. The final part will deal with various current approaches to religious experience. In the conclusion to the chapter I raise questions concerning negative religious experience and the possibilities and problems concerning the evaluation of religious experience and its contribution to the life of the individual and society.

EXPERIENCE OF GOD IN THE SCRIPTURES

Scripture does not speak directly of religious experience using precisely that terminology. However, each of its books testifies to some form of encounter with God, from the creation to the eschatological visions, and to the consequences of this encounter, such as conversion or judgment. In the Old and New Testaments, God speaks and acts. People are wit-nesses to this. Humanity, represented either by the chosen nation or by the church, is included in the dialogue with God.

Two Definitions of Experience of God as Religious Experience

In the chapter on divine revelation we have already spoken about knowing God in religious experience. We discussed the encounter with the hiddenness of God through Jacob's struggle with the unknown man, Moses' encounter with the Lord in the burning bush, and Elijah's meeting with God on Mount Horeb.[4] In addition we looked at the encountering of a God who allows human beings to know God in a way they can understand: God as Father, God born, crucified, and glorified in our humanity—the Son, God the Spirit—Guide, Advocate, Comforter.[5] We will understand religious experience here as meeting this God, but also in the wider sense of the word as meeting a different dimension of human life, one that usually remains hidden, but sometimes moves to the fore and reveals itself, even if often unnamed or even unnameable by any particular religious symbolic system.

In doing this I distinguish between narrow and broad definitions of religious experience. The narrow definition understands religious experience in terms of the concrete religion in which it takes place, and places it in the direct context of other recognized authorities of this religion (sacred stories, ritual, catechism, ethical principles, and institution).[6] It is then more accurate to talk about Jewish, Christian, Islamic, Buddhist, etc. spiritual experience. Here Christian spiritual experience means meeting the triune personal God, leading to a change in the human heart, called *metanoia* (conversion). This involves the hearing of the Word and seeing something of God's work and God's character. Slowly, step by step, this will transform a person's life, returning to him/her the lost image of God in which he/she was created, and the lost unity with God in which there is the salvation of humankind, the church, and the whole of creation.

The broad definition of religious experience stems from common elements, namely people's experiences of self and the world that are as yet unnamed and not evaluated by the categories of their religious systems. Any situation people describe as an encounter with mystery, miracle, wonder, or their fascination with something they have experienced as different from the world, transcending everything, eternal, holy will be

---

4. See Gen 32:25–32; Exod 3:1–14; 1 Kgs 19:4–13.

5. See von Balthasar, *Love Alone*, 6.

6. See the six dimensions of religion according to Smart, "Religion," 496–98.

taken as a religious experience.[7] It is important to note that both definitions concern the same reality. They only differ in their approach to it.
Both approaches can be found in the Scriptures and tradition. Both are
consciously or unconsciously applied when we try to reflect on our own
immediate experience.

In the following examples I will examine experience understood as
a test, as illumination, as a way of instruction, and as a deepening of our
inner understanding.

Experience as a Test

In the Old Testament we find examples of "testing"—when God tries
people, as well as when people "try" God. Here I will focus on those narratives where the "testing" leads to an experience of what God is like, how
God acts, how God manifests God's will and plans, and how people get to
know God and one another in this process. I also consider negative examples, when people project their interests into the experience of God.

PEOPLE TRIED BY GOD

The experience of God is often contrasted with human images of
God's judgment, of how God repays the wicked and blesses the righteous.[8]
This is most strikingly illustrated by the book of Job. Against the attempts
to hold on to the visibility of God's judgments and the assumption that,
if people experience misfortune in life, it is because they must be more
sinful than others,[9] Job speaks of his situation as a test: "What are human
beings, that you make so much of them, that you set your mind on them,
visit them every morning, test them every moment?" (Job 7:17–18) At
the same time Job challenges the Lord and is not willing to accept cheap
solutions. He complains to his friends:

> Look, my eye has seen all this, my ear has heard and understood it.
> What you know, I also know; I am not inferior to you. But I would
> speak to the Almighty, and I desire to argue my case with God. As

7. This broad definition of religious experience is influenced by the modern approach
to the topic in authors such as William James or Rudolf Otto.

8. See, e.g., Hab 1:2–4; Isa 59:14; Jer 14:9; Mic 7:2n. These texts question the assumption that the Lord's judgments are visible here and now as mentioned, e.g., in Gen 18:25;
Exod 6:6; 7:4; Num 33:4; Deut 32:41; 1 Chr 16:14; or Ps 105:7.

9. See the discourses of Job's friends who try to explain his suffering and are unable to
share his lament or his faith: Job 4–5; 8; 11; 15; 18; 20; 22; 25.

for you, you whitewash with lies; all of you are worthless physicians. If you would only keep silent, that would be your wisdom! Hear now my reasoning, and listen to the pleadings of my lips. Will you speak falsely for God, and speak deceitfully for him? Will you show partiality toward him, will you plead the case for God? Will it be well with you when he searches you out? (Job 13:1–9)

Although, when facing the Lord and being confronted with the abyss between human understanding and God's wisdom, Job is incapable of "explaining" God's counsel, ultimately he succeeds in the test. He is transformed by the process, and the direct experience of God deepens his faithfulness.[10] He becomes the epitome of the God-fearing man, who now participates in the transformation of his setting, in this case, his friends and their ideas about God.[11] His direct experience of God changes him from a good to a better man, and reveals possibilities of progressing in goodness, progressing from the Lord's original blessing through the period of trial to a more plentiful blessing.

GOD TRIED BY PEOPLE

In the Old Testament stories the testing of God is generally viewed negatively as indicating distrust, as, for example, in Exodus where Moses brings water out of the rock by striking it, for he is afraid that his thirsty people might stone him.[12] According to Numbers, which tells the same story, Moses and Aaron, who had had plenty of experience of the Lord, tempt the Lord with their unfaithfulness. The power of the word is not enough for Moses in this story; he needs the staff, something more visible and tangible to ensure that the Lord would act.[13]

There are, however, some situations where to ask questions concerning the Lord's presence amongst us, and whether it is really he who speaks, is not evaluated negatively as putting the Lord to the test. When Gideon, whom the Lord calls to become a judge, needs to know whether he has invented his calling or not and whether it is really the Lord sending him to bring the Israelites out from the hands of the Midianites, the Lord is tested in quite another way. Or rather, Gideon tests whether what he had heard

---

10. See Job 42:5.
11. See Job 42:7–9.
12. See, e.g., Ex 17:7.
13. See Num 20:7–13; compare to Num 27:14; Deut 1:37; 3:26; 4:21; 32:51.

really came from the Lord God, and thus he demands a sign three times.[14] The first time he brings a sacrifice under the sacred oak and this sacrifice is accepted. He is scared that he would die, because he has seen the angel of the Lord, but instead learns that the Lord is bringing him peace, because the Lord is peace. He builds him an altar with this name.[15]

Next, two "trials" take place after Gideon has destroyed Baal's altar and is preparing for battle against the Midianites and Amalek, the advocates of the cult of Baal. Gideon spreads out a fleece on the floor and first pleads to God to be shown a sign that God wants to save Israel by Gideon's hand, so that the next morning the dew will only be on the fleece and around it will be dry ground. This is what happens,[16] but Gideon is still not certain. This trial can be explained without God's intervention, without the demonstration of God's will. Fleeces soak up water and dry out the surroundings. It is necessary to repeat the same experiment with the opposite task: "Then Gideon said to God, 'Do not let your anger burn against me, let me speak one more time; let me, please, make trial with the fleece just once more; let it be dry only on the fleece, and on all the ground let it be dew.' And God did so that night. It was dry on the fleece, and on all the ground there was dew." (Judg 6:39–40)

Gideon sets out for war the next day, but before this the roles in "testing" are reversed—now the Lord tests who among Gideon's troops fears and cowers before the elements of nature. He sends a part of Gideon's army home, so that Israel could not say that they were delivered by their own hand, or put the victory down to someone else.[17]

The experience of the Lord as army leader is certainly problematic for us today. The subject of "holy war" in all fundamentalist traditions disgusts us, but at the same time it is a part of not only Islam, but also Judaism and Christianity, both in history and the present. Does the Lord really give power to some nation or group to beat another army or another nation? The task of interpreting our sacred texts and wrestling with their anti-cultural values from today's point of view is not over. Let us not concentrate on the issue of war, though, but rather on the issue of experience. To sum up, in our text people try if God is with them. God tries

14. Compare with the task of two or three witnesses who were to guarantee the credibility of the testimony at the court; Deut 17:6; 19:15; Num 35:30, and so on.

15. See Judg 6:17–24.

16. See Judg 6:36–38.

17. See Judg 7:1–7.

whether people are with God. Through God's trying of people we move to another difficult issue—human sacrifices.

ACTIVE OR PASSIVE GOD: THE PROBLEM OF HUMAN SACRIFICES

The Israelites despised human sacrifices as a pagan practice. Against them they advocated the protection of life.[18] There are, however, two cases where the subject of human sacrifice appears and the experience of the Lord reveals itself as conflictual. In the first instance it is a promise: "And Jephthah made a vow to the Lord, and said, 'If you will give the Ammonites into my hand, then whoever comes out of the doors of my house to meet me, when I return victorious from the Ammonites, shall be the Lord's, to be offered up by me as a burnt offering.'" (Judg 11:30–31) Jephthah is victorious and on his return his only daughter comes to welcome him. Jephthah makes an offering of her—physically[19] and symbolically—and even blames her for his foolish promise: "Alas, my daughter! You have brought me very low; you have become the cause of great trouble for me. For I have opened my mouth to the Lord, and I cannot take back my vow." (35)[20] Jephthah's daughter has no other response than agreement and lament in the story. Her cry then becomes that of Israelite girls, "for four days every year the daughters of Israel would go out to lament the daughter of Jephthah the Gileadite." (40) It seems as if humans tested themselves in this story. This trial creates a sacrifice. The Lord is attributed a passive role as the one who grants requests and receives sacrifices. The story shows the horror of the situation, but it does not criticize the solution of the conflict.

However, this type of critique can be found in the story of Abraham and Isaac, which begins even more radically. The sacrifice is not proposed by Abraham, but by the Lord, who tests Abraham: "'Abraham!' And he said, 'Here I am.' He said, 'Take your son, your only son Isaac, whom you love, and go to the land of Moriah, and offer him there as a burnt offering on one of the mountains that I shall show you.'" (Gen 22:1–2) Abraham obediently rises and goes to carry out this order. He does not argue, does

18. See the prohibition of human sacrifices in Deut 18:10 and the critique of pagan practice in 2 Kgs 3:26–27.

19. See Judg 11:39.

20. Compare with Num 30:2. A similar situation appears in the New Testament when Herod promised to the daughter of Herodias to grant her anything for dancing and she asked for the head of John the Baptist (see Matt 14:1–12; Mark 6:21–28). The fulfillment of the oath comes into conflict with the commandment not to kill and the folly of the one who decides the situation is demonstrated by being faithful to the oath.

not doubt, and is silent. On the way he answers Isaac's question about where the lamb for the burnt offering is by saying, "God himself will provide the lamb for a burnt offering, my son." On the mountain he binds his son Isaac and lays him on top of the wood and as he is about to kill his son with the sacrificial knife, he hears the Lord's angel calling from heaven, "'Abraham, Abraham!' He said, 'Here I am.' The angel said, 'Do not lay your hand on the boy or do anything to him; for now I know that you fear God, since you have not withheld your son, your only son, from me.'" (11–12) Abraham then sacrifices a ram that he finds caught in a bush and the Lord repeats his promise that Abraham's offspring will be as numerous as the stars of heaven and as the sand on the sea shore and in him all the peoples will be blessed.[21]

The Lord tests Abraham, but at the same time has an active role in the development of the narrative. In comparison to Jephthah, the main actor in the previous story, here the Lord interferes and from the point of view of Abraham, even changes his word.[22] Both Jephthah and Abraham are in the position of "fatherly" responsibility for the people entrusted to their care, both are God-fearing men, and yet the outcome of each narrative is very different: one ends with a ritual of lamentation over the death of Jephthah's daughter, the other by the restituted life of Isaac, for Christians a fore-image of Christ's resurrection. In the story of Jephthah and his daughter we are led to share a sense of God's absence, a "test" in which God was active neither at the beginning nor the end, and thus Jephthah's fear of God without the concomitant experience that God is the Lord of life culminates in sacrifice of life and is dominated by sorrow, emptiness, and fear. In the conclusion of the story of Abraham and Isaac, life dominates over death, and God reveals himself as the Lord who protects and multiplies life.

Experience as a Deepening of our Sensory Perception

We can now move from the narrative and dramatic approach to the illuminative and instructive approach, remembering that all four approaches are blended together and what we attempt here is no more than showing the

21. See Gen 22:15–18.

22. This story of Abraham is customarily interpreted in the New Testament as an archetype of Jesus' sacrifice on the cross and his resurrection. See Heb 11:17–19, John 3:16; further, with the commentary on Abraham's act of faith, which has the power to reveal future things, Rom 4:16–22; Jas 2:21–22.

emphasis. A classic example where all these approaches overlap is the disciples' encounter, first with the empty tomb, and then with the risen Lord. But before moving there, let us look at another type of experience testified both in the Old and New Testaments, namely seeing God face to face.

SEEING GOD FACE TO FACE

In the creation narratives we are told that our first mythical ancestors could communicate with God directly, meeting him in the Garden of Eden. This was lost with the Fall. And although in the lives of the Patriarchs there are many accounts of talking to God as one might to a visiting relative, there is also a growing awareness that in the state we are, we might not survive seeing God face to face.[23] The symbol of seeing God face to face, however, is used for Jacob's communication with the Unknown at the brook of Jabbok: "For I have seen God face to face, and yet my life is preserved." (Gen 32:30) In the case of Moses we read that on Mount Sinai "the Lord used to speak to Moses face to face, as one speaks to a friend." (Exod 33:11)

In both cases, however, the face to face experience preserves the sense of mystery. In Jacob's case it is expressed by the fact that the Unknown remains Unknown, does not reveal his name. It is Jacob who receives from him a new name. In the case of Moses, this is done by explaining that, despite the direct experience, Moses was allowed to see only the Lord's back: "See, there is a place by me where you shall stand on the rock; and while my glory passes by I will put you in a cleft of the rock, and I will cover you with my hand until I have passed by; then I will take away my hand, and you shall see my back; but my face shall not be seen." (Exod 33:21–23) The mystery has to be further protected by Moses' veiling his face, as it shone after he came down from the mountain and the Israelites were afraid to come near him.[24]

The experience symbolically described as seeing God face to face resurfaces in the prophets. Isaiah's account of his call includes an ecstatic experience of him being taken to heaven and seeing the Lord sitting on his throne, and when struck by fear, being purified by one of the seraphs.[25] In the narrative this is a preamble to the calling by the Lord and to the ac-

---

23. See Exod 33:20.
24. See Exod 34:29–35.
25. See Isa 6:1–6.

ceptance of the call by Isaiah. Moreover, "Go and say to this people . . . " is made legitimate by the experience.[26] The calling of the prophet Ezekiel begins similarly with a vision, this time of open heavens, where God reveals who God is and legitimates the prophet's mission.[27] Daniel speaks about visions of God. God sends his holy messengers to open the eyes and ears of people. These messengers reveal God's intentions expressed in human dreams, uncovering images of future things, and giving understanding and words of interpretation.[28] In these texts direct and mediated experience interpenetrate each other, and likewise God's presence and God's otherness remain interwoven. We can say that God presents Godself as the other, and the symbolic expression of seeing God face to face both carries the closeness involved and breaks it, because in the closeness the anthropomorphic images of God cannot hold who God is.

Despite the fact that in the New Testament the glory of God is revealed in his Son, we encounter a similar range of experiences.[29] First, perhaps like in Paradise, the disciples and the crowds are in the presence of the Lord, without experiencing it as seeing God face to face, as most of the time they do not know whom they are seeing. But there are exceptional experiences breaking through the ordinary ones, most especially the story of the transfiguration,[30] where Peter, James, and John are able to see and hear what they have only imagined before, Jesus' glory. Likewise, in some of the healing narratives those whose sight is renewed can see also spiritually, and recognize in Jesus the face of God.[31]

The Empty Tomb

Illuminative experiences in the New Testament do not only involve a straightforward transformation from blindness to seeing the world and God in their right order, as in the healing stories. Transformation of people happens also through seeing emptiness. This is most radically spelled out at the empty tomb.

After Jesus' crucifixion it seems that Mary, the other women round Jesus, and the other disciples are deprived even of his dead body. Physical

26. See Isa 6:8–9a.

27. See Ezek 1–2; compare Ezek 40:4.

28. See also Dan 7–12.

29. Compare to John 1:14; 14:7.

30. See Matt 17:1–9; Mark 9:2–9; Luke 9:28–36; also 2 Pet 1:17–18.

31. See Matt 9:27–28; 20:30–34; Mark 10: 46–52; Luke 18:35–43; John 9:13–41.

encounter with the remains of their beloved Son, Master, and Friend becomes impossible. This experience leads to a different stage of their faith, which, after the confrontation with their blindness, will be nourished by meeting the risen Lord. Although the Gospels are told from this perspective and from the experience of the church after having received the Holy Spirit, the ambivalence of the encounters with the Risen One is not removed. First, not everybody has such an experience, although all could see and hear the earthly Jesus if they coincided in the same place and time. The risen Jesus cannot be recognized at first sight: he is mistaken for a gardener, or for a stranger who does not know what has happened in Jerusalem.[32] He does strange things that do not belong to our spatiotemporal reality, like walking through closed doors, or disappearing. At the same time he is not a ghost, he eats with his disciples, they can see his wounds, and Thomas can even touch them.[33] Yet what it means to be in the stage where death has no more power remains mysterious, even for those who have the direct experience of encountering the risen Lord.

After Jesus' ascension these encounters take on a different form, but continue to be testified, as we read in Acts, especially in the story of Saul's conversion:

> Now as he was going along and approaching Damascus, suddenly a light from heaven flashed around him. He fell to the ground and heard a voice saying to him, 'Saul, Saul, why do you persecute me?' He asked, 'Who are you, Lord?' The reply came, 'I am Jesus, whom you are persecuting. But get up and enter the city, and you will be told what you are to do.' The men who were traveling with him stood speechless because they heard the voice but saw no one. Saul got up from the ground, and though his eyes were open, he could see nothing; so they led him by the hand and brought him into Damascus. For three days he was without sight, and neither ate nor drank. (Acts 9:3–9)

Here, too the new seeing is accompanied by temporary blindness, both physical and symbolic, as all of his previous certainties crumble. In their place, there is God's otherness and the radical claim on Saul's life, which he is yet to understand. Even much later, when, as Paul, the apostle to the gentiles, he writes to the Corinthians about faith, hope, and love, he says "For now we can see in a mirror, dimly, but then we will see face to face.

---

32. See Luke 24:13–35; John 20:11–18.
33. See John 20:19.26; compare to Luke 24:39–43; John 20:26–29.

Now I know only in part; then I will know fully, even as I have been fully known." (1 Cor 13:12)

PENTECOST AND THE NEED TO DISCERN THE SPIRITS

Another type of illuminative and instructive experience in the New Testament is Pentecost, and the different ways the Spirit is given to both the Jewish and Gentile disciples.[34] It is interesting that first we read about the collective experience of the sending of the Spirit, in which both individual participants and their relationships are further transformed in order to do mission. Now they can be what they were called for, the church, whose gates would not be breached even by the power of hell.[35] Even then, nevertheless, there is no guarantee of infallibility of understanding, or of following the right spirit.[36] This clarity is still to come, as Paul emphasizes, and while we are awaiting it and working towards it, it is healthy to accept that here and now, even if we have been given the Holy Spirit, our understanding is always only ever partial.

Likewise, in the Johannine tradition, which also knows ecstatic visions,[37] there is a similar emphasis on the partiality of our knowledge and on the possibility of wrong discernment. We are reminded that this ecstatic experience is possible because after the incarnation God's glory is visible where the Son of God is present.[38] The Johannine writings further rehabilitate what we may call the notion of common sense in experiencing reality: "Little children, let no one deceive you. Everyone who does what is right is righteous, just as he is righteous." (1 John 3:7) With the Spirit we still need to learn to see what is there to be seen, and not our spiritualized images of reality. If Christian experience is reduced to pious feelings and imagination, then it is a proof that the living God is elsewhere, as John says: "Whoever does not love, does not know God, for God is love . . . No one has ever seen God; if we love one another, God lives in us and his love is perfected in us." (1 John 4:8.12)

To conclude, the phenomenology of experience in the Scriptures is rich and varied, and it provides different ways of human transformation.

---

34. See, e.g., Acts 10:1–48.

35. See Acts 2:1–47; compare to the promise given to Peter in Matt 16:18.

36. See Paul's challenging Peter for not being fair to gentile Christians, Gal 2:11–14; or the stories of trying to manipulate the Spirit in Acts 5:1–10; 8:18–23.

37. See Rev 1:1; 4–22.

38. John 1:14.

The kind of experience we have focused on here is "direct experience," because it concerns people who claim that such things happened to them. But at the same time it is an interpreted experience. They relied on earlier symbolic language to carry the meaning for the events, and extended the possibilities of such language by their contributions. In the following parts we will examine both how the emphasis on the experience and how the symbolic mediation of it was elaborated within Christian traditions, became marginalized, and was then rediscovered in modern and postmodern times.

COMMUNICATION WITH GOD IN THE EASTERN AND WESTERN TRADITION

Having summarized some main types of experiencing God and the reality transformed by God in the Scriptures, let us move to tradition, and investigate how the need to discern and communicate the immediate encounter with the divine complemented and vivified its ecclesial mediations. We will look at two representative examples of Eastern and Western classics. The first is Symeon the New Theologian (949–1022), a Greek ascetic and mystic writer and founder of monasteries in Constantinople and its vicinity, who significantly influenced the movement called hesychasm.[39] The second is Ignatius of Loyola (1492–1556), a Basque pilgrim and founder of the Jesuits, whose *Spiritual Exercises* are part of a living tradition that has spread outside both the Society of Jesus and the Roman Catholic Church.[40]

Prayer and Spiritual Progress according to Symeon the New Theologian

The Eastern tradition does not make any sharp distinction between mysticism and theology, between personal experience and the church's dogmatic formulations. Everything together expresses the revealed truth, which nourishes and at the same transcends us, and which is to be lived so that we can understand it in order to be changed by it. In tenth- and

39. Hesychasm was a renewal movement in the Eastern Church that followed the example of the Desert Fathers and consisted of people who left for silent places to be able to pray and reach full union with God.

40. This text is partly based on my article, Noble, "Religious Experience—Reality or Illusion."

eleventh-century Byzantium, the time of Symeon the New Theologian, such unity was under threat as an over-strong accommodation by the church to the culture of the court removed the prophetic and spiritual alterity of the Christian way of life as testified in the Scriptures and lived by the early church. Symeon the New Theologian belonged to the ascetic church of the monks and of those who were dissatisfied with the accommodation. This church understood itself as a counterpart to "secular wisdom" and focused on the journey of deification. The dual emphases on the "otherworldliness" of God's kingdom and on the need for an unceasing direct communication with God were seen as necessary parts of that journey. Although they interpreted the divisions and conflicts in the church as coming from the opposition between the secular and the sacred, in examining Symeon's works *On Faith*, and *One Hundred and Fifty-Three Practical and Theological Texts*, as well as *The Three Methods of Prayer*, a treatise which comes from the circle of Symeon's disciples, we will see that underneath this polarized understanding a new and deeper form of integration was discernible. In order to understand that, we need to examine the way of spiritual progress as described by Symeon.

In his autobiographical book *On Faith* Symeon talks about the inner life of a young man George who, in the midst of his "worldly" life, has an ecstatic experience of the divine. In his vision of the divine light he meets an angelic figure penetrated by that light, and is given a short instruction and a book. Later we learn that it is a treatise *On the Spiritual Law* by Mark the Monk, which, when he comes back to full consciousness, is to give him directions on how to live a good life. Symeon's reader learns about its three main emphases, in the light of which the previous direct experience is filled with meaning for the first stage of the journey, where the reader may find himself or herself, just as George did. These are: (i) "If you desire spiritual health, listen to your conscience, do all it tells you, and you will benefit"; (ii) "He who seeks the energies of the Holy Spirit before he has actively observed the commandments is like someone who sells himself into slavery and who, as soon as he is bought, asks to be given his freedom, while still keeping his purchase-money"; (iii) "Blind is the man who cries out and says: 'Son of David, have mercy upon me'. (Luke 18:39) He prays with his body alone, and not yet with his spiritual knowledge. But when the man once blind received his sight and saw the

Lord, he acknowledged Him no longer as the Son of David but as the Son of God, and worshipped Him (cf. John 9:38)."[41]

Despite this ecstatic experience, George does not at first follow the path in which the eyes of his soul are to be opened. Instead, Symeon shows how the tension between the worldly and the spiritual remains for the next twelve years of his life, until he learns that to walk the path revealed by his earlier vision, he has to surrender his own will.[42] This point, difficult to interpret, is the key to entering again into intimacy with the divine light. The reader, together with George, needs to learn that such light cannot be controlled from our end, that if we are to be transformed by it, it has to happen on its terms, and not ours. For our part, we are helped by encountering our blindness and our sinfulness, and through that encounter we gain the humility needed to appropriate the experience of God.

Symeon also emphasizes that this journey does not happen in isolation, but in the church. The old man seen in the early vision has been praying for George all the time, Symeon says, and his petitions helped George in the struggle he could not undergo alone.[43] In order to grasp the meaning of the ecstatic experience of the divine, faith and purification are needed, so that one can move from faith to love, which then makes participation in God possible.[44]

---

41. Symeon the New Theologian, "On Faith," 17; compare St Mark the Ascetic, *On the Spiritual Law* §69; *On Those who Think that They are Made Righteous by Works* §64; *On the Spiritual Law* §13–14, in *Philokalia I,* 115, 130, 111.

42. Symeon the New Theologian, "On Faith," 23.

43. Symeon comments: "When I heard this story, I thought how greatly the intercession of this saint had helped the young man, and how God had chosen to show him to what heights of virtue the holy man had attained." Symeon the New Theologian, "On Faith," 18. The old man in the vision is an allusion to Symeon's own spiritual father, Symeon the Studite. See Palmer, "St Symeon the New Theologian," 12.

44. What is required at the beginning of the journey is "true faith and unhesitating expectation" ("On Faith," 18) and paying attention to what conscience says ("On Faith," 19). But, as Symeon says: "The young man had not observed long fasts or slept on the ground, worn a hair short or shaved his head." ("On Faith," 19) Along the journey one is confronted with temptation, and experiences the reality of one's weakness, which leads to humility and to the need for "great labours and many tears," prayer for the forgiveness of many sins, solitude, obedience and "many other rigorous practices and actions," ("On Faith," 23) to keep on the path of grace and to regain the vision. On this journey one moves from faith to love, which makes participation in God possible (see "On Faith," 24).

In *One Hundred and Fifty-Three Practical and Theological Texts* and later in *The Three Methods of Prayer* another theme emerges, namely that of a false experience of God, which blocks one's genuine spiritual progress. Symeon and his circle contrast the journey of deification with its fabrications. In *One Hundred and Fifty-Three Practical and Theological Texts* Symeon returns to what being inwardly enlightened by the light of the Holy Spirit means. This time, however, he takes a step further and examines what happens when one's unconverted intelligence and intellect lead the way and imitate the divine light. In such a case the human mind in its imagination projects what it wants to see.[45] In *The Three Methods of Prayer* the self-deception (and deception of others) is elaborated in two ways, corresponding to the first two methods. In the first case the heavenly world spreading out in front of one's inner eyes is an artifact of the human imagination of how such a world should look. People who wish to dwell in such a place with their souls filled by an imagined divine love not only prevent themselves from making true spiritual progress, but are in danger of losing their sanity.[46]

The second type of deception consists in wrongly assessing one's own role in an experience of something that is not, or at least not wholly, a fabrication. It is marked by an effort to guard oneself, but in fact leads to running from one area to another, struggling between guarding one's senses, examining one's thoughts, talking to God, and wandering off into captivating thought. The problem is when such a stage is regarded with self-esteem, and the person imagines they have reached the point where they can teach others, without realizing their own blindness.[47]

Only the third form leads to deification. It requires the practice of obedience to God through the spiritual father, pure conscience, and control over the abuse of material things. Then, after having cleared the ground, the intellect penetrates into the depth of the heart and in prayer encounters the love of Christ. The type of prayer that is proposed consists of an invocation of Jesus Christ, and so is also called the Jesus prayer.[48] On this journey all human faculties are gradually united in prayer and a person is once again capable of relating to the world in a manner that

---

45. Symeon the New Theologian, "*One Hundred and Fifty-Three Texts,*" 36.

46. See "*The Three Methods of Prayer,*" 67–68.

47. Ibid., 68–69.

48. Ibid., 70–73.

would include all that has been created into the process of deification. This deeper integration, however, comes only with the other gifts of transformation as sketched above. The previous two forms of deception are in fact results of embarking on the journey in an improper order. People who set off in this way are like those who, wanting to ascend a ladder, think that they can start at the top and climb down.[49]

The hesychast way of prayer and spiritual progress includes both an ecstatic encounter with the divine and a conscious relationship with Christ. In both cases the Holy Spirit enlightens people and initiates in them a process they cannot initiate themselves. And yet, each is a different stage of the process. The ecstatic stage lies at the bottom of the ladder from which one progresses by means of purification of one's senses, intellect, and will, by prayer based on the Scriptures, especially the Psalms, to becoming immersed in contemplation, where all that was at an earlier stage left behind is saved and as such is now included. In this process a new person emerges, the one in whom all physical and psychical energies are harmonized in prayer, and the image of Christ makes the person gradually Christ-like.

The Direct and the Mediated Relationship with God according to Ignatius of Loyola

In the western church of the sixteenth century, to which Ignatius of Loyola[50] belonged, mysticism represented a similar alternative to what we have seen with Symeon. As would later Teresa of Avila, John of the Cross, and other spiritual writers, Ignatius stressed the direct encounter between the Creator and the creature, and the fact that the meaning of such encounters is gradually revealed when a person follows the Christ of the gospels. These two emphases give shape to the inner life of prayer and to the mission that flows from it.[51] Ignatius' account of the different facets

---

49. See "*The Three Methods of Prayer,*" 73. The proposed sequence stands as follows: (i) cleansing the heart of the passions; (ii) singing Psalms to the Lord; (iii) contemplation. See "*The Three Methods of Prayer,*" 73–75.

50. Ignatius' original name was Iñigo Lopez de Recalde. He changed it to Ignatius out of respect for the early Christian martyr Ignatius of Antioch († after 110).

51. The church of Ignatius' time still tried to hang on to the medieval model of the political-religious unity of the world, a model that was exported to its new missionary locations outside Europe, though it had been strongly shaken on its home ground. Since as early as the twelfth century various movements within the church demanded reform and

belonging to the experience of God and to the discernment of whether such experience is genuine can be found in his *Autobiography, Spiritual Diary,* and in the *Spiritual Exercises,* which was written as a manual for those who accompany others on their path to conversion.[52]

Ignatius, like Symeon, knew ecstatic experience. In his *Autobiography,* however, it does not come at the beginning of the journey, but in the middle, when he had already decided to live a radically different life, and was struggling to bring to God's service all of his inner powers. But before we get there, let us examine where Ignatius sees the starting point of his conversion, namely in the awareness of two possible ways of life. Ignatius recollects a time when, having been wounded at a battle in Pamplona, he was convalescing in the castle of Loyola. Only two books were available in the library, *The Life of our Lord Jesus Christ* by Ludolf of Saxony, and the lives of the saints as recorded in the *Golden Legend* of Jacopo of Varazze. As he read them, he started to notice a difference between two types of attraction at work in him. One was to the life of a soldier-knight, nourished by reading of the courtly romances, and the other was inspired by reading about Jesus Christ and his saints. The first was impossible to put into practice, and left him dry and discontented. The second, despite its challenges, seemed possible, and left him content and happy, even if the spiritual journey used imagery similar to the knight's adventures, as he dreamt of going to Jerusalem barefoot and fasting and forcing the body to obedience even more strictly than the saints did, performing even greater actions of faith.[53]

---

represented a spiritual alternative. See, e.g., the work of Joachim de Fiore (c.1130–1202) or Gerhard Groote (1340–1384) who inspired the *Devotio moderna* movement, from where *The Imitation of Christ* ascribed to Thomas a Kempis came. These movements present the first spiritual background against which Ignatius appropriated his experience of God acting in human life, before he was educated in scholastic theology.

52. Unlike the *Spiritual Exercises* and *Spiritual Diary*, Ignatius' *Autobiography* was not written by Ignatius, but dictated to Gonçalves de Camara, a Portuguese Jesuit who considered the record of the founder of the order an important testimony for the healthy development of future generations of Jesuits. The testimony of these writings is supplemented by his letters and by the *Constitutions of the Society of Jesus*, where Ignatius, in contradistinction to his previous writings, does not act as a "mystic," but as a practical organizer of rules for the life of the order, oriented to mission and service. See Ganss, "Introduction," 275.

53. Ignatius, *Autobiography*, 1.6–7. The translation I use gives this the title "Reminiscences," 14–15.

Retrospectively, Ignatius understood that there were two spirits operating, the evil and the good, which could be discerned in all of his life-experience.[54] In the *Spiritual Exercises,* where he returns to the theme of discernment, he stresses this recognition, when he states that in our inner life we can learn to use our imagination as a space where the whole process of our thought can be examined. In order to understand where our desires and intentions come from, we need to track their beginning, their middle, as well as their end, as both the good and the evil spirit are discernible in the train of thought. Evil, then, is not only being led to do a bad or vain thing, but also losing one's peace of mind and spiritual joy.[55]

Ignatius is similar to Symeon in working with a dualist framework, yet even if he speaks about the vanity of the world and the greatness of holiness, the main opposition he works with is not the world and God, but the good and evil spirits. These two forces operate both in the soul and in the world. In both the soul and the world the drama of salvation takes place. The experience of God and the awakened inner life it leads to are, according to Ignatius, to bring a person to actively participate in this drama. To do this, the person first needs to understand who he or she is in relationship to God, i.e., their specific gifts and failings. Then, when the imagination is filled with insights into the life of Christ in the gospels and in his death and resurrection, people are helped to focus and invest their whole being in a life for the greater glory of God, and participate thus in the salvation of humankind.

Ignatius, like Symeon, is aware of the ability of the soul to deceive itself, and to ascribe to God things that do not come from him. His advice, though, is not to silence our dreams, but to scrutinize them, to learn what good and what evil lies in them, and how God talks to us within our soul. The otherness of the reality of God inbreaking into our lives completes the earlier intuition, and the knowledge arrived at by means of ascetic

54. See Ignatius, *Autobiography* 1.8; (= "Reminiscences," 15). Compare to the "Rules by which to perceive and understand to some extent the various movements produced in the soul: The good that they may be accepted and the bad that they may be rejected," *Spiritual Exercises* (n.30), §§ 313–27; and "Rules for the same purpose containing more advanced ways of discerning the spirits": Ignatius, *Spiritual Exercises,* §§ 328–36.

55. See Ignatius, *Spiritual Exercises* §§ 333–34 and "Toward Perceiving and Understanding Scruples and the Enticements of our Enemy the Following Notes are Helpful," *Spiritual Exercises,* §§ 345–51.

practices, studies of the Scriptures, and of theology.[56] The following of Christ gradually changes from external imitation to inner relationship.[57]

As with Symeon, Ignatius' understanding of the experience of God is not reduced to the moments of enlightenment, even if these are invaluable. It is a process that includes the use of reason, feeling, will, and human imagination, a process in which divine and human initiatives must be brought into harmony. This is then the source and foundation of the missionary activity in which one can speak from experience to experience and work towards the transformation of the church and the world from within the inwardly experienced relationships.

Both of the spiritual traditions give us a language of how to speak about the immediacy of the encounter with God, and about the true and the false mediations of it. These and other insights, however, found it very difficult to find a place in modern theology, until it was realized that they

56. After Ignatius had recovered from his injuries, he decided on a radical change in his life. He would do good deeds in God's service. He set off on a pilgrimage to the monastery of Montserrat near Barcelona and then he devoted himself to prayers and studies in the nearby town of Manresa. The demanding nature of the ascetic exercises that he prescribed for himself brought him to the edge of exhaustion. Here the experience by the river Cardoner served as a breakthrough. See Ignatius' retrospective account of his vision there, which changed him so radically "as if he was a different man" and yet at the same time confirmed the continuity of his journey of conversion. Ignatius of Loyola, *Autobiography* 2.30 (= "Reminiscences," 26–27).

57. Ignatius wanted to follow Christ to the extent of leaving for Jerusalem and staying there in order to serve Christ. In his *Autobiography* he says that on his first pilgrimage he was forced to return under the threat of excommunication by the Franciscan provincial (3: 46). After this pilgrimage Ignatius decided to become a priest. During the course of his studies he strove to share his spiritual experience, and organized spiritual exercises for his friends, but this brought him before the inquisition several times. Repeated controversies forced him to move from Barcelona to Salamanca and then to Paris. There he finished his studies and in 1534 he made promises of poverty and chastity together with six companions, hoping to serve the church. He tried to set off once more for the Holy Land with his companions. They received permission in Rome, but no ship was setting off to Jerusalem. The companions went to Rome instead where they offered their services to Pope Paul III and asked him to endorse their order: this permission was granted in 1540. Between 1541 and 1552 Ignatius, the first general of the order, worked on its *Constitution*. (see notes from *The Spiritual Diary*, esp. 22 (from February 23rd 1544). The order expanded quickly in Europe and overseas, and was directed especially to missionary and preaching activities. In the year of Ignatius' death (1556) it had around 1000 members in 13 provinces, with 110 houses, including Prague.

were indispensible for both understanding the sources of theology and for discriminating between faith and superstition.[58]

THE REHABILITATION OF RELIGIOUS EXPERIENCE IN MODERN TIMES

Just as in the late Middle Ages dissatisfaction with church politics contributed to the popularity of mysticism, so the modern celebration of rationality, science, and progress brought with it, as a side effect, a return to romantic religious feelings at the level of folk piety and, at the theological level, a search for the lost unity between humankind, the world, and God. The subject of religious experience emerged in both of these alternative pursuits and both contributed to the understanding of the types of religious experience with which contemporary theology works.

Renewal of Interest in the Subject

The theme of religious experience in the nineteenth and twentieth centuries appears with renewed urgency in the Protestant environment, which is perhaps why it was most radically rejected there.[59] The authors I will introduce here have something in common, namely that they experienced a religiously extreme environment from which they broke away, whilst trying to retain the experience they had had there. They use it as a starting point in their subsequent scientific research. Friedrich Schleiermacher and Rudolf Otto represent the German environment. Therefore I consider them together, although the American William James predates Otto.

SCHLEIERMACHER'S EMPHASIS ON RELIGIOUS FEELING

F. D. E. Schleiermacher (1768–1834), a German theologian from a Pietist background,[60] attempted an apology of Christianity in a world tired of

58. Compare to Trtik, *Vztah já–Ty*, 71; and Küng, *On Being a Christian*, 418.

59. David Hay points out that the subject of religious experience is also embedded in the very movement of reformation and is linked with an interest in the process of conversion that appeared in the sixteenth and seventeenth century among English Puritans and German Pietists. Hay, *Religious Experience Today*, 10.

60. Schleiermacher's parents converted from the Reformed Church to the Herrnhuter Unity of Brethren and brought their son up in a Christianity that was suspicious of doctrines and stressed "religious feeling." Schleiermacher admits that he inwardly experienced the power of this type of religion when he travelled as an adolescent boy to meetings of brothers with his father. However, he later broke with the Unity because its

Enlightenment rationalism. He reintroduced religious experience as one of the main topics of theology. Schleiermacher wanted to show that life without experience of God, without meaning and longing for eternity, is incomplete. Moreover, theology is impossible without them. In his work *On Religion: Speeches to its Cultured Despisers* (1799), inspired by German Romanticism, Schleiermacher presents the Enlightenment conflict between "natural" and "positive" religion.[61] All positive religions, Christianity among them, stem according to him from natural religion and refer to it. The key for this connection is not, though, a moral duty as in Kant, but intuition and feeling. Here Schleiermacher, influenced by his experience in the Reformed Church, stresses especially the feeling of total dependence on God. In his main work *The Christian Faith* (1821–22) Schleiermacher interprets Christianity as the high point of natural religion and founds this statement on the quality of experience of God. According to him it culminates in Jesus' knowledge of dependence on the Father, and continues in the sense of this dependence that abides among Christians in their personal lives and social structures.[62]

Schleiermacher was criticized for his romantic idea of Christianity as a religion of feelings,[63] perhaps simply on account of his choice of the unfortunate term *Gefühl*. Tillich warned that Schleiermacher's "feeling" has to be translated as "intuition," for he is not interested in subjective emotions but in experiencing God.[64] Similarly, I think that we can better understand Schleiermacher's intention if we translate his concept of "total dependence" as "radical relation."[65] This type of reading, however, was ahead of its time because the end of the nineteenth and the beginning of

---

teaching was too narrow for him. He was ordained in the Reformed Church in Berlin in 1794, where he also came into closer contact with Romanticism, something that reopened for him the subject of intuition and feelings in regard to religion.

61. Kant develops this topic in the opposite direction to Hegel, for whom "natural" religion comes from human nature, while the "positive" religion, represented by Judaism or Christianity, stands against nature—it suppresses human freedom and stands against reason. See Hegel, *On Christianity*, 134–63.

62. See Schleiermacher, *On Religion*, 18–54.

63. Schleiermacher was criticized especially by the Barthians. Barth himself tried to write a well-balanced evaluation of his work in Barth, *Protestant Theology in the Nineteenth Century*.

64. See Tillich, *Perspectives*, 96.

65. See Schleiermacher, *The Christian Faith*, I, §34.

the twentieth century deal with religious experience in reference to "feeling" as a completion of and counterbalance to reason.

OTTO'S IRREDUCIBLE CATEGORY OF THE HOLY

The German Lutheran theologian Rudolf Otto[66] (1869–1937) follows Schleiermacher and develops his emphasis on religious feeling and puts it into the context of his study of the various concrete forms of worshipping the divine in which the "sense of the numinous" appears.[67] Otto talks about God's presence filling human minds with wonder. This state of mind, totally different from anything else, cannot, according to Otto, be reduced to anything else. His key work *The Idea of the Holy* (1917) concentrates on the methodology implemented while examining the numinous. As the subtitle of the book—*An Inquiry into the Non-rational Factor to the Idea of the Divine and Its Relation to the Rational*—emphasizes, the methodology includes working beyond the limits of the rational. Where it is possible to speak about the aspects of the numinous clearly, we need to use precise concepts and accurate descriptions, as rational science demands. The scientific approach will lead us to its limits, to the boundaries of what can be rationally explained.[68]

The non-rational factors are to be approached by the analysis of symbols, and in particular of the feelings that are left in place in the symbolic mediation, even after the concepts either run into contradictions or fail to name the numinous phenomena altogether.[69] Otto's analysis here goes in the following direction. The experience with the numinous appears in six forms: (i) as something that evokes a feeling of "having been created"; (ii) as something that appears in its inaccessibility, evoking feelings of

---

66. Otto came from a large North German family with an orthodox Lutheran background. Theology studies in Erlangen and especially in Göttingen shook the certainties of his first tradition and drew him more towards the Protestant liberalism of Ritschl. His main interest in "truth" concerning religious experience brought him out from an exclusivism, where the Catholic and Jewish tradition were perceived as dangerous, to the very open recognition that any religious tradition rejoices in and testifies the one God in some way. Many of Otto's travels contributed to the formation of this attitude, including journeys to Greece, Galilee, Palestine, Syria, Mount Athos, India, Japan, China, Russia, North America, and the investigation of the holy places and rituals of local religions.

67. The word 'numinous' comes from the Latin *numen*, meaning 'signal', 'power', and used in addressing an emperor.

68. See Otto, *The Idea of the Holy*, 1–4.

69. Ibid., vii.

terror; (iii) as something that appears in its sublimity, evoking feelings of being dazzled with irresistible power; (iv) as energy, having an impact with its urgency, evoking feelings of all-consuming love, anger, etc. ; (v) as something quite different from anything we know; (vi) as something totally fascinating.[70] In these six aspects Otto tried to express a twofold experience with the numinous: there is in it something that repels and attracts at the same time, *mysterium tremendum et fascinans*.

The goal of Otto's works is to show that religion cannot be reduced either to a question of reason or to morality. The "Holy" is according to Otto a basic religious category. It is a category that does not have a synonym and cannot be fully interpreted by any category of value.[71] It is a category *sui generis* and cannot be understood outside the experience that testifies it.

Variety and Levels of Religious Experience in James

The interest in religious experience in New England can be traced as far back as the eighteenth century. It was first connected with the experience of conversion that was often motivated by colorful Puritan sermons and from there moved to what was to become the psychology of religion.[72] The American psychologist and religious thinker William James (1842–1910) came from this New England background.[73] In his work *The Varieties of Religious Experience* (1902) he dealt with phenomena that testified to human contact with a power that transcended the conscious "I" and at the same time significantly influenced the person's feelings and work. James rejected the hypothesis that religious experience has its origins in suppressed human sexuality.[74] Similarly to Otto's later view, he advocated that we have to approach religious experience as something *sui generis* and non-reducible. James' pragmatic view stressed in addition that religious experience cannot be judged according to its origin—because inquiries of this type lie outside of our experience, and thus outside of our abilities to evaluate.

---

70. See Otto, *The Idea of the Holy*, 8–41.

71. Ibid., 52–61.

72. See, e.g., Edwards, *Treatise Concerning Religious Affections*.

73. His father Henry James intended to become a Presbyterian pastor, but he left the seminary because it seemed insufficiently pious for him there. Later he broke with Calvinism as such, but retained the piety, a topic his son later related with the tools of empirical psychology.

74. See James, *Varieties of Religious Experience*, chapter 1, "Religion and Neurology," esp. 33.

Concentrating on extreme cases, where, he says, the reality of the invisible that becomes a subject of the human consciousness is seen most clearly, he demonstrates that this "subject" is radically different from other "subjects" of consciousness. It captures in many varieties quite a specific presence (called or not called the presence of God), and is often accompanied with feelings of unreality. What this subject is can be identified only indirectly, according to James, by what it does to the person in question and to his or her environment.[75]

James approaches religion from what he sees as its subjective level, and contrasts it to the objective level of the teaching and institution. He is partly aware of the vulnerability of his position, as religious experience does not stand in isolation, and if the subjects testifying religious experience are separated from one form of doctrinal and institutional religion, they soon create their own superstitions, their own myths, creeds, metaphysics, and even institutional frameworks, in other words, analogies to what they separated themselves from.

For him, it is not possible to omit the question of objectivity, but it is necessary to look at it from a different angle. James substitutes the "objectivity" of religious tradition with the "objectivity" of science. At the same time he makes the objectivity of science dependent on the material of experience.[76] Here we encounter a typical ideal of James's time, an objective, impartial science that is to supplement the uncensored plurality and depth of human subjectivity, and as such take the place of the objective level of religion that no longer plays a positive role. This ideal, as the chapter on method showed, was subjected to criticism. Today's inquiry into religious experience should not work by substituting the objective aspect of religion with the objective aspect of science assumed by James, but use them both critically.

James played a positive role in opening up the possibilities of the scientific research of religious experience, whether from a psychological, sociological, philosophical, or religious studies perspective.[77] Now we will examine how the inner space of religious experience was re-appropriated in theology.

75. See James, *Varieties of Religious Experience*, 74–86. For his pragmatic criterion, see 41.

76. Ibid., 416.

77. These were further developed by, among others, Hardy, *The Spiritual Nature of Man*; Hay, *Religious Experience Today*.

Theological Approaches to Religious Experience

Religious experience has always been part of theology, even if under different names, as we have seen in the part on Symeon the New Theologian and Ignatius of Loyola. However, it has not always been recognized as a subject theology should examine. The interest that modern philosophy, psychology, sociology, and religious studies invested into religious experience needed to find its theological counterparts. The theological discussion involved questions of how religious experience and divine revelation are related, whether Christianity can legitimately operate with the concept of immanence without losing the emphasis on the transcendent God, as well as whether religious experience differs from other types of experiences, or represents a holistic perception of life from a religious point of view. In the following pages we will examine some of the key elements of these discussions, focusing first on Tyrrell's struggle to differentiate between immanence and immanentism so as to safeguard the place of God from being taken by human projection. Then we will examine Tillich's rules of symbolic mediation in which religious experience can become part of a wider tradition, and finally Lonergan's threefold notion of conversion, in which the unity and the tension between the religious, the moral, and the intellectual dimensions of our experiencing reality are preserved.

THE DIFFERENCE BETWEEN IMMANENCE AND IMMANENTISM IN TYRRELL

I want now to return to something introduced in the third chapter on authority, where I examined the difficulties that theologians appropriating tradition in modern times encountered. I already mentioned Tyrrell in that context, and in particular the two types of relationship to immanence he analyzed. The first approach considered the developing human situation as an environment where God's revelation was taking place. To use Tyrrell's language, immanence was seen as a space where transcendence could be encountered. The other approach was found in the official Vatican documents from that time. These talked about "immanentism" as a denial of transcendence. In order to examine the place of religious experience as a subject theology should investigate, we need to look into this distinction in more detail.

The anti-modernist documents mention the expression "immanentism" alongside "agnosticism," and see in them the two main heresies of a Catholic intellectual culture that, in their view, was undermining Christian faith. "Agnosticism" is defined as refusing the validity of rational argument in religious matters, and "immanentism" as taking "vital immanence" as a source and a teacher of religion:

> It is thus that the religious sense, which through the agency of vital immanence emerges from the lurking-places of the subconsciousness, is the germ of all religion, and the explanation of everything that has been or ever will be in any religion. This sense, which was at first only rudimentary and almost formless, under the influence of that mysterious principle from which it originated, gradually matured with the progress of human life, of which, as has been said, it is a certain form.[78]

To use our present language, "immanentism," according to the antimodernists, presupposed an anthropology that did not rely on God as the transcendent other.[79] The Modernists use the method of immanence in theology, according to the Encyclical *Pascendi Dominici Gregis*, as follows: "The philosopher has declared: The principle of faith is immanent; the believer has added: This principle is God; and the theologian draws the conclusion: God is immanent in man. Thus we have theological immanence."[80] The Encyclical professes itself unsure what the Modernists mean when they say that God is immanent for human beings, whether they mean that God acts in human interiority, or that God is in everything, even human interiority.[81] Another problem concerns the relationship between natural religiosity, stemming from human subconsciousness, and a particular religious system that its adherents believe to be based on revelation, such as Catholicism. As the Encyclical puts it: "They [the Modernists] endeavor, in fact, to persuade the non-believer that down in

78. Pascendi §10.

79. "Now the doctrine of immanence in the Modernist acceptation holds and professes that every phenomenon of conscience proceeds from man as man." Pascendi §39.

80. Pascendi §19.

81. "Concerning immanence it is not easy to determine what Modernists precisely mean by it, for their own opinions on the subject vary. Some understand it in the sense that God working in man is more intimately present in him than man is even in himself; and this conception, if properly understood, is irreproachable. Others hold that the divine action is one with the action of nature, as the action of the first cause is one with the action of the secondary cause; and this would destroy the supernatural order. Others, finally, explain it in a way which savors of pantheism, and this, in truth, is the sense which best fits in with the rest of their doctrines . . ." Pascendi §19.

the very depths of his nature and his life lie hidden the need and the desire for some religion, and this not a religion of any kind, but the specific religion known as Catholicism . . ."[82] Only at this point does the Encyclical agree with Tyrrell's concept of immanence.

The experiencing of God is the beginning of faith for Tyrrell. Everyone has a sense for God or a religious sense inside.[83] There we can see God at work within us as well as outside of us all the time.[84] Immanence does not reject transcendence, but it is a space where we can perceive transcendence as something that is not entirely unfamiliar to us. Tyrrell puts the emphasis on immanence in a twofold sense. On the one hand, if religion is to be communicable for a contemporary person, it has to be an organic part of civilization and culture, and not an alien entity that fell from on high. It needs to grow together with culture and civilization from the same root. On the other hand, God is immanently present in human spirit. Any other form of belief brings growing alienation.[85]

But people do not create religion. The emphasis on immanence does not mean that we are the authors of our own experience. The experience of God is embedded in the whole of life. It has grown and developed with life in many often inharmonious forms. Immanence is, though, dependent on reference:

> Religion too can be set before us under different presentations, all true in their way, but none, nor all together, exhaustive of reality. We can recognise under various descriptions a face that we have once seen; but if we have never seen it, no description can bring its full individuality home to us.[86]

Tyrrell is neither an anti-realist, nor a relativist, nor a pantheist. Those views are true that correspond with real human experience of the self-revealing God. A "familiar face" can be recognized on the basis of various descriptions. Tyrrell says that, if this face is truly "familiar," it will correspond with some of our previous experiences, our relationships, close or distant. Tyrrell criticizes liberal Protestantism for losing this very

---

82. Pascendi §37.

83. See, for example, Tyrrell, *Religion as a Factor*, 2–13.

84. Tyrrell, *Nova et Vetera*, 235.

85. See Tyrrell, *Through Scylla and Charybdis*, 383.

86. Tyrrell, *Lex Orandi: Or, Prayer and Creed*, v.

dimension of transcendent reference, and reducing itself to reason and moral duty.[87]

Tyrrell's conception of immanence enabled him to understand religious experience in terms of the whole of human experience. Instead of taking away from the religious experience the reference to God preceding and transcending this world and human life, this reference was extended to the rest of human experience. The division of "sacred" and "secular" experience disappeared. The whole of experience could be captured from the religious point of view.

Cheap or Precious Symbol according to Tillich

Our next question is how such experience can be communicated within a particular religious tradition, so that its overflowing meaning and inner cohesion are not betrayed. Paul Tillich, whose concept of the relationship between theology and culture I examined in the previous chapter, rehabilitates the symbolic mediation of revelation. This can also be applied to the realm of experience. According to him both revelation and experience share in one ground of being and participate in the ultimate concern. If a communication of both is to function, we need to maintain a distinction between cheap and expensive symbols, as symbols are the bearers of meaning in each instance.

Tillich builds his understanding of symbol on the theory of mediation, which starts with religion. According to him every religion attempts to personify the holiness that emerges through human religious experience. Thus every religion is faced with the problem of how to mediate something that is ultimate through what is available to us as finite human beings. The fact that this must be done does not devalue the religious experience or even the holy emerging in the experience, provided that the non-ultimate does not take the place of the ultimate. For Tillich, everything can become bearer of the ultimate meaning, but not everything is the ultimate meaning. People used to communicate revelation of the divine mystery through nature as well as through culture. All that exists at some point took on the mediating role and with it, according to Tillich, gave the divine mystery a personal face.[88]

---

87. See Tyrrell, *Christianity at the Cross-roads*, 65.
88. See Tillich, *Biblické náboženství a ontologie*, 19.

Against the background of universal religion, Tillich interprets biblical personalism and the symbols it works with.[89] He distinguishes two functions. The first is the substitute function. A symbol symbolizes something it is not identical with, and participates in the power of what it symbolizes. The second and main function of symbol is to disclose the levels of reality that would otherwise remain hidden, as they cannot be approached in any other way.[90] Religious symbol has, according to Tillich, a transcendent and immanent level.[91] This means that it is born in the meeting of the divine and the human. People do not create symbols on their own. We can say that symbols are born out of the encounter with a reality that is other, different, marked simultaneously by the presence of the holy and by its transcendent absence.

Symbols, including religious symbols, can also die, Tillich argues. This happens when they lose their mediating function, when they no longer open up the dimension of depth for human beings.[92] If we took this vulnerability away from symbols, they would become idols. Symbols cannot substitute the "ultimate reality."[93] If we want to use them for such a purpose, if we want to give them an unconditional validity, what is to be defended is killed by the same movement. Symbols lose their value and become cheap. In Tillich a cheap "symbol" is a reduction of symbol to something that does not mediate anything. This is either because we do not expect anything from it or because it replaces what it ought to mediate. A precious symbol stands and falls with mediation.

In the Protestant tradition, Tillich's symbolic mediation was further developed by Paul Ricoeur. In the Catholic tradition, as we saw in the chapter on revelation, symbolic theology concentrates on the understanding of sacrament and sacramentality, and sees religious experience as a part of, and a corrective to, the sacramental vision of the world in God.

89. Ibid., 21–22.

90. See Tillich, *Biblické náboženství a ontologie*, 115–16.

91. "There are two levels in all religious symbols: the transcendent level which *exceeds* the empirical reality we encounter, and the immanent level that we find in the very *encounter* with reality." Tillich, *Biblické náboženství a ontologie*, 119.

92. See Tillich, *Biblické náboženství a ontologie*, 117–18.

93. Ibid., 124–25.

THE PROCESS OF CONVERSION IN LONERGAN

In what sense, then, is religious experience corrective of our previous religious convictions, whether or not expressed in sacramental categories? Bernard Lonergan offers an answer to this question through examining different aspects of conversion. According to him, conversion is a process involving all our relationships, experiences, ideas, and intentions, which are gradually, with the help of the symbols that are available to us, transformed into something good and life-giving. Lonergan focuses his attention on the notions of identity and communication, and from this point of view approaches a human person and his or her conversion. He develops this theme in an essay entitled "First Lecture: Religious Experience,"[94] which starts with a definition of people as "symbolic animals:"

> Traditionally man was defined with abstract generality as the *zoon logikon*, the *animal rationale*, the rational animal. More concretely today he is regarded as the symbolic animal, whose knowledge is mediated by symbols, whose actions are informed by symbols, whose existence in its most characteristic features is constituted by a self-understanding and by commitments specified by symbols. On the abstract view man was understood as nature. On the relatively recent view man is understood as historic: for the symbols that inform his being vary with the cultures into which he is born, and the cultures themselves change with the passage of time. They emerge, they develop, they flourish, they influence one another, they can go astray, vanish with their former carriers, only to reappear with fresh vitality and vigor grafted upon new hosts. [95]

Lonergan understands religious[96] experience as what cultivates human authenticity and increases the sensitivity of recognition of what is not authentic. He characterizes religious experience as God's love poured into our hearts. We experience it as a human experience that needs to be put into a relationship with other things in our consciousness. Religious experience forms an "infrastructure" in this way. It can be in harmony

94. Lonergan, "First Lecture: Religious Experience."

95. Ibid., 115.

96. Lonergan understands religion in two ways: as an integral part of social order with its institutional tradition whose explicit form is like a tree trunk, nation, or church; but also as something that precedes this, since behind the institutionalization there is the religion of the previous period. See Lonergan, "First Lecture: Religious Experience," 120. This latter aspect was developed by, among others, Mircea Eliade who concentrated on archaic symbolism and mythology. See, e.g., Eliade, *The Sacred and the Profane*.

or in discord with the rest of our consciousness. It can develop over the course of a human life. It is cultivated in the "immanent context."[97] "The cultivation of religious experience is its entry into harmony with the rest of one's symbolic system, and as symbolic systems vary with the culture and civilization, so too does the cultivation of religious experience."[98] Religious experience belongs to the infrastructure of our life, and operates within it, impacting on other elements of life. In this context Lonergan pays attention to conversion, which he understands as a lifelong process. In *Method in Theology* he writes:

> Conversion is a matter of moving from one set of roots to another
> . . . It occurs only inasmuch as a man discovers what is inauthentic
> in himself and turns away from it, inasmuch as he discovers what
> the fullness of human authenticity can be and embraces it with his
> whole being.[99]

The change of roots, however, needs further interpretation. Lonergan did not have a negative anthropology, according to which there was hardly anything good left in the human race after the Fall. The change of roots does not involve turning one's back on the past, but rather, turning one's back on inauthenticity, while accepting all that has been good from a deeper awareness of it and clearer discernment. A primary impulse to the change of roots might feel disharmonious—conversion may and often does represent a time of crisis, when the old symbolic appropriation of the world and oneself is no longer valid, and the new one has not yet arrived. Lonergan distinguishes three aspects of conversion: religious, moral, and intellectual.[100] He develops each of them to the extent that they gradually touch the roots of our humanity, where the person is enlightened by meeting the living God.[101]

Conversion is then something positive in its very principle. It implies a change from worse to better. Lonergan does not solve the question as to what happens if the change of roots implies a change from better to worse, nor is he concerned with the problem of how to determine criteria

---

97. See Lonergan, "First Lecture: Religious Experience," 125.

98. Lonergan, "First Lecture: Religious Experience," 127.

99. Lonergan, *Method in Theology*, 271.

100. See Lonergan, *Method in Theology*, 270.

101. See Soskice, *Metaphor and Religious Language*, 138.

for what is "better" or "worse." He only says that this decision-making greatly depends on the angle from which we evaluate these matters.[102]

New Tools for Analyzing Religious Experience

The inquiry into religious experience brings us back to the first chapter, where I dealt with the use of phenomenology, hermeneutics, and epistemology in theology. Today in the area of religious experience we usually begin with phenomenology, since it allows us to focus on phenomena, without having to develop a consistent theory about where the phenomena came from. We have seen this in James. In what follows, I first present Brentano's criteria for evaluation of experience, and how Husserl and his successors worked with these criteria. Then I will briefly consider questions of interpretation of religious experience in contemporary culture, where I will offer a critical reading of Ricoeur. In the end I will at least outline what contribution we can expect of epistemology while working with negative religious experience.

POSSIBILITIES OF PHENOMENOLOGICAL ANALYSIS

If we want to talk about a phenomenological analysis of religious experience, we have to return before Husserl, to the Austrian thinker and psychologist Franz Brentano (1838–1917), who first examined the ingredients of what we call experience, and what is as such stored in our mind. In his work *Psychology from an Empirical Standpoint* (1874) Brentano defines experience as a mental phenomenon to which we have access in our inner consciousness in three ways: (i) in the presentation (here the question of truth and untruth has not been formulated yet—it is at the level of encounter with the subject of our experience); (ii) in the judgment we make concerning what was presented; (iii) in the movement of our will and feelings (the basic attitudes in our mental structure are like-dislike, love-hate, etc.)[103]

A good analysis of experience must refer to all three elements, and in the proper order, trying to go beyond the later to the earlier, from the movements of the will and feelings to judgment, and from judgment to the presentation. This order belongs to the actual presentation of the phe-

---

102. Lonergan hints at this issue at least marginally when he talks about the impossibility of neutral research in the realm of religion, but of a positive or negative predisposition. See "First Lecture: Religious Experience," 128.

103. See Brentano, *Psychology*, 198.

nomena. We can say that the presentation is then as important as the yet unevaluated event, as a reference point we come back to again and again when the later two elements may either fossilize, or develop in other directions than where they started. In this sense it is the bedrock of our experience. The question of truth is asked only at the second level. It is an evaluation of what happened in our mind. It was difficult for Brentano to find an appropriate term for the third level. He did not find one word to describe it and in the end settled for the movement of two human powers together, will and feelings, pushing people in different directions, liberating them or paralyzing them with fear, making them generous or selfish. The word "movement" signifies the openness of this process.

Brentano's pupil Edmund Husserl (1859–1938) introduced a distinction of levels between (i) the mind (as a set of mental phenomena), (ii) events and experience, and (iii) the subjects (objects) that our mind intends. The third level was considered the basic one for the investigation of the matter as it appears "phenomenologically." A mental experience according to Husserl can be reduced to a phenomenon by reflection on it. For example, meeting a big strange dog without a muzzle and without its owner, and being frightened, is my mental experience. At the moment of realizing my fear, the fear becomes a phenomenon and as such can be analyzed. The analysis must be directly related to the experience in order not to name more things than the person experiences, so that the evaluative judgment does not become an escape from the direct level of experience, and the experience is not reduced to knowledge or defense against the movement of will and feelings that, according to Brentano, also belong to the fullness of our mental life.

Husserl develops a similar approach to Schleiermacher, although using more accurate terminology. He does not speak of feelings in the first place, but of intuition, which he founds on his principle of donation.[104] Knowing is, for him, possible on the basis of intuition and of observing the phenomena. This is the way to approach religious experience, too. The fact that people have spoken about having religious experience throughout the centuries, and do so even now, makes it possible to look at it as a phenomenon and as such analyze it, without first establishing whether it is true or not, whether we want it or not, or how we feel about it. It has to be taken into account because it appears and we have to allow it to

---

104. See Marion "Metaphysics and Phenomenology," 287.

reveal itself with the values it contains, the relationships it is interwoven with, movements of will and feelings, as Brentano would say, but also with social structures that re-establish within it the relationship to tradition, institution, and doctrine.

Here Husserl is insufficient. We cannot overload the experience in such a way that we could count with its uncovering knowledge unconditioned by time and space, or with the infallibility of our intuition. The strict exclusion of presupposition with which Husserl starts and his requirements that from the beginning to the end all that we take into account in our analysis must be phenomenologically documented,[105] does not allow his method to take advantage of the tradition, in which we learn discernment between what is true, good, beautiful, and just—and what is not so. This we learn from previous experiences and from previous judgments, our own as well as those transmitted to us by traditions to which we belong, and against which we interpret our life as a whole, however fallible and imperfect they are.

Phenomenology might help in analyzing the meaning of religious experience as well as in an analysis of the presuppositions that stand in the way of seeing it.[106] The phenomenological interpretation is not speculative, but works with the interpretation of what is given. It does not form meaning, but finds it.[107] Phenomenological analysis of experience, including religious experience, teaches us that we are neither the owners, nor the protectors of the meaning. In this sense meaning is no longer subjective. We can intend it in our intuition, but, as Patočka says, it is always dependent on the "original," on the whole of natural life.[108]

Similarly Scheler's analysis of the "religious act" combines "the principle of donation" as knowledge enabled by observing the phenomena, and by the principle of suspension of judgment, *epoche*. He wants to rehabilitate the act of faith, devotion, and service where God and the natural world are present directly and the believer recognizes both on the basis of intuition.[109] The transcendent present is then viewed in immanent experience.

---

105. Husserl, *Logische Untersuchungen*, II, 19.

106. See Husserl's conception of *epoche*, chapter 1, 3.1.1.

107. Husserl, *Karteziánské meditace*, 145.

108. See Patočka, "Husserlova fenomenologie," 175–76.

109. See Scheler, *He the Eternal*, 134.

Dupré, in addition, stresses the need for symbolic representation. Religion is experienced with the help of symbols, as in Tillich, including the whole spectrum of the finite images taken from the natural world and human enterprises. They help us to head towards a transcendent goal, being both embedded in and reaching beyond their spatio-temporal mode.[110] The strongest symbol is then word—the Word that has become flesh. At the same time Dupré shows the limits of the phenomenological method. For a believer the transcendent God is not reducible to a phenomenon, even if the phenomenon is endowed with meaning testifying the transcendent God.[111]

A more positive evaluation of the phenomenological method can be found in Luciana O'Dwyer. For her, the phenomenological method still works with a realist presumption. Reality is not something we could create ourselves on the basis of our longing for meaning. It is given.[112] Our perception of reality flows like a river, whose banks are widening from perception of ourselves to perception of others, to the perception of the whole world. Self-transcendence deepens who we are and at the same time rids us of abstract images.[113] According to O'Dwyer, it is not possible to separate "reality" and "how reality appears." We have no other access to "reality" than through phenomena, but we can recognize various forms in the way reality appears to us. O'Dwyer writes: "A person who has the experience of seeing a spring of water in the desert does *really* have the experience of that illusion."[114] Illusion is not raised to reality by this, though. The spring is not what is real, but the experience of the person who believed they saw the spring and later found out that they only dreamt they saw it.

In the area of religious experience we also need to work with this level of reality. Moreover, the assessment whether, for example, someone heard

110. Dupré, *Religious Mystery*, 7–8.

111. Compare Dupré, *Religious Mystery*, 6.10.

112. According to O'Dwyer, Husserl and Heidegger refuse the so-called naturalist scientific realism where it is possible to separate the "idea of reality" from the "reality itself," and the "reality itself" ought to serve as a base for the certainty of the idea that "represents" or "expresses" it. According to Husserl it is not possible to further "anchor" our experience of reality. Reality cannot be anchored from outside, as though it was an outside object for us, but only in our conscience, where it is real for us. Subjectivity here is extended to intersubjectivity. See O'Dwyer, "Reality," 45.

113. See O'Dwyer, "Reality," 47.

114. O'Dwyer, "Reality," 50.

the voice of God's angel speaking to them, or whether they dreamt it, can often be more difficult than the assessment of the spring in the desert. The authenticity of the experience, suggests O'Dwyer, is not given by the fact that "the spring was really there," by the so-called objective reality of the experience. Thus:

> . . . an illusion can be an authentic phenomenon only if it presents itself in a real, living context in which a person finds himself specifically placed and in a determined relationship to the place and surroundings where the person is located when the illusion arises. In this perspective, an illusion is one of the manners in which the actual relationship of an individual to his surroundings expresses itself in a definite situation. That relationship is grounded on the intentionality of consciousness; it is not grounded on the physical presence of the object . . . [115]

According to O'Dwyer every authentic experience has its form of reality. Various forms of reality do not equal one another, though. They differ in their level of authenticity and their depth.

The analysis of religious experience can take the approach advocated by O'Dwyer, enriched partly by taking into account the experiences we somehow doubt, but mainly by analyzing something else in them than whether they correspond with our picture of reality. In this approach the web of relations in which the experience is embedded becomes real, a person's reaction becomes real, God will be real in relation to me, to my neighbors, to my world, but the nature of this reality may be different from what was originally expected. Thus, for example, an experience of meeting the speaking angel can be a religious experience, even if its reality might lie in something else than we had originally thought. Here I am already touching on two other topics I wish to deal with: the question of the development of the interpretation of an experience in different periods of life and the issue of negative religious experience and its interpretation.

A Reinterpretation of Ricoeur's Hermeneutical Circle

In the chapter on method we saw how Ricoeur further developed Heidegger's emphasis on our being thrown into the world and Gadamer's emphasis on speech. He was interested in the process of understanding, and examined it through the development in our relation to symbols,

---

115. O'Dwyer, "Reality," 50.

the bearers of our experience. In the chapter on revelation we saw that Ricoeur talks about three basic stages of this development.[116]

Ricoeur's analysis can also be used for the development of the interpretation of religious experience, but it corresponds only with those situations where a person has experienced the uncritical immediacy of faith and afterwards the period of critical doubt. In the chapter on revelation I dealt with Ricoeur's next step, namely the distinction between an interpretation that is a reflection of reality and one that distorts reality by not relating to it in the right way.[117] Here, however, I want to look at an issue that Ricoeur's analysis does not address directly.

This situation is relatively typical for many adult converts, whose development could be described in Ricoeur's categories as a move from a hermeneutic of suspicion to the first naivety. People who grew up in a non-religious environment adopted the categories of critical reason and only later underwent a religious experience. This experience—and the world of faith and meaning that comes with it—is interpreted as the overcoming and rejection of critical reason. People at this stage are vulnerable to fundamentalism as well as to breaking the ties with their life before that period of faith and meaning. When the "loss of naivety" is not the mediating stage but the initial stage, does it mean that such people come back to the hermeneutics of suspicion in time—in a new fuller form—and that from there they might move to the second, critical immediacy? Or is this journey too long and is it necessary for something else to take on the mediating role, something present in the newly-found, non-critical immediacy?

Here it is necessary to complete Ricoeur's analysis and seek, in Lonergan's terminology, the way to human authenticity through whatever it is that mediates this further development. When critical thinking is made into a taboo, two other aspects of the process of conversion—religious and moral—remain.[118] If at least one of them relates to reality in a non-distorted way, it ceases to be "reductive" and becomes "restorative."[119] And through that area and its symbols, authenticity and wholeness can flow into other areas. Even in this scenario, though, Ricoeur's remark that not every one of us can achieve an adult authenticity and wholeness,

---

116. See chapter 2, 78–84.

117. See Ricoeur, *The Conflict of Interpretations*, 467; *Interpretation Theory*, 19–22.

118. See Lonergan, *Method in Theology*, 270.

119. See Ricoeur, *Symbolism of Evil*, 350.

certainly not in all areas of life, is valid. Growing into maturity is an open-ended process, at least from this side of history. Moreover, it is necessary to emphasize that in terms of Christian theology it is necessary to understand the Ricoeurian hermeneutic circle (in its original and alternative forms) as a process that is initiated, accompanied, and completed through God's grace, inviting human beings to cooperate.

NEGATIVE RELIGIOUS EXPERIENCE FROM THE EPISTEMOLOGICAL STANDPOINT

There are two important questions that I have already touched on indirectly in this chapter. First, whether in the process of growing towards human maturity and wholeness, religious experience may initiate both progress and regress; and second, whether we can meaningfully speak about a negative religious experience, or whether it is a contradiction in terms. If we take as a starting point a religious sense present in the inwardness of every human person, then religious experience would be seen as grasping the goodness that has been given to us at the roots of our being, and as appropriating this goodness as a result of the experience. In such an understanding, religious experience would always be good, initiating progress on our way towards becoming who we are meant to be. What leads to regress would be expressed in terms of human idolatry (falsifying the holy), or demonology (experiencing negative spiritual forces and their impact on human life). F. W. Dillistone, who advocates the uniqueness of religious experience, and like Schleiermacher, James, or Otto pleads for distinguishing it from other experiences—artistic or scientific, for example—nevertheless recognizes the plurality within religious experience that includes the negative experience. Any religious experience, Dillistone insists, is not a human creation, because it is a transcendent experience. Transcendence, however, can be divine but also demonic, psychedelic, hysteric, or hypnotic.[120]

Then, there is the second question, to which I will pay more attention now, namely what contributes to a wrong understanding and appropriation of experience in its positive givenness by God, and hence leads to human regress. If we take religious experience as a depth dimension of every human experience perceived from a religious point of view, the negativity would be seen not in terms of a non-divine transcendence, but in terms of

---

120. See Dillistone, "Experience, Religious," 205.

distorted human immanence. As Raymond Studzinski stresses, genuine religious experience is conditioned by the possibility of the subject to be open to a new world of meaning, new self-understanding, and understanding of reality in relation to the holy.[121]

Both of the positions, that of Dillistone and that of Studzinski, appear in a new light if we take into account O'Dwyer's insistence that every authentic experience has its form of reality, even if they differ in their level of authenticity and their depth. Here authenticity and non-authenticity are not measured either by the source of the experience or by the human intellectual and moral disposition, but by means of our whole relation to reality, including an adequate perception and judgment of what has happened in the experience.[122] O'Dwyer writes that the authenticity of an experience is not given by equating what we experience with what things are "objectively," but by the things presenting something real in the vital context in which we find ourselves.[123]

Thus, what may be from a disengaged position seen as inauthentic experience, can become a way to authenticity for a person who has undergone that experience. Yet, it may be an experience of something else than what was originally expected. I remember an example of a student of mine, who told me about his enlightenment, which took place once when he was invited to a charismatic meeting. When there were prayers in tongues, his friends as well as he himself desired that he be baptized by the Spirit: he closed his eyes, concentrated deeply, and at one point he started feeling light and warmth coming to him. When he opened his eyes, he saw that he was looking into a light bulb. This experience did not teach him anything objective about the possibilities or impossibilities of the gifts of the Spirit such as were displayed in that community, yet for him it was an important insight into his own ability to be mistaken. In this sense it was a religious experience, helping him not to take without

---

121. See, e.g., Studzinski, "Experience, religious," 370; this understanding is indebted to Schillebeeckx's way of working with the concept of the dimensionality in theology. See Schillebeeckx, *Christ*.

122. See O'Dwyer, "Reality," 50.

123. "In this perspective, an illusion is one of the manners in which the actual relationship of an individual to his surroundings expresses itself in a definite situation. That relationship is grounded on the intentionality of consciousness; it is not grounded on the physical presence of the object . . ." O'Dwyer, "Reality," 50.

discernment as divine anything which makes such claims, whether from without or from within us.

O'Dwyer's approach can teach us that even an experience of what is not what it is supposed to be can become a way to enter more deeply into reality. In this sense, the loosening of our grip on the question of what is the essence of things, and analyzing what appears consistently from the engaged point of view, can show us a way from error to truth.

CONCLUSION

In this chapter I have tried to examine in what sense religious experience can be not only a source of theology, but a source that can also be studied. Although we work with immediate and mediated experience in theology (through Christian holy stories, rituals, teachings, ethical principles, and the institution),[124] this chapter intended to deal more with religious experience in its immediate form. Or, to be more precise, I should say with the immediate dimensions of the experiences testified in the Scriptures and tradition as well as in modern and postmodern writers, which can by means of analogy help us to find direction in our interior life. If there is no theology without immediate religious experience, as Tillich claimed,[125] without at least some understanding of our inner life we would always approach the discipline of theology as outsiders. In order to take religious experience (of others and our own) seriously, we need to engage in discernment as was described in this chapter with the help of different authors.

The content of the experience never stood in isolation from the whole web of ways a person or a group of people related to God, to each other, and to the world in which they lived. Already in the Scriptures, when I spoke about experience as a test, we could see how God's trying the person in order to find out what is inside, included also people trying if God was really with them.[126] The story of Jephthah's sacrifice of his own daughter shows the terrible consequences that can arise from human ideas of faithfulness to what is promised God when taken in isolation from other promises, also those of God to us.[127]

---

124. See six dimensions of religion according to Smart, "Religion," 496–98.

125. See Trtik, *Vztah já-Ty*, 71.

126. See, e.g., Job 7:17–18 and Exod 17:7.

127. See Judg 11:30–40.

By analyzing the call of Isaiah, the prophecy of Ezekiel, and the conversion of Saul, I demonstrated experience as a shift of certainties and as a deepening of understanding in relationships, as mentioned above. The more at home with the Lord the prophets or the apostles were, the fewer finite images of God were needed. In the intimacy with the Lord, from which they were sent to speak out to their people, there were no claims to entire or infallible knowledge of the Lord or his will. We have also been told about human desires to hold onto something that can be understood and managed, but these parts of the narratives remained a shadow accompanying both the Old and the New Testament accounts of genuine religious experience, even that of Christ's resurrection and of Pentecost. We could also see that even with the biblical narratives, evaluation of what was experienced changed over time and left space for further interpretation, as the people of God in different times were to remember these testified experiences.[128]

The plurality of religious experiences in the Scriptures, even if not described in this precise terminology, entered into the Christian tradition, and provided us with different analyses of human interiority being both initiated and completed by God. Both Symeon and Ignatius were aware of human beings' capacities to deceive themselves on their spiritual journey. While their ways of discernment corresponded to their personality types as well as to the cultural setting in which their own experiences took place, they did not encourage us to imitate them. Instead, they encouraged us to learn discernment in invoking Jesus while undertaking the purifying journey into our own hearts.[129]

Symeon and his pupils contrasted the "profane" and the "spiritual" life because they experienced the church making itself too much at home in the political status quo, and they needed a language of distance from what they saw as an unsatisfactory model of Christian life. Besides criticizing them for their dualism, we can, however, learn from them how contextualized is each interpretation of our experiences. It can inspire a consistent contextualization of our own convictions then, which would significantly broaden what we see as authentic.

Ignatius's desire to speak from experience to experience, while assuming that the creator works specifically not only with each culture, but

---

128. See, for example, Saul's conversion as reflected in differently dated writings, or Abraham's testing and its interpretation in the Old and New Testament.

129. See Symeon the New Theologian, "The Three Forms of Prayer," 31–32.

with each person he has created,[130] can fall on fruitful ground if we assume a similarly extended horizon of authenticity. Then, even if we know that Ignatius himself had negative experiences with the Inquisition that contributed to how he expressed loyalty to the church, that he did not know the Reformers, and did not understand their cause, we still should not judge his authenticity by our measures, but allow him to speak about the following of Christ in language which our differently configured experience can benefit from.

Following religious experience both as a source and as a subject of theology, I had to track how the subject was reintroduced in modernity by Schleiermacher, Otto, and James, and which theological issues were at stake when appropriating their insights. Studying religious experience as plural in form and irreducible to other experiences, even if not entirely separated from them, at a time when European and American societies were no longer predominantly Christian, needed further specifications of the roles of natural religiosity and the symbolic Christian tradition. It was not surprising that no agreement was reached on whether this religiosity was a starting point or an obstacle to a life transformed by the holy narratives as testified in the Scriptures. Different positions in this area have as long a history as Christian theology itself. In the modern times the debate on religious experience also included a striving for a non-reductionist understanding of human immanence.

Theologians like Tyrrell or Tillich stressed that immanence is a space where we encounter the transcendent other, which is both testified in Christian symbolism, but precisely as the transcendent other coming to our immanence, and in Jesus Christ transforming us by the Spirit in the relationship of love. A language of conversion, as employed by Lonergan, was helpful for connecting together the anthropologically general and the religiously specific aspects of growing into what we have been created for, authentic human beings in relationship with God, with other people, and with our world.

At the close of the chapter I returned to the methods that I considered in the first chapter of this book. Now I tried to show in more detail how phenomenology, hermeneutics, and epistemology can help contemporary theology in working with the multilayered subject of religious experience. I showed how O'Dwyer's phenomenological approach enables

130. Ignatius of Loyola, *Spiritual Exercises* 15.

us to work with the experience of illusion without denying that such an experience itself is a real experience.

However, this approach also teaches us that examination of the structure of experience, the values it bears, the levels of reality it relates to, what is at work when its reality might rest in something else than we originally expected, is always done from an engaged perspective, which in a good analysis we both have to recognize and to put in brackets. The hermeneutical method helped me to deal with the development of the interpretation of religious experience through different life periods, especially in a culture that has been religiously uprooted, and where people often do not enter the first immediate state of faith as children. In the epistemological method I focused on how to work with negative religious experience and how to interpret its negativity. In both cases I asked what initiates growth into greater human authenticity while confronting non-divine transcendence or disfigured human interpretations of what is taking place.

As a final comment to this chapter, I should add that in my analysis of religious experience different models of divine-human cooperation have emerged. These range from God's action and human beings' reception of it, however passive, to the human search for God, experiencing what God is not, and in this sense, at least negatively, learning something about the divine reality. If either the divine or the human pole of the relationship was undervalued, the interpretation of religious experience suffered from reductionism. For a good analysis of religious experience as a source and as a subject of theology, insights from all the previous chapters were needed, which is why this is the concluding chapter of the book. Theological methods teach us how to combine the non-scientific and the scientific aspects of our investigations without confusing them. The examination of claims to divine revelation prepared the ground for approaching the divine mystery precisely as self-revealing mystery, and understanding the symbolic categories in which the mystery is carried, not as its replacement, but as windows to it. Looking into different concepts and types of authority helped us to ground the notion of authenticity, and so did the exploration of the role of the historical and cultural context. The subject of religious experience cannot be isolated from the previous themes, and yet it adds to them an irreducible dimension of "understanding the realities profoundly and . . . savoring them interiorly." [131]

131. Ignatius of Loyola, *Spiritual Exercises*, 121.

Conclusion

Having come to the end of this ecumenical introduction to theology, it is possible to see that its foundations (the *fundamentum*—the word from which fundamental theology is derived) are relational. The theological methods introduced in the first chapter tried to comprehend how relationships with God, with our fellow human beings, and with the whole of the created world are imprinted in the Christian texts. We have investigated how these relationships and the multitude of questions they raise, the narratives that attempt to capture these relationships, especially in their transitional moments, or perhaps we could say moments of conversion, can be interpreted and passed on.

Theology begins when a person wants to understand his/her life-journey and realizes that, for it to be complete, it has to include a spiritual dimension and, moreover, that this spiritual dimension is a source of life for all other dimensions of our existence. In this book I have spoken about religious immediacy, or religious experience, reflecting, in Pauline language, the trinity of faith, hope, and love.[1] We have seen that such reflection does not happen in isolation. Theology is not an isolated subject, finding its fulfillment in an isolated God. Some form of community is needed, where the relationships that are reflected are lived as reality, and not only thought as ideal modes of being. Likewise, there needs to be an access to the wisdom accumulated in tradition, and its symbolic forms of meaning that allow the reading of one's life journey as a journey with others towards God's kingdom.

It was, however, also necessary to point out that there is a difference between devout reflection and theology, that theology is both a spiritual journey and a science with all the requirements that makes on it. Theological reflection needs to be, or at least needs to struggle to be, historically accurate, terminologically correct, systematically unconfused, and clear in its interpretation. Theologians are challenged by these

1. See 1 Cor 13:3; 1 Thes 1:3; 5:8; Eph 1:15–18; Col 1:4–5.

requirements that theology shares with other sciences and that remain valid whether we do confessional theologies or an ecumenical theology. With them we have to seek the specific nature of theology and its specific contribution to the other human ways of searching for and finding knowledge.

In this book I have used three classical concepts of theology as a science to illustrate what its scientificity can mean in different historical, cultural, and even confessional contexts: Augustine's existential understanding of science as wisdom, Thomas's dialectic understanding of science as rationality, and Schleiermacher's understanding of "positive" science. The different modes of the science of theology, however, showed family resemblances in their dependence on some spiritual journey and on the community of faith, hope, and love from which they came, and on which they offered a developing reflection. Then I introduced three significant current methods—phenomenology, hermeneutics, and epistemology—and showed how they are employed in theological work. Throughout the book, the phenomenological method has been used when we needed to approach as closely as possible the immediacy of revelation, as well as encounters with its authoritative interpretation, or when we concentrated on religious experience in its multilayered character.[2] The hermeneutical method was employed when we focused on the texts, their meaning, and on the different strands of tradition of interpretation. All the themes examined in the book benefited from a hermeneutical analysis.

The epistemological method helped us to raise the question of truth not only historically and culturally, but more generally, to test the adequacy of the certainties that were claimed, and to safeguard their theoretical-practical nature. At the same time reflecting on the themes from an epistemological point of view proved useful when relational and open-ended knowledge was replaced by ideological security and desires to control even the transcendent. By naming what has gone wrong, the epistemological method helped theologians to return within the scope of their symbolic knowledge and appreciate the symbolic non-knowledge as a part of knowledge. This helped us to see that transcendence would be always transcendent, and God would stay God, loving but also supreme, active, but also in ways beyond our understanding and beyond our reach.

---

2. See O'Dwyer's approach in chapter 5, 226–27.

The open dialectics, or to use a phrase I borrow from my husband, non-synthesizing dialectics[3] between knowledge and non-knowledge with regards to God came back in more detail in the chapter on revelation. We have approached revelation in two ways: the transcendent dimension of revelation, where we have to deal with the radical otherness of God that claims our life and calls us to conversion, as a response of faith in the situation in which we find ourselves; and the immanent dimension of revelation that is inter-subjective, relating our hearts to the structures of humanity, and the human community in which understanding and interpretation are mediated.

In the first instance we could talk about the way in which the revelation of God's mystery contains both revelation and mystery. This was seen, for example, in the revelation given to Moses and the ancestors. But it is also evident in Paul. The story of his conversion on the road to Damascus frequently stresses the clarity of his vision, but less frequently the fact that he also lost his sight. Moreover, even the new sight he received also carried with it an inability to see clearly.[4]

The second dimension of revelation—its immanence—was displayed in those biblical stories that showed that the questions concerning God are raised always already in some form of relationship to God, to the people around us, and to the world in which we live. Abram, who met God on the way to Shechem, accepted the promise and worshipped God, understood this revelation in relation to his people.[5] The revelation given to Moses, Elijah, and possibly also to Thomas, who was unable to believe that the Lord had risen from the dead,[6] works with human values and relationships. God's transcendence lets us experience God immanently— we would not be able to understand in any other way. Our structures of understanding are human. We find our direction in life according to what we perceive as pleasant or unpleasant, what we agree or disagree with, what we accept or refuse. Immanence then stands or falls with trust that the Holy Spirit works in us, and breathing the breath of life into us, converting and illuminating us in our relationships, leads us to Jesus, where we are purified and made once again capable of following on the journey

3. See Tim Noble, *Keeping the Window Open*, 279.

4. "For now we see in a mirror, dimly, but then we will see face to face." (1 Cor 13:12a).

5. See Gen 12:6–7.

6. See John 20:24–29.

he showed us, the journey to the Father. On this journey we learn to be authentically human when we exercise solidarity and compassion, when we share love, hope, and faith, in taking other people, and eventually all the created world, with us. This is what we mean when in doctrinal terms we say that in the Christian symbolic system revelation is a part of the economy of salvation of the Holy Trinity.

Communication with God is not about pondering the theoretical possibility of God's existence, but encountering the reality that is often not so much a question as a basic certainty that makes sense of everything else. This may of course seem somewhat incomprehensible to those who have never had a similar encounter.[7] The experience with God and God-transformed reality is not what Williams called epistemological security,[8] the belief that our knowledge cannot ultimately deceive us because it is embedded in God's revelation. Here all immanent certainties are subject to the transcendent otherness of God and God's kingdom. The Church Fathers were well aware of this. So, for example, both Justin and Gregory of Nyssa were very careful not to use absolute categories, not even for our dynamic life, or our knowledge of God. At the same time these Church Fathers, as well as the theologians of the Alexandrian and the Antiochian schools, dealt with how to interpret God's revelation and how to hand down the experience of a self-revealing God, without pushing aside the aspects we do not understand.

Belief in revelation is developed in relation to the spiritual progress of humankind in contemporary theology (Lossky and Ricoeur), and with regard to an understanding of sacraments, the sacramental character of the church and the world, where everything is a sign of God's love to us, and of a desire for this love to be reciprocated, and to spread through creation (Chauvet). Especially the second development may at first appear as alienating to Christians from churches without a strong emphasis on the sacraments. But the desire to understand others may bring home some of the insights that stress that, even in the sacramental mediation, the point is not to "own" God, but to belong to God, and thus to belong to each other as witnesses of God's life that transcends all boundaries, including the boundary of death. And this emphasis may shed a different

---

7. The king of Moab, Balak, who hired Balaam to curse Israel, does not understand what happens to Balaam. (Num 23:11) Those who accompanied Saul to Damascus "stood speechless because they heard the voice but saw no one." (Acts 9:7)

8. See Williams, *On Christian Theology*, 142.

light on whether or how the rest of the Christian tradition that makes use of sacramental categories can be appropriated.

While talking about divine revelation in the Christian context, we need to bear in mind not only that there are others who claim that their religion is revealed and that God appears differently in their symbolic mediation of revelation, but also that such facts must have a place in our theology of revelation. It does not mean that we have to make a synthesis of all the claims to divine revelation in different religions, and behave as if all of them were waiting for us to come and judge and divide between true and wrong. Instead, a Christian theology of revelation, as presented in this book, needs to make space not only for ecumenical dialogue (which I would argue lies within the Christian theology of revelation already), but also for inter-religious dialogue, and thus to the fact that we are not the exclusive recipients of revelation.

The position I outlined did not want to deprive faith of its specific characteristics. It is indeed carried by the traditions of its holy stories, by its rituals, dogmas, ethical codes, experiences, and institutions.[9] However, at the same time it is aware that all has been and is being formed in relationship to others whose faith is carried by different religious traditions. If we say that the truth of revelation is not guaranteed by coherency only, it must follow that there is also a transcendent reference to be adopted. We cannot try to measure this reference from an ultimate perspective, simply because none of us is God, but we can follow how it is imprinted in the practices of the claimants. In other words, the truth leaves tracks in the manner in which people's actions, beliefs, and convictions testify to the God to whom they refer. There is a visibility of truth (always incomplete and always including the possibility of error on our part) along with its fruits.

The third chapter showed how Christian tradition works with the concept of authority. A distinction was introduced between divine authority, which alone is absolute and non-mediated, and the plurality of mediated and mediating authorities, such as the Scripture, tradition, the church (external authorities), and human reason and conscience (internal authorities). While in different Christian traditions there are different emphases on what and who can legitimately mediate divine authority, they have this transcendent reference in common. Likewise, all traditions

---

9. See six dimensions of religion according to Smart, "Religion", 496–497.

share a fragility that comes from the fact that they are not the ultimate, and if they try to avoid this fragility, they run the risk of self-referentiality. In the realm of the pre-ultimate judgments, they also struggle with the fact that the necessary plurality of the external and internal authorities is not always in harmony. There are tensions, conflicts, and aporias.

Traditions grow and become more nuanced in response to them. They impoverish and at times even kill the treasure of faith if they try to defend it by reducing rights to truth-claims only to some voices. Yet lived faith and reflection also have the power of germinating. As we have seen with Hus, Newman, or Tyrrell, what is excluded in one generation may become a tool of renewal in the next.

The third chapter was not devoted solely to individual discernment of what to believe in and how to act, but also to the experience of the church and its corporate discernment. In the history of theology this discernment received a particular name, apostolic succession. Broadly understood, the churches' search for ways to follow Christ faithfully involved the whole issue of how to preserve the continuation of the apostolic teaching and the apostolic ways of life in future generations. In this light the current ecumenical discussion concerning who "has" and who "has not" apostolic succession has become more nuanced. Following the early patristic concepts we found a need to preserve the historical continuity of the episcopal (presbyteral)[10] ordination, expressed in the laying on of hands, symbolizing the handover of the commission to serve, and providing the power and gifts of the Holy Spirit that enable this service.

Historical continuity, though, was not the only criterion. It was accompanied by an eschatological concept that stressed that the fullness of our Christian life comes from the future, from the kingdom of God. We can taste this future as the Spirit makes it present in the Eucharistic gathering, and wherever "the blind receive their sight, the lame walk, the lepers are cleansed, the deaf hear, the dead are raised, and the poor have good news brought to them," (Matt 11:5) in other words where we experience the healing power of God.[11] Both understandings of apostolic succession are important, and while in the history of theology we have seen different attempts at their synthesis, we could also consider taking them as two poles that need to remain in dialectical tension. This would make it

10. See Jorissen, "Behindert die Amtsfrage die Einheit der Kirche?"
11. See Zizioulas, *Being As Communion*, 176.

more possible for those Christian traditions that have emphasized much more one of these poles (often at the expense of the other) to integrate the other without feeling disowned in their previous attempts to grasp what a faithful following of Christ may mean. Such an approach may be more ecumenically beneficial than a synthesis between the historically tangible and the transcendentally subversive elements of ecclesial identity. Cyprian's attempt to pin down where the genuine church was to be found needed to be revised by Augustine because in the Donatist controversy it proved to be a source of further divisions and animosity. Nevertheless, it did show that if the dialectical poles are deprived of their power, the church tends either to totality or to disintegration.

These two poles re-emerged in the following chapter, dedicated to the contextuality of theology. When we investigated the nature of the time-frame within which theological reflection occurs, we found out that it was not given by history alone, but also by the eschatological expectation present in a given period. Historical time and eschatological time together formed memory and supported hope in the promised future. An anamnetic approach to time (as making the past present in our memory) needed to be complemented by the epicletic approach (invocation of the Holy Spirit to re-tell us the past from the point of view of the future, of the fullness in God). References to "God's memory" thus reached beyond claims that God remembers all the good and the bad we have done, and included the revelation of the yet unrealized possibilities of life.[12] Our experiences of encountering God's memory here and now—individual and collective—were always interpreted against the background of a particular historical period, which imprinted on the symbolic forms in which the experiences were carried its own convictions and values. The referential nature of such experiences also involved, however, the relativization of these convictions and values, reminding us that the divine memory is something that we do not possess, but which possesses us.

I worked similarly with the coordinates of space. I argued that our experience is not formed only by the culture of the specific places we inhabit, but also by a utopian culture of that which has not yet been realized, and in the world in which we live cannot be fully realized, that which we dream of and where we set our hopes. Each cultural context in which theology is done carries what has been realized in it, but also what is still

---

12. See Metz, *Faith in History and Society*, 202.

unrealized. Furthermore, a Christian hope, which is also testified in the cultures, is both mediated by the various utopias (as a vision of how a better world where God is in the center may look) and subverts utopias (as none of the mediations are identical with the Kingdom of God).

The extended concept of time and space forming the context in which we interpret our experience of God and reflect upon it enabled us to overcome the post-Enlightenment tensions between the ideal of progress and the experience of regress, and between the church and culture. At the same time, however, other issues came to the fore. These included how to work with the idea of contextuality, so that we did not use it to assert our interests of power, and how to work with tradition, so that it would not become dead, a restored certainty of the past, or even of some time that never existed.[13]

The final chapter focused on religious experience as a subject of theological inquiry, including both experiences that are seen as related to explicitly Christian themes and experiences with what people might call the transcendent, the sacred, or the holy. After having demonstrated that already in the Scriptures there is a plurality of ways in which God and divinely-transformed reality are experienced, and a plurality of styles and symbolic forms of how to grasp and interpret the experience, I concentrated on two themes that kept re-emerging throughout the scriptural accounts. The first one was how to integrate individual experiences into the life-process of maturing in relationships with God as well as with people and with the created world. The second theme involved both questions of how to discern between an authentic and inauthentic religious experience, and how to remain flexible and allow for growth in our understanding of what has been experienced, and what can be learnt from what was previously categorized either as an authentic or an inauthentic experience. Here we found that also in a spiritual life what might have been an inauthentic experience of one thing (such as a well in the desert) can be integrated as an authentic experience of another thing (such as a mirage).[14] These themes, addressed by the classics of both Western and Eastern Christianity, have returned with a new urgency in our contemporary, largely post-secular, and post-Christian setting.

13. See Küng, *Christianity*, 650.

14. Here I use the examples of O'Dwyer discussed in chapter 5, 226–27.

To understand present approaches to religious experience and to the issues it raises we also had to track the post-Enlightenment journey of the theme through psychology, sociology, and religious studies back to theology. While theology could learn from the other sciences a methodological exactness that nevertheless gives space to the transcendent other as the transcendent other and to the sacred as the sacred, theologians needed to make their own road in re-connecting this much more pluriform experience to the Christian tradition and to the community of faith where the tradition lives. They had to find answers to why such a task should be undertaken in the first place, and why they should not be satisfied with dealing with religious experience just as psychologists, sociologists, or religious studies specialists do. While arguing against the privatization of religious experience, often taken for granted in the other sciences, they opened up new ways of integrating Christian symbolic heritage to the debate concerning forms of relationship between the transcendent and the immanent reality. Furthermore, their emphasis on religious experience being but one part of the whole process of conversion towards God rehabilitated the communal aspect of religious experience without losing the personal one.

To conclude, the dynamics between the communal and the personal aspects of reflecting on religious immediacy has been of special interest to me in this book. As my task was to present an ecumenical fundamental theology, I concentrated on the different communities contributing to the communal symbolic wealth of Christianity. What might have perhaps disappointed the reader was the fact that I did not compare the traditions I relied on in terms of which is better and which is worse in each particular aspect. But this was not my task. Moreover, to be frank, I do not think that this is a standpoint from which an ecumenical theology could be done. If we are to be able to learn from each other, such a process requires a genuine openness and reciprocity, and cannot be organized by any tradition, denominational or ecumenical institution, or by any theologian, as if from above. To be within this process of learning and teaching and common search, we need to take seriously that within the common journey our personal life-story is important. Its messiness, relying on finding life where life is to be found, its letting go of what is dead, and its often multiple belonging, where life can be shared, is of an indispensable value. Our life-stories ground our theology, but at the same time, make generalizations very difficult.

Thus, in the end, ecumenical fundamental theology relies on the dynamics between the communal and the personal reflection on a life of faith, hope, and love. Within this dynamics we figure out what divine revelation means—as well as learn what it means when we get this wrong. Here the external and the internal authorities exercise their ministerial roles in order to allow God to be God and God's loved creation to be God's loved creation. What it means and requires may differ in various contexts, but, if it is missing, our lives become disoriented. Yet, throughout the centuries, there have been voices calling us home, and healing energies making transitions in life possible. Tracking God is at the same time tracking the narratives of salvation, of moving from being lost to being found, and tracking a desire to penetrate this mystery still deeper.

Bibliography

Adams, J. L. "Introduction." In Troeltsch, E. *The Absoluteness of Christianity and the History of Religions*. Richmond: John Knox, 1971.

Adorno, T. *Aesthetic Theory*. London: Routledge & Kegan Paul, 1984.

———. and M. Horkheimer. *The Dialectic of Enlightenment*. New York: Herder and Herder, 1972.

Alfaro, J. "Faith." In *Encyclopedia of Theology*, edited by Karl Rahner, 500–514. Tunbridge Wells: Burns & Oates, 1986.

Arnold, M. *Culture and Anarchy*. Oxford: Oxford University Press, 2006.

Balthasar, H. U. von. *Love Alone: The Way of Revelation*. London: Sheed and Ward, 1992.

———. "On the Tasks of Catholic Philosophy in our Time." *Communio* 20 (1993) 147–87.

Baptism, Eucharist and Ministry. WCC, Geneva, 1982.

Churches Responses to BEM: Official Responses to the "Baptism, Eucharist and Ministry" Text. Vol. I, edited by M. Thurian. Geneva: WCC, 1986.

Barth, K. *Protestant Theology in the Nineteenth Century: Its Background and History*. London: SCM, 1972.

———. *The Word of God and the Word of Man*. New York: Harper and Row, 1957.

Baur, F. Ch. *Paul, the Apostle of Jesus Christ*, Peabody: Hendrickson, 2003.

Bindney, D. "The Concept of Value in Modern Anthropology." In *Anthropology Today: An Encyclopedic Inventory*, edited by O. Billig et al., 682–99. Chicago: University of Chicago Press, 1953.

Bloch, E. *The Principle of Hope*. Cambridge, Mass.: MIT, 1996.

Brentano, F. *Psychology from an Empirical Standpoint*. London—New York: Routledge, 1995.

Brown, P. *Augustine of Hippo: A Biography*. London: Faber, 1967.

Brown, R. and R. F. Collins. "Canonicity." In *The New Jerome Biblical Commentary*, edited by Raymond E. Brown et al., 1034–54 (=66:§§1–101). London: Geoffrey Chapman, 1993

Brueggemann, W. *Israel's Praise. Doxology against Idolatry and Ideology*. Philadelphia· Fortress, 1988.

Brunkhorst, H. *Adorno and Critical Theory*. Cardiff: University of Wales Press, 1999.

Cady, L. E. "Loosening the Category That Binds: Modern 'Religion' and the Promise of Cultural Studies." In *Converging on Culture: Theologians in Dialogue with Cultural Analysis and Criticism*, edited by D. Brown et al., 17–40. Oxford: Oxford University Press, 2001.

Carter, Stephen. *The Culture of Disbelief: How American Law and Politics Trivialize Religious Devotion*. New York: Basic Books, 1993.

Castelot, J. J. and A. Cody. "Religious Institutions of Israel." In *The New Jerome Biblical Commentary*, edited by R.E. Brown et al., 1253–83. London: Geoffrey Chapman, 1993.

Cavanaugh, W. T. *Torture and Eucharist.* Oxford: Blackwell, 1998

Ceresko, A. R. *Introduction to the Old Testament: A Liberation Perspective.* Maryknoll: Orbis Books, 1997.

Chauvet, L.-M. "The Liturgy in its Symbolic Space." *Concilium* (1995/3) 29–39.

———. *Symbol and Sacrament: A Sacramental Reinterpretation of Christian Existence.* Collegeville: Liturgical Press, 1995.

Clarkson, J. F., et al. *The Church Teaches: Documents of the Church in English Translation.* Rockford, Illinois: Tan Books, 1973.

Clayton, J. "Introducing Paul Tillich's Writings in the Philosophy of Religion." In Paul Tillich, *Main Works IV: Writings in the Philosophy of Religion*, edited by John Clayton, 9–28. New York—Berlin: De Gruyter—Evangelisches Verlagswerk, 1987.

Cyprian. *The Unity of the Catholic Church.* London: The Manresa Press, 1924.

Danielou, J. *Grégoire de Nysse, La Vie de Moise.* Paris : Sources Chrétiennes 1, 1955.

———. *The Christian Today.* New York, Tournay, Paris, Rome: Desclee Company, 1960.

Davies, B. *Aquinas.* London, New York: Continuum, 2002.

Davis, C. "Revelation and Critical Theory." In *Divine Revelation*, edited by P. Avis, 87–111. London: Darton, Longman & Todd, 1997.

Descartes, R. *Discourse on the Method and Meditations on First Philosophy.* New Haven: Yale University Press, 1996.

Dillistone, F. W. "Experience, Religious." In *A New Dictionary of Christian Theology*, edited by A. Richardson and J. Bowden, 204–7. London: SCM, 1987.

Dolejšová (Noble), I. *Accounts of Hope: A Problem of Method in Postmodern Apologia.* Bern, Berlin, Bruxelles: Peter Lang, 2001.

———. "Wittgenstein's Account of Religion as a Desire to Become a Different Man." In *Passion for Critique: Essays in Honour of F. J. Laishley*, edited by H. B. Browne and G. Griffith-Dickson, 219–33. Praha: Sít, 1997.

Domenach, J. M. "Voyage to the End of the Sciences of Man." In *Violence and Truth: On the Work of René Girard*, edited by P. Dumouchel, 152–59. London: Athlone Press, 1987.

Dunn, J. D. G. "Biblical Concept of Divine Revelation." In *Divine Revelation*, edited by P. Avis, 1–22. London: Darton, Longman & Todd, 1997.

———. *The Theology of Paul the Apostle.* Edinburgh: T. & T. Clark, 1998.

Dupré, L. "*Religious Mystery and Rational Reflection.* Grand Rapids: Eerdmans, 1998.

Dupuis, J. "Interreligious Dialogue." In *Dictionary of Fundamental Theology*, edited by R. Latourelle and R. Fisichella, 518–23. New York: Crossroad 2000.

———. *Jesus Christ and the Encounter of World Religions.* Maryknoll: Orbis, 1991.

———. *Towards a Christian Theology of Religious Pluralism.* Maryknoll: Orbis, 1997.

Eagleton, T. *Ideology: An Introduction.* London, New York: Verso, 1994.

Eliade, M. *The Sacred and the Profane.* New York: Harcourt, Brace & World, 1959.

Edwards J. *A Treatise Concerning the Religious Affections.* Edinburgh: Banner of Truth Trust, 1986. (First published 1746).

Evdokimov, P. "La culture et l'eschatologie." *Semeur* 50 (1947) 15–24.

———. *L'art de l'icone. Théologie de la beauté.* Paris: Desclée de Brouwer, 1970.

———. *Orthodoxie.* Neuchâtel—Paris: Delachaux et Niestle, 1959.

Fiorenza, F. S. "Religion and Society: Legitimation, Rationalisation, or Cultural Heritage." *Concilium* (1979/5) 24–32.

Fries, H. *Fundamental Theology*. Washington: The Catholic University of America Press, 1996.

Gadamer, H. G. "Hermeneutics and Social Science." *Cultural Hermeneutics 2* (1975) 307–16.

———. *Truth and Method*. New York: Crossroad, 1979

Gallagher, M. P. *Clashing Symbols: An Introduction to Faith and Culture*. London: Darton, Longman and Todd, 1997.

Ganss, G. E. "Introduction to 'Selections from the *Constitutions of the Society of Jesus*.'" In *Ignatius of Loyola: Spiritual Exercises and Selected Works*, edited and translated by G. E. Ganss, 275–82. Mahwah: Paulist Press, 1991.

Geertz, C. *The Interpretation of Cultures*. New York: Basic Books, 1973.

Geffré, C. and W. Jeanrond. "Introduction: Why Theology? How Theologians Today Understand Their Work." *Concilium* 6 (1994/6), vii–x.

Grant, R. M. *The Letter and the Spirit*. London: SPCK, 1957.

Gregory of Nyssa. *The Life of Moses*. New York: Paulist Press—Toronto: Ramsey, 1978.

———. *Treatise on the Inscription of the Psalms*. Oxford: Clarendon Press, 1995.

Gunton, C. E. *The Promise of Trinitarian Theology*. Edinburgh: T. & T. Clark, 1997.

Haag, H. "Die Buchwerdung des Wortes Gottes in der Heiligen Schrift." In *Mysterium Salutis: Grundriss heilsgeschichtlicher Dogmatik* Vol 1, edited by Johannes Feiner and Magnus Löhrer, 289–428. Einsiedeln, Zürich, Köln: Benziger Verlag, 1965.

Habermas, J. *Hermeneutik und Ideologiekritik*. Frankfurt: Suhrkamp, 1971.

———. *Knowledge and Human Interests*. Boston: Beacon Press, 1972.

Hardy, A. *The Spiritual Nature of Man: A Study of Contemporary Religious Experience*. Oxford: Clarendon Press, 1979.

Harnack, Adolf von. *What is Christianity?* London: Williams & Norgate, 1904.

Hay, D. *Religious Experience Today: Studying the Facts*. London: Mowbray, 1990.

Hegel, G. W. F. *Fenomenologie ducha*. Československá akademie věd, Brno, 1960.

———. *On Christianity: Early Theological Writings by Friedrich Hegel*. New York: Harper & Brothers, 1961.

———. *Philosophy of History*. London—New York: Colonial Press, 1900.

Heidegger, M. *Being and Time*. London: Blackwell, 1962

———. *Was ist Metaphysik?* Frankfurt: Klostermann, 1965.

Husova výzbroj do Kostnice. Edited by F. M. Dobiáš and A. Molnár. Praha: Kalich, 1965.

Hus, J. *Magistri Johannis Hus Opera omnia: Spisy latinské I*. Praha: Bursik, 1904.

———. "Odpověd M. Jana Husi k 42 článkům, od M Štěpána z Pálče komisařům koncila proti němu předloženým." In Jan Hus, *Magistri Johannis Hus Opera omnia: Spisy latinské I*. 75–93. Praha: Bursik, 1904.

———. "O šesti bludiech." In *Drobné spisy české Opera Omnia IV*. 271–96. Praha: Academia, 1985.

———. *Řeč o míru*. Praha: Kalich, 1963.

———. "Výklad víry." In *Výklady: Opera omnia I*, Praha: Academia, 1975.

Husserl, E. *Karteziánské meditace*. Praha: Svoboda, 1993

———. *Logische Untersuchungen*. Tubingen: Max Niemeyer, 1968.

———. "Phenomenology": No Pages. Online: http://www.hfu.edu.tw/~huangkm/phenom/husserl-britanica.htm (Taken from *Journal of the British Society for Phenomenology* 2 (1971) 77–90; also in Husserl, E. *Husserl: Shorter Works*, edited by Frederick Elliston and Peter McCormick. 21–35. Notre Dame: University of Notre Dame Press, 1981, and in *Encyclopedia Britannica* (1927).

Ignatius of Loyola. "Reminiscences." In *Saint Ignatius of Loyola: Personal Writings*, edited and translated by Joseph Munitiz and Philip Endean, 1–64. London: Penguin, 1996.

———. *Spiritual Exercises and Selected Works*. Mahwah: Paulist Press, 1991.

Inwood, M. J. "Jaspers, Karl." In *The Oxford Companion to Philosophy*, edited by Ted Honderich, 428. Oxford: Oxford University Press, 1995.

James, W. *The Varieties of Religious Experience: A Study of Human Nature*. Glasgow: Collins, 1979.

Jaspers, K. "Philosophical Autobiography." In *The Philosophy of Karl Jaspers*, edited by P. A. Schilpp. New York: Tudor Publishing, 1957.

Jorissen, H. "Behindert die Amtsfrage die Einheit der Kirche? Katholisches. Plädoyer für die Anerkennung der reformatorischer Ämter." In *Eucharistische Gastfreundschaft: ein Plädoyer evangelischer und katholischer Theologen*, edited by J.Brosseder and H-G. Link, 85–97. Neukirchen—Vluyn: Neukirchener Verlag, 2003.

Kant, I. *Critique of Practical Reason and Other Works on the Theory of Ethics*. London: Longmans, Green, 1963.

Karfikova, L. "'Celé pole plné rozmanitých bylin' (Origenova biblická hermeneutika podle *Peri archon* IV.1–3)." In *Studie z patristiky a scholastiky*, 9–37. Praha: Oikoumené, 1997.

Ker, I. *Newman on Being a Christian*. Notre Dame – London: University of Notre Dame Press, 1990.

Kerr, F. *After Aquinas: Versions of Thomism*. Oxford: Blackwell, 2002.

Kuhn, T.S. *The Structure of Scientific Revolutions*. Chicago: Chicago University Press, 1970.

Küng, H. *Christianity: The Religious Situation of Our Time*. London: SCM, 1995.

———. *Global Responsibility. In Search of a New World Ethic*. London – New York: SCM, 1991.

———. *On Being a Christian*. Glasgow: Fount, 1978.

———. *Theology for the Third Millennium*. New York – London: SCM, 1991.

Lampe, G. W. H. "The Origins of the Creeds." In *The Nature of Christian Faith and Its Expressions in Holy Scripture and Creeds. A report by the Doctrine Commission of the Church of England*, 52–61. London: SPCK, 1976.

Lash, N. "Modernism, *Aggiornamento* and the Night Battle." In *Bishops and Writers: Aspects of the Evolution of Modern English Catholicism*, edited by A. Hastings, 51–79. Wheathampsted: Anthony Clarke, 1977.

Lechte, J. *Fifty Key Contemporary Thinkers*. London, New York: Routledge, 1994.

Leeming, B. *Principles of Sacramental Theology*. London: Longmans, 1963.

Leibniz, G. W. *Neue Abhandlungen uber den menschlichen Verstand*. Leipzig: Felix Meiner, 1915.

Leonard, E. *George Tyrrell and the Catholic Tradition*. London: Darton, Longman and Todd, 1982.

Lessing, G. E. *Schriften 2: Antiquarische Schriften: Theologische und philosophische Schriften*. Frankfurt: Insel, 1967.

Levi, S. M. "Suffering and Post-Modern Consciousness: The Imaginative Appropriation of Tradition in Contemporary Culture." *Anglican Theological Review* 3 (1998) 320–37.

Lewis, C. S. *Four Loves*. London: Fount, 1998.

Libanio, J. B. "Hope, Utopia, Resurrection." In *Systematic Theology. Perspectives from Liberation Theology*, edited by J. Sobrino and I. Ellacuría, 279–90. London: SCM, 1996.

———. "The Current State of Theology in Latin America". In *The Month* 9/10 (2000), 351–56.

Loisy, A. *The Gospel and the Church*. Philadelphia: Fortress, 1976.

Lonergan, B. 'First Lecture: Religious Experience', in *A Third Collection: Papers by Bernard Lonergan SJ*, edited by F. E. Crowe, 115–28. London: Geoffrey Chapman—Mahwah: Paulist, 1985.

———. *Method in Theology*. London: Darton, Longman and Todd, 1972.

Lossky, V. *Orthodox Theology: An Introduction*. Crestwood: St Vladimir's Seminary, 1978.

Lubac, H. de. *Letters of Etienne Gilson to Henry de Lubac*. San Francisco: Ignatius Press, 1988

———. *Surnaturel: Etudes historiques*. Paris: Aubier, 1946.

———. «Typologie et allegorisme.» *Recherches de science religieuse* 34 (1947) 180–226.

Lyotard, J.-F. *The Differend*. Manchester: MUP, 1986.

———. *The Postmodern Condition. A Report on Knowledge*. Manchester: MUP, 1994.

———, and J. L. Thebaud. *Just Gaming*. Manchester: MUP, 1985.

Macquarrie, J. *Two Worlds Are Ours: An Introduction to Christian Mysticism*. London: SCM, 2004.

Malherbe, A. J. "Introduction." In Gregory of Nyssa. *The Life of Moses*, 1–23. New York: Paulist Press—Toronto: Ramsey, 1978.

Marcuse, H. *El final de la utopia*. Barcelona, 1968.

Marion, J. L. "Metaphysics and Phenomenology: A Summary for Theologians." In *The Postmodern God: A Theological Reader*, edited by G. Ward, 279–96. Oxford: Blackwell, 1997.

Markus, R.A. *Saeculum: History and Society in the Theology of St Augustine*. Cambridge: CUP, 1970.

Men, A. (writing as Abbot Pol). *Zamysel Božij i čudesa ěgo miloserdnoj ljubvi*. Brussels: Foyer Oriental Chrétien, 1990.

Metz, J. B. "Anamnestic Reason: A Theologian's Remarks on the Crisis in the *Geisteswissenschaften*." In *Cultural Political Interventions in the Unfinished Project of the Enlightenment*, edited by A. Honneth et al., 189–94. Cambridge, Mass.—London: MIT, 1992.

———. *Faith in History and Society: Toward a Practical Fundamental Theology*. London: Burns & Oates, 1980.

Meyendorff, J. "Apostolic Continuity and Orthodox Theology: Towards a Synthesis of Two Perspectives." *St Vladimir Theological Quarterly* 19 (1975) 75–108.

———. *Byzantine Theology: Historical Trends and Doctrinal Themes*. New York: Fordham University Press, 1979.

———. *Catholicity of the Church*. Crestwood: St Vladimir's Seminary Press, 1983.

———. "Preface." In Gregory of Nyssa. *The Life of Moses*. New York: Paulist Press—Toronto: Ramsey, 1978.

Milbank, J. "Postmodern Critical Augustinianism: A Short Summa in Forty-two Responses to Unasked Questions." In *The Postmodern God: A Theological Reader*, edited by G. Ward, 265–78. Oxford: Blackwell, 1997.

———. *Theology and Social Theory*. Oxford: Blackwell, 1990.

Molnár, A. *Na rozhraní věků* . Praha: Vyšehrad, 1985.

Moltmann, J. *God in Creation*. London: SCM, 1985.

————. *Theology of Hope: On the Grounds and the Implications of a Christian Eschatology.* London: SCM, 1974.

————. *The Spirit of Life: A Universal Affirmation*. London: SCM, 1992.

Newman, J. H. *An Essay in Aid of a Grammar of Assent*. Oxford: Clarendon Press, 1985.

————. *An Essay on the Development of Christian Doctrine*. Harmondsworth: Penguin, 1973.

————. *Apologia pro vita sua*. London: Dent & Sons, 1955.

————. *Certain Difficulties Felt by Anglicans in Catholic Teaching*. London: Basil Montagu Pickering, 1876 (1990).

————. *Sermons Preached on Various Occasions*. London: Burns, Oates, & Co., 1874.

————. *The Via Media*. Oxford: Clarendon Press, 1990.

Niebuhr, R. *Christ and Culture*. New York: Harper, 1956.

Nietzsche, F. *Thus spake Zarathustra*. London: Dent—New York: Dutton, 1958.

Noble, Ivana. "Religious Experience—Reality or Illusion: Insights from Symeon the New Theologian and Ignatius of Loyola", In *Encountering Transcendence: Contributions to a Theology of Christian Religious Experience*, edited by L. Boeve et al., 375–93. Leuven: Peeters, 2005.

————. "The Apophatic Way in Gregory of Nyssa." In *Philosophical Hermeneutics and Biblical Exegesis*, edited by P. Pokorný and J. Roskovec, 323–39. Tübingen: Mohr Siebeck, 2002.

————. *Theological Interpretation of Culture in a Post-Communist Context: The Central and East European Search for Roots*. Farnham: Ashgate, forthcoming.

————. see also under Dolejšová, Ivana

Noble, Tim. *Keeping the Window Open: The Theological Method of Clodovis Boff and the Problem of the Alterity of the Poor*. Prague: IBTS, 2009.

O'Collins, G. *Fundamental Theology*. Mahwah: Paulist Press, 1981.

O'Dwyer, L. "Reality in Husserl and in Heidegger." In *A Hundred Years of Phenomenology: Perspectives on a Philosophical Tradition*, edited by R. Small, 43–51. Aldershot: Ashgate, 2001.

Otto, R. *The Idea of the Holy: An Inquiry into the Non-rational Factor to the Idea of the Divine and Its Relation to the Rational*. London, Edinburgh, Glasgow: Humpley Milford—Oxford University Press, 1925.

Palmer, G. E. H. et al. "St Symeon the New Theologian: Introductory Note." In *The Philokalia IV: The Complete Text Compiled by St Nikodimos of the Holy Mountain and St Makarios of Corinth,* edited by G. E. H. Palmer et al., 11–15. London: Faber & Faber, 1998.

Pannenberg, W. "Introduction." In *Revelation and History*, edited by W. Pannenberg, 3–21. London: Sheed and Ward, 1979.

————. "La signification de l'eschatologie pour la compréhension de l'apostolicité et de la catholicité de l'Eglise." *Istina* 14 (1969) 154–70.

Pascal, Blaise. *Pensées*. Harmondsworth: Penguin, 1977.

Patočka, J. "Husserlova fenomenologie, fenomenologická filosofie a 'Karteziánské meditace'." In Husserl, E., *Karteziánské meditace*, Praha: Svoboda, 1993.

Phan, P.C. *Culture and Eschatology: The Iconographical Vision of Paul Evdokimov*. New York, Bern, Frankfurt: Peter Lang, 1985.

Pickstock, C. *After Writing: On The Liturgical Consummation of Philosophy*. Oxford: Blackwell, 1998.

Pixley, J. "Las utopias principales de la Biblia." In *La esperanza en el presente de America Latina*, edited by R. Vidales and L. Rivera, 313–30. San José: DEI, 1983.

———. and C. Boff. *The Bible, the Church, and the Poor.* Maryknoll: Orbis, 1986.

Price, R. "'Hellenization' and Logos Doctrine in Justin Martyr." *Vigiliae Christianae* 42 (1988) 18–23.

Rahner, K. "Christianity and the Non-Christian Religions." In *Theological Investigations* Vol. V, 115–134. London: Darton, Longman and Todd, 1966.

———. *Foundations of Christian Faith: An Introduction to the Idea of Christianity.* London: Darton, Longman & Todd, 1978.

Ranke, L. von. *Geschichten des romanischen und germanischen Volker von 1494 bis 1514.* Leipzig: Dunder und Humbolt, 1874 (first edition 1824).

Rendtorff, R. "The Concept of Revelation in Ancient Israel." In *Revelation and History*, edited by W. Pannenberg, 23–53. London: Sheed and Ward, 1979.

Ricoeur, P. *Gravity and Grace.* London: RPK, 1952.

———. *Interpretation Theory: Discourse and the Surplus of Meaning.* Fort Worth: Texas Christian University, 1976.

———. *Symbolism of Evil.* Boston: Beacon, 1967

———. *The Conflict of Interpretations: Essays in Hermeneutics.* Evanston: Northwestern University Press, 1974.

———. *Time and Narrative.* Chicago: College of Chicago Press, 1984.

Russell, N. *Doctrine of Deification in the Greek Patristic Tradition.* Oxford: Oxford University Press, 2004.

Šandera, P., "Alexandrijská a Antiochejská škola", Praha: Pracovní texty Institutu ekumenických studií v Praze, 1999.

Sanneh, L. *Religion and the Variety of Cultures: A Study in Origin and Practice.* Valley Forge, Pennsylvania: Trinity Press International, 1996.

Scheler, M. *He the Eternal in Man*, New York: Harper and Brothers, 1960.

Scheller, M. *Die Stellung des Menschen im Kosmos.* Munich: 1947.

Schillebeeckx, E. *Christ: The Experience of Jesus as Lord.* New York: Seabury, 1980.

Schleiermacher, F. *Brief Outline on the Study of Theology.* John Knox, Richmond, Virginia, 1970. (Edinburgh: T. & T. Clark, 1850).

———. *On Religion: Speeches to Its Cultured Despisers.* New York: Frederick Ungar Publishing Co., 1955.

———. *The Christian Faith*, Edinburgh: T. & T. Clark, 1928.

Smart, N. "Religion." In *The New Dictionary of Christian Theology*, edited by A. Richardson and J. Bowden, 496–98. London: SCM, 1983.

Sobrino, Jon. *Jesus the Liberator: A Historical-Theological Reading of Jesus of Nazareth.* Translated by Paul Burns and Francis McDonagh. Tunbridge Wells: Burns and Oates, 1993.

———. *La fe en Jesucristo: Ensayo desde las víctimas.* Madrid: Trotta, 1999

Soskice, J. M. *Metaphor and Religious Language.* Oxford: Clarendon, 1985.

Strauss, D. F. *The Life of Jesus Critically Examined.* Philadelphia: Fortress, 1973.

Studzinski, R. "Experience, religious." In *The New Dictionary of Theology*, edited by Mary Collins et al., 369–74. Wilmington: Michael Glazier, 1987.

Symeon The New Theologian. "*One Hundred and Fifty-Three Practical and Theological Texts.*" In *The Philokalia IV: The Complete Text Compiled by St Nikodimos of the Holy Mountain and St Makarios of Corinth,* edited by G. E. H. Palmer et al., 25–66. London: Faber & Faber, 1998.

——. "On Faith." In *The Philokalia IV: The Complete Text Compiled by St Nikodimos of the Holy Mountain and St Makarios of Corinth,* edited by G. E. H. Palmer et al., 16–24. London: Faber & Faber, 1998.

——. "The Three Methods of Prayer." In *The Philokalia IV: The Complete Text Compiled by St Nikodimos of the Holy Mountain and St Makarios of Corinth,* edited by G. E. H. Palmer et al., 67–75. London: Faber & Faber, 1998.

Theodore of Mopsuestia. *Commentary on Galatians 4:24.* In *Documents in Early Christianity,* edited by M.Wiles and M.Santer, 151–52. Cambridge: CUP, 1993.

Thompson, J. B. *Study in the Theory of Ideology.* Cambridge: Polity Press—Oxford: Blackwell, 1984.

Tillich, P. *A History of Christian Thought.* New York: Harper and Row, 1968.

——. *Biblical Religion and the Search for Ultimate Reality.* Chicago: The University of Chicago Press, 1955.

——. *Biblické náboženství a ontologie,* Praha: Kalich, 1990.

——. *Dynamics of Faith.* London: Allen & Unwin, 1957.

——. *Perspectives on 19th and 20th Century Protestant Theology.* New York, Evanston, and London: Harper & Row, 1967.

——. "Philosophy and Theology", "The Two Types of Philosophy of Religion", "The Problem of Theological Method", "Biblical Religion and the Search for Ultimate Reality", 279–88; 289–300; 301–12; 357–88. In Paul Tillich, *Main Works IV.* Berlin—New York: De Gruyter—Evangelisches Verlag, 1987.

——. "Rechtfertigung und Zweifel." In *Main Works VI.* Edited by John Clayton. chapter 4, 83–98. Berlin—New York: De Gruyter—Evangelisches Verlag, 1992.

——. *Theology and Culture.* New York: Oxford University Press, 1959.

Topfer, B. "Lex Christi Dominum a církevní hierarchie u Jana Husa ve srovnání s jejich pojetím u Jana Viklefa." In *Jan Hus mezi epochami, národy a konfesemi,* edited by J. B. Lášek, 96–103. Praha—Bayreuth: Křesťanská akademie, 1995.

Tracy, D. *The Analogical Imagination: Christian Theology and the Culture of Pluralism.* New York: Crossroad, 1981.

Trakatellis, D. C. *The Pre-existence of Christ in the Writings of Justin Martyr: An Exegetical Study With Reference to Humiliation and Exaltation Christology.* Missoula, Montana: Scholar Press, 1976.

Trtik, Z. *Vztah já–Ty a křesťanství.* Praha: Blahoslav, 1948.

Tylor, E. B. *Primitive Culture: Researches into the Development of Mythology, Philosophy, Religion, Language, Art and Custom.* Vol.1 New York: Henry Holt, 1874

Tyrrell, G. *Christianity at the Cross-roads.* London: Longmans, Green and Co., 1909.

——. *Lex Orandi.* London: Longmans, Green & Co., 1904.

——. *Medievalism: A Reply to Cardinal Mercier.* London: Longmans & Green, 1908.

——. *Nova et Vetera.* London, New York: Longmans, Green and Co., 1900.

——. *Religion as a Factor of Life.* Exeter: William Pollard and Co., 1902.

——. *Through Scylla and Charybdis.* London: Longmans, Green & Co., 1907.

Vawter, B. "Introduction to Prophetic Literature." In *The New Jerome Biblical Commentary,* edited by R.E. Brown et al., 186–200. London: Geoffrey Chapman, 1993.

Ventura, Václav. "Teologie jako duchovní cesta." In *Úvod do teologického myšlení,* 31–34. Praha: IES Working Texts, 1997.

Weber, M. *The Theory of Social and Economic Organization.* New York: Free Press, 1964.

Westphal, M., et al. (eds.), *Modernity and its Discontents.* New York: Fordham College Press, 1992.

Williams, R. *Arius: Heresy and Tradition*. London: Darton, Longman & Todd, 1987.
———. *On Christian Theology*. Oxford: Blackwell, 2000.
Wittgenstein, L. *On Certainty*, Oxford: Blackwell, 1969.
———. *Remarks on Frazer's Golden Bough*. Retford: Brynmill, 1979.
Zizioulas, J. *Being as Communion: Studies in Personhood and the Church*. Crestwood: St Vladimir's Seminary Press, 1993.

Subject/Name Index